Praise for
TEACH YOUR KIDS TO CODE

"The text is clear, the graphics are engaging, and the apps are awesome. This is the programming guide for parents and kids to enjoy together."
—Aaron Walker, Cybersecurity Expert, NASA

"The energy and excitement Bryson brings to teaching is captured perfectly in *Teach Your Kids to Code*, with colorful, captivating games and graphics that help develop real-world skills."
—Bindy Auvermann, Executive Director, Next Generation Youth Development, Inc.

"An easy five stars . . . kids (and adults) will have a solid foundation from which to jump to more advanced programming books."
—James Floyd Kelly, *GeekDad*

"Provides the building blocks of a great future in the rapidly changing world of technology."
—JoAnne Taylor, former Vice President, Global Telecommunications, IBM

"The concepts in *Teach Your Kids to Code* can help any young person enhance their college prospects and expand their career opportunities."
—Dr. Raj Sunderraman, Department Chair of Computer Science, Georgia State University

"Every child on the planet should have this book, and so should every parent."
—James E. Daniel, Jr., Founder, App Studios, LLC

"An innovative, motivating guide . . . Builds skills that can last a lifetime."
—Dr. Steven Burrell, Vice President for Information Technology & CIO, Georgia Southern University

"The kind of book I wish I'd had as a kid."
—Scott Hand, Software Engineer, CareerBuilder

TEACH YOUR KIDS TO CODE

TEACH YOUR KIDS TO CODE

A PARENT-FRIENDLY GUIDE TO PYTHON PROGRAMMING

BY BRYSON PAYNE

no starch press

San Francisco

TEACH YOUR KIDS TO CODE. Copyright © 2015 by Bryson Payne.

Printed in USA

Third printing

19 18 17 16 15   3 4 5 6 7 8 9 10

ISBN-10: 1-59327-614-1
ISBN-13: 978-1-59327-614-0

Publisher: William Pollock
Production Editor: Riley Hoffman
Cover Illustration: Josh Ellingson
Illustrator: Miran Lipovača
Developmental Editors: Tyler Ortman and Leslie Shen
Technical Reviewers: Michelle Friend and Ari Lacenski
Copyeditor: Rachel Monaghan
Compositor: Riley Hoffman
Proofreader: Paula L. Fleming
Indexer: BIM Indexing & Proofreading Services

For information on distribution, translations, or bulk sales, please contact No Starch Press, Inc. directly:
No Starch Press, Inc.
245 8th Street, San Francisco, CA 94103
phone: 415.863.9900; info@nostarch.com
www.nostarch.com

Library of Congress Cataloging-in-Publication Data

Payne, Bryson.
  Teach your kids to code : a parent-friendly guide to Python programming / by Bryson Payne. -- 1st edition.
      pages cm
  Includes index.
  Summary: "A guide to teaching basic programming skills for parents and teachers, with step-by-step explanations, visual examples, and exercises. Covers programming concepts including loops, lists, functions, and variables, and how to build games and applications"-- Provided by publisher.
  ISBN 978-1-59327-614-0 -- ISBN 1-59327-614-1
  1. Python (Computer program language)--Study and teaching (Elementary) 2. Computer programming--Study and teaching (Elementary) 3. Python (Computer program language)--Study and teaching (Middle school) 4. Computer programming--Study and teaching (Middle school) I. Title.
  QA76.73.P98P39 2015
  005.13'3--dc23
                                            2015006794

To Alex and Max,
my two favorite coders

ABOUT THE AUTHOR

Dr. Bryson Payne is a tenured professor of computer science at the University of North Georgia, where he has taught aspiring coders for more than 15 years. His students have built successful careers at Blizzard Entertainment, Riot Games, Equifax, CareerBuilder, and more. He was the first department head of computer science at UNG, and he holds a PhD in computer science from Georgia State University. In addition, he works extensively with K–12 schools to promote technology education.

Dr. Payne has been programming for more than 30 years. The first program he sold was to *RUN* magazine (Commodore 64) for their "Magic" column in 1985, for $10.

Dr. Payne lives north of Atlanta, Georgia, with his wife, Bev, and two sons, Alex and Max.

ABOUT THE ILLUSTRATOR

Miran Lipovača is the author of *Learn You a Haskell for Great Good!*. He enjoys boxing, playing bass guitar, and, of course, drawing. He has a fascination with dancing skeletons and the number 71, and when he walks through automatic doors he pretends that he's actually opening them with his mind.

ABOUT THE TECHNICAL REVIEWER

Ari Lacenski is a developer of Android applications and Python software. She lives in San Francisco. She writes about Android programming at *http://gradlewhy.ghost.io/*, mentors with Women Who Code, and plays songs about space pirates on guitar.

BRIEF CONTENTS

CONTENTS IN DETAIL

3
NUMBERS AND VARIABLES: PYTHON DOES THE MATH   31

4
LOOPS ARE FUN (YOU CAN SAY THAT AGAIN)   53

7
FUNCTIONS: THERE'S A NAME FOR THAT 141

8
TIMERS AND ANIMATION: WHAT WOULD DISNEY DO? 175

9
USER INTERACTION: GET INTO THE GAME   207

10
GAME PROGRAMMING: CODING FOR FUN   231

ACKNOWLEDGMENTS

This book would not have been possible without the exceptional support of the No Starch Press team. Thanks especially to Bill Pollock for believing in the project; to Tyler Ortman for championing and editing; and to Leslie Shen, Riley Hoffman, Lee Axelrod, Mackenzie Dolginow, Serena Yang, and Laurel Chun for their indefatigable editing, reviewing, marketing, and production prowess and for the countless ways they helped me improve this book from my original manuscript. And thanks to Rachel Monaghan and Paula Fleming for their help copyediting and proofreading.

Thanks to Michelle Friend and Ari Lacenski for their thoughtful and thorough technical review, and to Conor Seng for being the first to read the book and try out the programs—at 10 years old.

Thanks to Miran Lipovača for his amazing illustrations—they bring the kind of life to the text that I could only have dreamed of.

Thanks to my father-in-law, Norman Petty, a retired IBM'er, who began teaching himself Python using an early draft of the book.

Special thanks to my wife and best friend, Bev, for her constant support, and to my amazing sons, Alex and Max, for helping test every program and suggesting improvements. This book and my entire life are infinitely better because of the three of you.

Finally, thanks to my mom, Esta, who encouraged me to love learning and solving puzzles.

INTRODUCTION

WHAT IS CODING AND WHY IS IT GOOD FOR YOUR KIDS?

Computer programming, or *coding*, is a crucial skill every child should be learning. We use computers to solve problems, play games, help us work more effectively, perform repetitive tasks, store and recall information, create something new, and connect with our friends and the world. Understanding how to code puts all this power at our fingertips.

Everyone can learn to code; it's just like solving a puzzle or a riddle. You apply logic, try a solution, experiment a little more, and then solve the problem. The time to start learning to code is *now*! We are at an unprecedented time in history: never before could billions of people connect with one another every day like we do now with computers. We live in a world of many new possibilities, from electric cars and robot caregivers to drones that deliver packages and even pizza.

If your children start learning to code today, they can help define this fast-changing world.

WHY SHOULD KIDS LEARN TO CODE?

There are many great reasons to learn computer programming, but here are my top two:

- Coding is fun.
- Coding is a valuable job skill.

CODING IS FUN

Technology is becoming a part of everyday life. Every company, charitable organization, and cause can benefit from technology. There are apps to help you buy, give, join, play, volunteer, connect, share—just about anything you can imagine.

Have your children wanted to build their own level for their favorite video game? Coders do that! What about create their own phone app? They can bring that idea to life by programming it on a computer! Every program, game, system, or app they've ever seen was coded using the same programming building blocks they'll learn in this book. When kids program, they take an active role in technology—they're not just *having* fun, they're *making* something fun!

CODING IS A VALUABLE JOB SKILL

Coding is *the* skill of the 21st century. Jobs today require more problem-solving ability than ever before, and more and more careers involve technology as an integral requirement.

The US Bureau of Labor Statistics predicts that more than 8 million technology jobs will be created in just the next five years. Seven of the ten fastest-growing occupations in the

2014–2015 Occupational Outlook Handbook that do not require master's or doctoral degrees are in the computer science or information technology (IT) fields.

Mark Zuckerberg was a college student working from his dorm room when he developed the first version of Facebook in 2004. Just 10 years later, 1.39 billion people were using Facebook *every month* (source: *http://newsroom.fb.com/company-info/*). Never before in history had an idea, product, or service been able to engage a billion people in under a decade. Facebook demonstrates the power of technology to reach more people, faster, than ever before.

WHERE CAN KIDS LEARN TO CODE?

This book is only the beginning. There are more places than ever to learn programming; websites like Code.org, Codecademy (see Figure 1), and countless others teach basic to advanced programming in a variety of in-demand programming languages. Once you've completed this book with your kids, your children can take free courses through websites like EdX, Udacity, and Coursera to extend their learning even further.

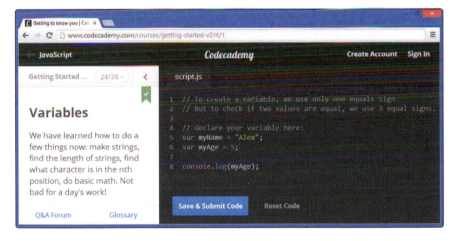

Figure 1: Codecademy teaches you how to program step by step in a variety of languages.

"Coding clubs" are a great way to have fun learning with friends. Getting a college degree in a relevant field is still one of the best ways to prepare for a career, but even if college isn't an option at the moment, your kids can begin building a programming portfolio and demonstrating their skills as a programmer and problem-solver today.

HOW TO USE THIS BOOK

This book isn't just for kids—it's for parents, teachers, students, and adults who want to understand the basics of computer programming, both to have fun and to gain access to new jobs in the high-tech economy. No matter what your age, you can have a great time learning the basics of programming. The best way to do this is to experiment and work together.

EXPLORE!

Learning to program is exciting if you're willing to try new things. As you and your kids follow along with the programs in this book, try changing numbers and text in the code to see what happens to the program. Even if you break it, you'll learn something new by fixing it. In the worst case, all you have to do is retype the example from the book or open the last saved version that worked. The point of learning to code is to try something new, learn a new skill, and solve problems in a new way. Make sure your kids are playing around—testing their code by changing something, saving the program, running it, seeing what happens, and fixing any errors.

The point of learning to code is to try something new, learn a new skill, and solve problems in a new way. Test your code by changing something, saving the program, running it, seeing what happens, and fixing errors if needed.

For example, I wrote some code to make a colorful drawing (Figure 2) and then went back, changed some numbers here and there, and tried running the program again. This gave me another drawing that was completely different but just as amazing. I went back again, changed some other numbers, and got yet another beautiful, unique drawing. See what you can do just by playing around?

Figure 2: Three colorful spiral drawings I created by trying different values in a line of code in one program

DO IT TOGETHER!

Experimenting with code is a great way to learn how programs work, and it's even more effective if you work with someone else. Whether you're teaching a child or student or studying for yourself, it's not just more *fun* to play with code together—it's also more *effective*.

For example, in the Suzuki Method of music instruction, parents attend lessons with their child and even study ahead so they can help their child between lessons. Starting early is another hallmark of the Suzuki Method; kids can start formal study by the age of three or four.

I began introducing my two sons to programming when they were two and four, and I encouraged them to have fun by changing small parts of each program, like the colors, shapes, and sizes of shapes.

I learned to program at the age of 13 by typing program examples from books and then modifying them to make them do something new. Now, in the computer science courses I teach, I often give students a program and encourage them to play around with the code to build something new.

If you're using this book to teach yourself, you can work with others by finding a friend to work through examples with you or by starting an after-school or community coding club (see *http://coderdojo.com/* or *http://www.codecademy.com/afterschool/* for ideas and tips). Coding is a team sport!

ONLINE RESOURCES

All the program files for this book are available at *http://www.nostarch.com/teachkids/*, as well as sample solutions for the Programming Challenges and other information. Download the programs and experiment with them to learn even more. Use the sample solutions if you get stumped. Check it out!

CODING = SOLVING PROBLEMS

Whether your child is 2 years old and learning to count or 22 and looking for a new challenge, this book and the concepts it introduces are a great pathway to a rewarding, inspiring pastime and better career opportunities. People who can program—and thus solve problems quickly and effectively—are highly valued in today's world, and they get to do interesting, fulfilling work.

Not all of the world's problems can be solved with technology alone, but technology can enable communication, collaboration, awareness, and action at a scale and speed never before imagined. If you can code, you can solve problems. Problem-solvers have the power to make the world a better place, so start coding today.

1

PYTHON BASICS:
GET TO KNOW YOUR ENVIRONMENT

Just about anything could have a computer in it—a phone, a car, a watch, a video game console, an exercise machine, a medical device, industrial equipment, a greeting card, or a robot. Computer programming, or *coding*, is how we tell a computer to perform a task, and understanding how to code puts the power of computers at your fingertips.

Computer programs—also called *applications*, or *apps*—tell computers what to do. A web app can tell the computer how to keep track of your favorite music; a game app can tell the computer how to display an epic battlefield with realistic graphics; a simple app can tell the computer to draw a beautiful spiral like the hexagon in Figure 1-1.

Figure 1-1: A colorful spiral graphic

Some apps are composed of thousands of lines of code, while others may be just a few lines long, like the program *NiceHexSpiral.py* in Figure 1-2.

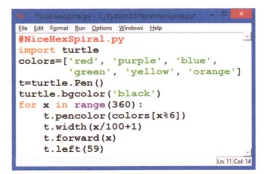

```
#NiceHexSpiral.py
import turtle
colors=['red', 'purple', 'blue',
        'green', 'yellow', 'orange']
t=turtle.Pen()
turtle.bgcolor('black')
for x in range(360):
    t.pencolor(colors[x%6])
    t.width(x/100+1)
    t.forward(x)
    t.left(59)
```

Figure 1-2: NiceHexSpiral.py, a short Python program that draws the spiral in Figure 1-1

This short program draws the colorful spiral shown in Figure 1-1. I wanted a pretty picture to use as an example in this book, so I decided to solve that problem using a computer program. First I sketched out an idea, and then I started coding.

In this chapter, we'll download, install, and learn to use the programs that will help us write code to build any kind of app you can imagine.

GETTING STARTED WITH PYTHON

To begin coding, we have to speak the computer's language. Computers need step-by-step instructions, and they can only understand certain languages. Just like a person from Russia might not be able to understand English, computers only understand languages made for them. Computer code is written in programming languages like Python, C++, Ruby, or JavaScript. These languages allow us to "talk" to our computer and give it commands. Think about when you teach a dog to do tricks—when you give the "sit" command, he sits; when you say "speak," he barks. The dog understands those simple commands, but not much else you say.

Likewise, computers have their own limitations, but they can do whatever you tell them to do in their language. The language we'll use in this book is *Python*, a simple, powerful programming language. Python is taught in introductory computer science courses in high school and college, and it's used to run some of the most powerful apps in the world, including Gmail, Google Maps, and YouTube.

To get you started using Python on your computer, we'll go through these three steps together:

1. Download Python.
2. Install Python on your computer.
3. Test Python with a simple program or two.

1. DOWNLOAD PYTHON

Python is free and easy to get from the Python website, shown in Figure 1-3.

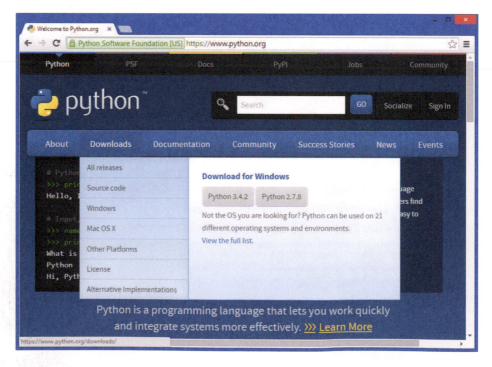

Figure 1-3: The Python website makes it easy to download Python.

In your web browser, go to *https://www.python.org/*. Hover your mouse over the **Downloads** menu button near the top and click the button that begins with **Python 3**.

2. INSTALL PYTHON

Find the file you just downloaded (it's probably in your *Downloads* folder) and double-click it to run and install Python and the IDLE editor. IDLE is the program we'll use to type and run our Python programs. For detailed installation instructions, see Appendix A.

3. TEST PYTHON WITH A PROGRAM

In your Start menu or *Applications* folder, find the IDLE program and run it. You'll see a text-based command window like the one shown in Figure 1-4. This is called the Python shell. A *shell* is a window or screen that lets the user enter commands or lines of code.

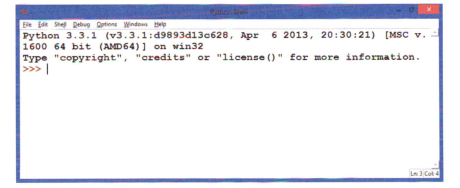

Figure 1-4: The IDLE Python shell—our command center for learning Python

The >>> is called a *prompt*, and it means that the computer is ready to accept your first command. The computer is asking you to tell it what to do. Type

```
print("Hello, world!")
```

and press ENTER or RETURN on your keyboard. You should see the Python shell respond by printing the text in quotes that you entered inside the parentheses: Hello, world!. That's it—you've written your first program!

WRITING PROGRAMS IN PYTHON

You'll usually want to write programs that are longer than a single line, so Python comes with an *editor* for writing longer programs. In IDLE, go to the **File** menu and select **File ▸ New Window** or **File ▸ New File**. A blank screen will pop up, with *Untitled* at the top.

Let's write a slightly longer program in Python. In the new, blank window, type the following three lines of code:

```python
# YourName.py
name = input("What is your name?\n")
print("Hi, ", name)
```

The first line is called a *comment*. Comments, which begin with a hash mark (#), are programming notes or reminders that the computer ignores. In this example, the comment is just a note to remind us of the program's name. The second line asks the user to input their name and remembers it as name. The third line prints "Hi, " followed by the user's name. Notice that there's a comma (,) separating the quoted text "Hi, " from the name.

RUNNING PROGRAMS IN PYTHON

Go to the **Run** option on the menu above your program and select **Run ▸ Run Module**. This will *run*, or carry out, the instructions in your program. It will first ask you to save the program. Let's call our file *YourName.py*. This tells your computer to save the program as a file called *YourName.py*, and the *.py* part means this is a Python program.

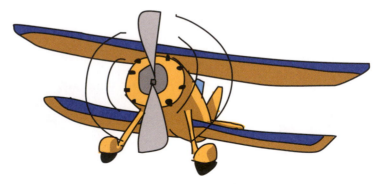

When you save the file and run it, you'll see your Python shell window start the program by showing the question What is your name?. Type your name on the next line and press ENTER. The program will print Hi, followed by the name you typed. Since this is all that you asked your program to do, the program will end, and you'll see the >>> prompt again, as shown in Figure 1-5.

```
                                    Python Shell                      _  □  ×
File  Edit  Shell  Debug  Options  Windows  Help
Python 3.3.1 (v3.3.1:d9893d13c628, Apr  6 2013, 20:30:21) [MSC v.
1600 64 bit (AMD64)] on win32
Type "copyright", "credits" or "license()" for more information.
>>> ================================ RESTART ====================
============
>>>
What is your name?
Bryson
Hi, Bryson
>>> |
                                                                Ln: 8 Col: 4
```

Figure 1-5: The computer knows my name!

For younger learners, like my three-year-old son, it's fun to explain that the program is asking them to type their name. Max knows the letters in his name, so he types *m-a-x* on the keyboard, and he loves it when I tell him the program said Hi, max back to him. Ask your young learner if she'd like the program to say something different. Max said "Hello," so I edited the earlier program on the third line to say Hello, instead of Hi,.

Then I changed the third line to read:

```
print("Hello, ", name, name, name, name, name)
```

Max loved it when the program replied to him with Hello, max max max max max. Try experimenting with the second and third lines of the program to have the computer ask different questions and print different answers.

WHAT YOU LEARNED

Learning to code is like learning to solve puzzles, riddles, or brainteasers. You start with a problem, apply what you know, and learn new things along the way. By the time you finish, you've exercised your mind, and you've answered a question. Hopefully, you've also had fun.

In this chapter, we solved our first major problem: we installed the Python programming language on our computers so that we could start coding. It was as easy as downloading a file, installing it, and running it.

In the chapters that follow, you'll learn how to solve problems using code. You'll start with simple visual puzzles, like drawing shapes on the computer screen (or a tablet or phone), and then find out how to create simple games like Guess a Number, Rock-Paper-Scissors, and Pong.

From the foundation you'll build in these first programs, you can go on to code games, mobile apps, web apps, and more.

At this point, you should . . .

- Have a fully functional Python programming environment and text editor.
- Be able to enter programming commands directly into the Python shell.
- Be able to write, save, run, and modify short programs in IDLE.
- Be ready to try more advanced, fun programs in Chapter 2.

PROGRAMMING CHALLENGES

At the end of each chapter, you can practice what you've learned—and make even cooler programs!—by trying a couple of challenges. (If you get stuck, go to *http://www.nostarch.com/teachkids/* for sample answers.)

#1: MAD LIBS

The simple *YourName.py* app has all the necessary components for us to build a much more interesting program, like the old-fashioned Mad Libs word games (go to *http://www.madlibs.com/* if you've never tried one before).

Let's modify the program *YourName.py* and save it as *MadLib.py*. Instead of asking for the user's name, we'll ask for an adjective, a noun, and a past-tense verb and store them in three different variables, just as we did for name in the original program. Then, we'll print out a sentence like "The *adjective noun verb* over the lazy brown dog." Here's what the code should look like after these changes.

MadLib.py

```python
adjective = input("Please enter an adjective: ")
noun = input("Please enter a noun: ")
verb = input("Please enter a verb ending in -ed: ")
print("Your MadLib:")
print("The", adjective, noun, verb, "over the lazy brown dog.")
```

You can enter any adjective, noun, and verb you wish. Here's what you should see when you save and run *MadLib.py* (I've entered smart, teacher, and sneezed):

```
>>>
Please enter an adjective: smart
Please enter a noun: teacher
Please enter a verb ending in -ed: sneezed
Your MadLib:
The smart teacher sneezed over the lazy brown dog.
>>>
```

#2: MORE MAD LIBS!

Let's make our Mad Lib game a little more interesting. Start a new version of *MadLib.py* by saving it as *MadLib2.py*. Add another input line that asks for a type of animal. Then, change the print statement by removing the word dog and adding the new animal variable after the end of the quoted sentence (add a comma before your new variable inside the print statement). You can change the sentence more, if you'd like. You could wind up with The funny chalkboard burped over the lazy brown gecko—or something even funnier!

2
TURTLE GRAPHICS: DRAWING WITH PYTHON

In this chapter, we'll write short, simple programs to create beautifully complex visuals. To do this, we'll use *turtle graphics*. In turtle graphics, you write instructions that tell a virtual, or imaginary, turtle to move around the screen. The turtle carries a pen, and you can instruct the turtle to use its pen to draw lines wherever it goes. By writing code to move the turtle around in cool patterns, you can make it draw amazing pictures.

Using turtle graphics, not only can you create impressive visuals with a few lines of code, but you can also follow along with the turtle and see how each line of code affects its movement. This will help you understand the *logic* of your code.

OUR FIRST TURTLE PROGRAM

Let's write our first program using turtle graphics. Type the following code into a new window in IDLE and save it as *SquareSpiral1.py*. (You can also download this program, and all the others in the book, at *http://www.nostarch.com/teachkids/*.)

SquareSpiral1.py

```
# SquareSpiral1.py - Draws a square spiral
import turtle
t = turtle.Pen()
for x in range(100):
    t.forward(x)
    t.left(90)
```

NOTE   *Notice the capital* P *in* t=turtle.Pen().

When we run this code, we get a pretty neat picture (Figure 2-1).

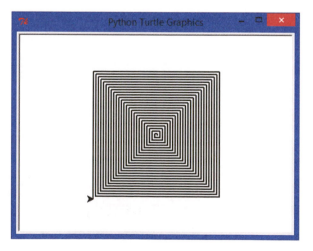

Figure 2-1: A hypnotic square spiral, created with the short program SquareSpiral1.py

HOW IT WORKS

Let's break the program down line by line to see how it works.

The first line of *SquareSpiral1.py* is a comment. As you learned in Chapter 1, a comment begins with a hash mark (#). Comments allow us to write notes in our programs to ourselves or to other humans who might read the program later. The computer doesn't read or try to understand anything after the hash mark; the comment is just for us to write something about what the program is doing. In this case, I've put the name of the program in the comment, as well as a brief description of what it does.

The second line *imports* the ability to draw turtle graphics. Importing code that's already been written is one of the coolest things about programming. If you program something interesting and useful, you can share it with other people and even reuse it yourself. Some cool Python programmers built a *library*—a reusable set of code—to help other programmers use turtle graphics in Python, even though turtle graphics are originally from the Logo programming language of the 1960s.[1] When you type import turtle, you're saying that you want your program to be able to use the code that those Python programmers wrote. The little black arrow in Figure 2-1 represents the turtle, drawing with its pen as it moves around the screen.

The third line of our program, t = turtle.Pen(), tells the computer that we'll use the letter t to stand for the turtle's pen. This will allow us to draw with the turtle's pen as the turtle moves around the screen just by typing t.forward() instead of writing out turtle.Pen().forward(). The letter t is our shortcut for telling the turtle what to do.

The fourth line is the most complex. Here we're creating a *loop*, which repeats a set of instructions a number of times (it *loops* through those lines of code over and over again). This particular loop sets up a range, or list, of 100 numbers from 0 to 99.

---

1. The Logo programming language was created in 1967 as an educational programming language, and five decades later, it's still useful for learning the basics of coding. Cool, huh?

(Computers almost always start counting at 0, not 1 like we usually do.) The loop then steps the letter x through each of the numbers in that range. So x starts as 0, and then it becomes 1, then 2, and so on as it counts all the way up to 99, for a total of 100 steps.

This x is called a *variable*.[2] (In the program *YourName.py* in Chapter 1, name was a variable.) A variable stores a value that can change, or vary, as we move through our program. We'll be using variables in almost every program we write, so it's good to get to know them early.

The next two lines are indented, or spaced over from the left. That means that they are *in the loop* and go with the line above, so they'll be repeated each time x gets a new number in the range from 0 to 99, or 100 times.

WHAT HAPPENS

Let's see what happens the first time Python reads this set of instructions. The command t.forward(x) tells the turtle pen to move forward x dots on the screen. Because x is 0, the pen doesn't move at all. The last line, t.left(90), tells the turtle to turn left by 90 degrees, or a quarter turn.

Because of that for loop, the pro-gram continues to run, and it goes back to the starting position of our loop. The computer adds 1 to move x to the next value in the range, and since 1 is still in the range from 0 to 99, the loop continues. Now x is 1, so the pen moves forward 1 dot. The pen then moves again to the left by 90, because of t.left(90). This continues again and again. By the time x gets to 99, the last time through the loop, the pen is draw-ing the long lines around the outside of the square spiral.

---

2. Younger readers may recognize x as the *unknown*, like when they solve $x + 4 = 6$ to find the unknown x. Older readers may recognize x from an algebra class or another mathematics course; this is where early programmers borrowed the concept of a variable from. There's a lot of good math in coding: we'll even see some cool geometry examples as we move forward.

Here is a step-by-step visual of the loop as x grows from 0 toward 100:

```python
for x in range(100):
    t.forward(x)
    t.left(90)
```

Loops 0 to 4: The first four lines are drawn (after x = 4).

Loops 5 to 8: Another four lines are drawn; our square emerges.

Loops 9 to 12: Our square spiral grows to 12 lines (three squares).

The dots, or *pixels*, on your computer screen are probably too tiny for you to see them very well. But, as x gets closer to 100, the turtle draws lines consisting of more and more pixels. In other words, as x gets bigger, t.forward(x) draws longer and longer lines.

The turtle arrow on the screen draws for a while, then turns left, draws some more, turns left, and draws again and again, with longer lines each time.

By the end, we have a hypnotizing square shape. Turning left 90 degrees four times gives us a square, just like turning left four times around a building will take you around the building and back where you started.

The reason we have a spiral in this example is that every time we turn left, we go a little farther. The first line that's drawn is just 1 step long (when x = 1), then 2 (the next time through the loop), then 3, then 4, and so on, all the way through 100 steps, when the line is 99 pixels long. Again, the pixels are probably so tiny on your screen that you can't easily see the individual dots, but they're there, and you can see the lines get longer as they contain more pixels.

By making all the turns 90-degree angles, we get the perfect square shape.

TURTLE ON A ROLL

Let's see what happens when we change one of the numbers in the program. One way to learn new things about a program is to see what happens when you change one part of it. You won't always get a pretty result, but you can learn even when something goes wrong.

Change just the last line of the program to t.left(91) and save it as *SquareSpiral2.py*.

SquareSpiral2.py

```
import turtle
t = turtle.Pen()
for x in range(100):
    t.forward(x)
    t.left(91)
```

I mentioned that a 90-degree left turn creates a perfect square. Turning just a little more than 90 degrees—in this case, 91 degrees every turn—throws the square off just a bit. And because it's already off a bit when it makes the next turn, our new shape looks less and less like a square as the program continues. In fact, it makes a nice spiral shape that starts to swirl to the left like a staircase, as you can see in Figure 2-2.

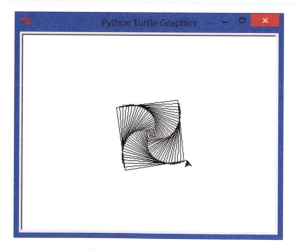

Figure 2-2: The square spiral program with one tiny change becomes a spiral staircase.

This is also a nice visual to help you understand how being off by just one number can drastically change the result of your program. One degree doesn't seem like a big deal, unless you're off by one degree 100 times (which adds up to 100 degrees), or 1,000 times, or if you're using a program to land an airplane . . .

If you don't know how degrees work yet, don't worry about it for now. Just play with the numbers and see what happens. Change the number of lines the program draws to 200, or 500, or 50, by changing the value in parentheses after range.

Also try changing the angle in the last line to 91, 46, 61, or 121, and so on. Remember to save the program each time. Then run it to see how your changes affect what the program draws. Older readers who know a bit of geometry will see some familiar shapes based on the angles used and may even be able to predict the shape based on the angle before the program runs. Younger readers can just enjoy changing things up a bit, and this exercise might come back to them when they're in a geometry class someday.

TURTLE ROUNDUP

Speaking of geometry, turtle graphics can draw lots more interesting shapes than just straight lines. We'll come back to the square shape again in the next section, but let's take a short detour to check out more of the Python Turtle library.

Let's change one more line of code: `t.forward(x)`. We saw earlier that this command, or *function*, moves the turtle's pen forward x pixels and draws a straight line segment; then the turtle turns and does it again. What if we changed that line of code to draw something more complex, like a circle?

Fortunately for us, the command to draw a circle of a certain size, or *radius*, is as simple to code as the command to draw a straight line. Change `t.forward(x)` to `t.circle(x)`, as shown in the following code.

CircleSpiral1.py

```python
import turtle
t = turtle.Pen()
for x in range(100):
    t.circle(x)
    t.left(91)
```

Wow! Changing one command from t.forward to t.circle gave us a much more complex shape, as you can see in Figure 2-3. The t.circle(x) function tells the program to draw a circle of radius x at the current position. Notice that this drawing has something in common with the simpler square spiral shape: there are four sets of circle spirals just like there were four sides to our square spiral. That's because we're still turning left just a little over 90 degrees with the t.left(91) command. If you've studied geometry, you know that there are 360 degrees around a point, like the four 90-degree corners in a square (4 × 90 = 360). The turtle draws that spiral shape by turning just a little more than 90 degrees each time around the block.

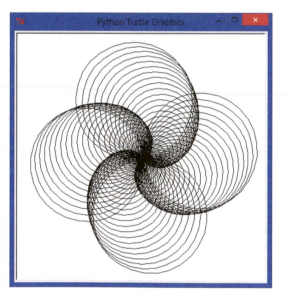

Figure 2-3: Just one more change gives us a beautiful set of four spiraling circles.

One difference you'll see is that the circle spiral is larger than the square spiral—about twice the size, in fact. This is because t.circle(x) is using x as the *radius* of the circle, which is the distance from the center to the edge, or one-half of the circle's width.

A radius of x means that the *diameter*, or total width, of the circle will be two times x. In other words, t.circle(x) draws a circle 2 pixels across when x is equal to 1, 4 pixels across when x is 2, all the way up to 198 pixels across when x is 99. That's almost 200 pixels across, or twice the size of our biggest side in the square, so the circle spiral is about double the size of our square spiral—and maybe twice as cool, too!

ADDING A TOUCH OF COLOR

These spirals are nice shapes, but wouldn't it be cooler if they were a bit more colorful? Let's go back to our square spiral code and add one more line to our program, right after the t = turtle.Pen() line, to set the pen color to red:

SquareSpiral3.py

```
import turtle
t = turtle.Pen()
t.pencolor("red")
for x in range(100):
    t.forward(x)
    t.left(91)
```

Run the program, and you'll see a more colorful version of our square spiral (Figure 2-4).

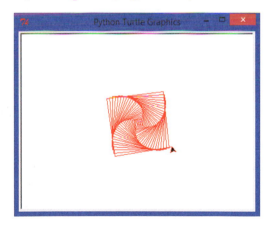

Figure 2-4: The square spiral gets a little more colorful.

Try replacing "red" with another common color, like "blue" or "green", and run the program again. You can use hundreds of different colors with the Turtle library, including some weird ones like "salmon" and "lemon chiffon". (Visit *http://www.tcl.tk/man/tcl8.4/TkCmd/colors.htm* for a full list.) Making the whole spiral a different color is a nice step, but what if we wanted to make each *side* a different color? That's going to take a few more changes to our program.

A FOUR-COLOR SPIRAL

Let's think through the *algorithm*—that is, the set of steps—that will turn our one-color spiral into a four-color spiral. Most of the steps are the same as in our previous spiral programs, but there are a few added twists:

1. Import the turtle module and set up a turtle.
2. Tell the computer which colors we'd like to use.
3. Set up a loop to draw 100 lines in our spiral.
4. Pick a different pen color for each side of the spiral.
5. Move the turtle forward to draw each side.
6. Turn the turtle left to get ready to draw the next side.

First, we need a *list* of color names instead of a single color, so we're going to set up a list variable called colors and put four colors in the list, like this:

```
colors = ["red", "yellow", "blue", "green"]
```

This list of four colors will give us one color for each side of our square. Notice we put the list of colors inside square brackets, [and]. Make sure that each color name is inside quote marks just like the words we printed out in Chapter 1, because these color names are *strings*, or text values, that we will pass to the pencolor function shortly. As noted, we're using a variable called colors to store our list of four colors, so whenever we want to get a color from the list, we'll use the colors variable to stand for the color of the pen. Remember, variables store values that change. It's right in their name: they vary!

The next thing we need to do is change the pen color *every time* we step through the drawing loop. To do this, we need to move the t.pencolor() function into the group of instructions under the for loop. We also need to tell the pencolor function that we want to use one of the colors from the list.

Type the following code and run it.

ColorSquareSpiral.py

```
import turtle
t = turtle.Pen()
colors = ["red", "yellow", "blue", "green"]
for x in range(100):
    t.pencolor(colors[x%4])
    t.forward(x)
    t.left(91)
```

The list of four colors makes sense, and we can see them in the running example (Figure 2-5). So far, so good.

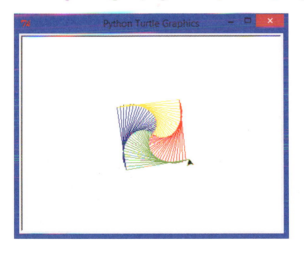

Figure 2-5: A much more colorful version of our square spiral program

The only new part is the (colors[x%4]) in the pencolor function. The x inside the statement is the same variable we're using elsewhere in the program. So x will continue to grow from 0 to 99, just like we've seen before. The colors variable name inside the parentheses tells Python to choose a color from the list of color names called colors that we added earlier in the program.

The [x%4] part tells Python that we will use the first four colors in the colors list, numbered 0 through 3, and rotate through them every time x changes. In this case, our color list only has four colors, so we'll rotate through these four colors over and over:

```
colors = ["red", "yellow", "blue", "green"]
           0       1        2       3
```

The % symbol in [x%4] is called the *modulo*, or *mod*, operator and represents the *remainder* in long division (5 ÷ 4 equals 1 with a remainder of 1, because 4 goes evenly into 5 once with 1 left over; 6 ÷ 4 has a remainder of 2; and so on). The mod operator is useful when you want to rotate through a certain number of items in a list, like we're doing with our list of four colors.

In 100 steps, colors[x%4] will loop through four colors (0, 1, 2, and 3, for red, yellow, blue, and green) a total of 25 times. If you have the time (and a magnifying glass), you could count 25 red, 25 yellow, 25 blue, and 25 green segments in Figure 2-5. The first time through the drawing loop, Python uses the first color in the list, red; the second time, it uses yellow; and so on. Then the fifth time through the loop, Python goes back to red, then yellow, and so on, and always cycles back around to red after every fourth pass through the loop.

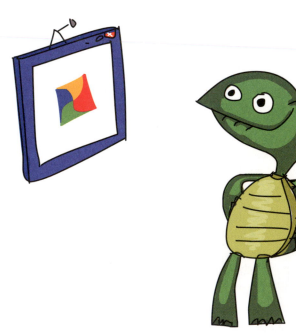

CHANGING BACKGROUND COLORS

Let's mix things up a bit again to see if we can create something even more beautiful than Figure 2-5. For example, as my five-year-old son Alex pointed out, the yellow sides are hard to see. That's because, just like yellow crayons on white drawing paper, the yellow pixels on the screen don't show up well against the white background color. Let's fix that by changing the background color to black. Type the following line of code anywhere after the `import` line in our program:

```
turtle.bgcolor("black")
```

Adding this one line gives us an even neater picture: all of the colors now stand out on the black background. Notice that we're not changing anything about the turtle's pen (represented by the variable t in our program). Instead, we're changing something about the turtle screen, namely the background color. The `turtle.bgcolor()` command allows us to change the color of the entire drawing screen to any of the named colors in Python. In the line `turtle.bgcolor("black")`, we've chosen black as the screen color, so the bright red, yellow, blue, and green show up nicely.

While we're at it, we can change the `range()` in our loop to 200, or even more, to make larger squares in our spiral. See Figure 2-6 for the new version of our picture with 200 lines on a black background.

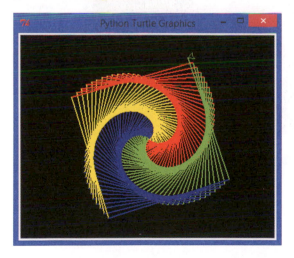

Figure 2-6: Our square spiral has come a long way from its simple beginnings.

Always willing to help make my programs more awesome, Alex asked for one more change: what if we replaced the line segments with circles now? Wouldn't that be the coolest picture of all? Well, yes, I have to agree—it is even cooler. Here's the full code.

ColorCircleSpiral.py

```python
import turtle
t = turtle.Pen()
turtle.bgcolor("black")
colors = ["red", "yellow", "blue", "green"]
for x in range(100):
    t.pencolor(colors[x%4])
    t.circle(x)
    t.left(91)
```

You can see the result in Figure 2-7.

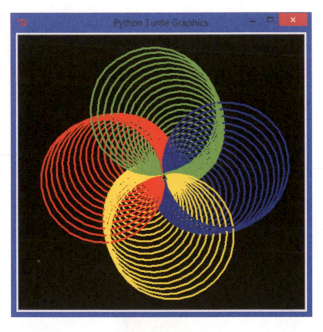

Figure 2-7: Alex's awesome color circle spiral—
eight lines of code, simple and elegant

ONE VARIABLE TO RULE THEM ALL

So far, we've used variables to change the color, size, and turning angle of our spiral shapes. Let's add another variable, `sides`, to represent the number of sides in a shape. How will this new variable change our spiral? To find out, try this program, *ColorSpiral.py*.

ColorSpiral.py

```
import turtle
t = turtle.Pen()
turtle.bgcolor("black")
# You can choose between 2 and 6 sides for some cool shapes!
sides = 6
colors = ["red", "yellow", "blue", "orange", "green", "purple"]
for x in range(360):
    t.pencolor(colors[x%sides])
    t.forward(x * 3/sides + x)
    t.left(360/sides + 1)
    t.width(x*sides/200)
```

You can change the value of `sides` from 6 down to 2 (one side's not very interesting, and you won't be able to use bigger numbers unless you add more colors to the list in the sixth line of the program). Then save and run the program as many times as you'd like. Figure 2-8 shows the pictures created with `sides = 6`, `sides = 5`, all the way down to `sides = 2`, which is the weird, flat spiral shown in Figure 2-8(e). You can change the order of the colors in the list, and you can use bigger or smaller numbers in any of the functions in the drawing loop. If you break the program, just go back to the original *ColorSpiral.py* and play some more.

The *ColorSpiral.py* program uses one new command, `t.width();` this changes the width of the turtle's pen. In our program, the pen gets wider (its lines get thicker) as it draws larger and larger shapes. We'll revisit this program and others like it in Chapters 3 and 4 as you learn the skills needed to create programs like this from scratch.

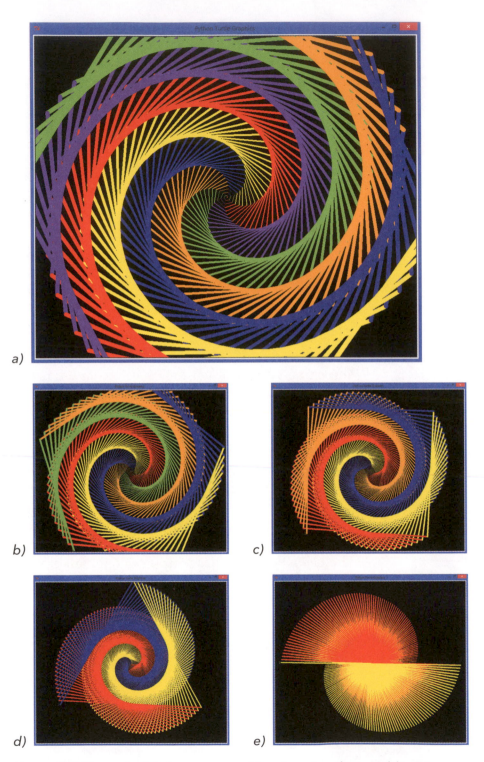

Figure 2-8: Five colorful shapes created by changing the variable *sides* from 6 (a) down to 2 (e)

WHAT YOU LEARNED

In this chapter, we drew impressive, colorful shapes in Python using the Turtle library of tools. We brought this library into our program by using the `import` command, and you learned that reusing code in this way is one of the most powerful things about programming. Once we've written something useful, or borrowed code that someone else has been kind enough to share, we not only save time but can also use that imported code to do neat new things.

You've also been introduced to variables like x and `sides` in our programs. These variables store, or remember, a number or value so that you can use it multiple times in a program and even change the value as you go. In the next chapter, you'll learn more about the power of variables and how Python can even help you do your math homework!

At this point, you should be able to do the following:

- Draw simple graphics with the Turtle library.
- Use variables to store simple number values and strings.
- Change, save, and run programs in IDLE.

PROGRAMMING CHALLENGES

Try these challenges to practice what you've learned in this chapter. (If you get stuck, go to *http://www.nostarch.com/teachkids/* for sample answers.)

#1: CHANGING THE NUMBER OF SIDES

We used a variable, sides, in the *ColorSpiral.py* program on page 25, but we didn't vary it much or change its value except for editing, saving, and running the program again. Try changing the value of sides to another number, say 5. Save and run the program to see how this affects your drawing. Now try 4, 3, 2, and even 1! Now, add two or more colors, in quotes, separated by commas, to the list of colors in the sixth line of the program. Increase the value of sides to use this new number of colors—try 8 or 10 or more!

continued

#2: HOW MANY SIDES?

What if you want to let a user decide the number of sides while the program runs? Using what you learned in Chapter 1, you can ask the user for a number of sides and store that input in the variable sides. Our only extra step is to *evaluate* the number the user enters. We can find out which number the user typed with the eval() function, like this:

```
sides = eval(input("Enter a number of sides between 2 and 6: "))
```

Replace the line sides = 6 in *ColorSpiral.py* with the preceding line. Your new program will ask how many sides the user wants to see. Then, the program will draw the shape the user asks for. Give it a try!

#3: RUBBER-BAND BALL

Try changing the *ColorSpiral.py* program into a more tangled and abstract shape just by adding an extra turn inside the end of the drawing loop. Add a line like t.left(90) to the bottom of the for loop to make the angles sharper (remember to indent, or space over, to keep the statement in the loop). The result, shown in Figure 2-9, looks like a geometric toy or perhaps a ball made of colored rubber bands.

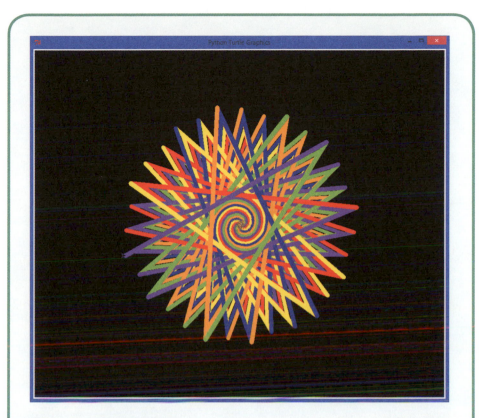

Figure 2-9: Adding an extra 90 degrees to each turn in ColorSpiral.py turns it into RubberBandBall.py.

Save this new version as *RubberBandBall.py*, or go to *http://www.nostarch.com/teachkids/* and find the program in the source code for Chapter 2.

3

NUMBERS AND VARIABLES: PYTHON DOES THE MATH

We've used Python to do really fun things, like make colorful pictures in just a few lines of code, but our programs have been limited. We just ran them and watched them make pictures. What if we wanted to *interact* with our Python programs? In this chapter, we'll learn how to have Python ask the user's name and even offer to do the user's math homework!

VARIABLES: WHERE WE KEEP OUR STUFF

In Chapters 1 and 2, we used a few *variables* (you might remember name from our first program in Chapter 1 or x and sides from Chapter 2). Now let's look at what variables really are and how they work.

A *variable* is something you want the computer to remember while your program is running. When Python "remembers" something, it's storing that information in the computer's memory. Python can remember *values* of several types, including number values (like 7, 42, or even 98.6) and strings (letters, symbols, words, sentences, or anything you can type on the keyboard and then some). In Python, as in most modern programming languages, we *assign* a value to a variable with the equal sign (=). An assignment like x = 7 tells the computer to remember the number 7 and give it back to us anytime we call out x. We also use the equal sign to assign a string of keyboard characters to a variable; we just have to remember to put quotation marks (") around the string, like this:

```
my_name = "Bryson"
```

Here, we assign the value "Bryson" to the variable my_name. The quotation marks around "Bryson" tell us that it is a string.

Whenever you assign a value to a variable, you write the name of the variable first, to the left of the equal sign, and then write the value to the right of the equal sign. We name variables something simple that describes their contents (like my_name when I'm storing my name) so we can easily remember them and use them in our programs. There are a few rules to keep in mind as we make up names for variables.

First, we always begin variable names with a letter. Second, the rest of the characters in the variable name must be letters, numbers, or the underscore symbol (_); that means you can't have a space inside a variable name (for example, my name will give you a syntax error because Python thinks

you've listed two variables separated by a space). Third, variable names in Python are *case sensitive*; that means that if we use all *lowercase* letters in a variable name (like abc), then we can only use the value stored in the variable if we type the variable name exactly the same way, with the same capitalization. For example, to use the value in abc, we have to write abc; we can't use *uppercase* letters like ABC. So My_Name is not the same as my_name, and MY_NAME is a different variable name altogether. In this book, we'll use all lowercase letters in our variable names, separating words with the _ symbol.

Let's try a program using some variables. Type the following code in a new IDLE window and save it as *ThankYou.py*.

ThankYou.py

```
my_name = "Bryson"
my_age = 43
your_name = input("What is your name? ")
your_age = input("How old are you? ")
print("My name is", my_name, ", and I am", my_age, "years old.")
print("Your name is", your_name, ", and you are", your_age, ".")
print("Thank you for buying my book,", your_name, "!")
```

When we run this program, we're telling the computer to remember that my_name is "Bryson" and that my_age is 43. We then ask the user (the person running the program) to enter their name and age, and we tell the computer to remember these as the variables your_name and your_age. We're using Python's input() function to tell Python that we want the user to enter (or *input*) something with the keyboard. *Input* is what we call information that's entered into a program while it's running—in this case, the user's name and age. The part in quotes inside the parentheses, ("What is your name? "), is called the *prompt* because it prompts the user, or asks them a question requiring their input.

In the last three lines, we tell the computer to print out the value we stored in my_name and the other three variables. We even use your_name twice, and the computer remembers everything correctly, including the parts the user typed as input.

This program remembers my name and age, asks the user for theirs, and prints a nice message to them, as shown in Figure 3-1.

Figure 3-1: A program with four variables and the output it creates

NUMBERS AND MATH IN PYTHON

The computer is great at remembering values. We can use the same variable hundreds or thousands of times in the same program, and the computer will always give us the right value as long as we've programmed it correctly. Computers are also great at performing calculations (addition, subtraction, and so on). Your computer is able to perform over *one billion* (1,000,000,000, or a thousand million) calculations every *second*!

That's much faster than we can compute numbers in our heads; although we're still better than computers at some tasks, fast math is a contest the computer will win every time. Python gives you access to that mathematical computing power with two main types of numbers, and it also lets you use a whole set of symbols to do math with those numbers, from + to - and beyond.

PYTHON NUMBERS

The two primary types of numbers in Python are called *integers* (whole numbers, including negatives, like 7, -9, or 0) and *floating-point numbers* (numbers with decimals, like 1.0, 2.5, 0.999, or 3.14159265). There are two additional number types that we won't use much in this book. The first is *Booleans*, which hold true or false values (sort of like the answers on a "true or false" test at school), and the second is *complex numbers*, which hold even imaginary number values (this might excite you if you know some advanced algebra, but we're keeping it real here—pun intended).

Integers, or whole numbers, are useful for counting (our variable x in Chapter 2 counted the number of lines as we drew the spiral) and for basic math (2 + 2 = 4). We usually state our age in whole numbers, so when you say you're 5 or 16 or 42, you're using an integer. When you count to 10, you're using integers.

Floating-point, or decimal, numbers are great when we want fractions, like 3.5 miles, 1.25 pizzas, or $25.97. Of course, in Python, we don't include the units (miles, pizzas, dollars), just the number with the decimal. So if we want to store a variable with the cost of our pizza (cost_of_pizza), we might assign it as follows: cost_of_pizza = 25.97. We'll just have to remember that the units we're using there are dollars, euros, or some other currency.

PYTHON OPERATORS

The math symbols like + (plus) and - (minus) are called *operators* because they operate, or perform calculations, on the numbers in our equation. When we say "4 + 2" aloud or enter it on our calculator, we want to perform addition on the numbers 4 and 2 to get their sum, 6.

Python uses most of the same operators that you would use in a math class, including +, -, and parentheses, (), as shown in Table 3-1. However, some operators are different from what you may have used in school, like the multiplication operator (the asterisk, *, instead of ×) and the division operator (the forward slash, /, instead of ÷). We'll get to know these operators better in this section.

Table 3-1: Basic Math Operators in Python

Math symbol	Python operator	Operation	Example	Result
+	+	Addition	4 + 2	6
−	-	Subtraction	4 - 2	2
×	*	Multiplication	4 * 2	8
÷	/	Division	4 / 2	2.0
4^2	**	Exponent or power	4 ** 2	16
()	()	Parentheses (grouping)	(4 + 2) * 3	18

DOING MATH IN THE PYTHON SHELL

This is a great time to give Python math a try; let's use the Python shell this time. As you might remember from Chapter 1, the Python shell gives you direct access to Python's power without writing a whole program. It's sometimes called the *command line* because you can type commands line by line and instantly see the result. You can type a math problem (called an *expression* in programming) like 4 + 2 directly at the command prompt (the >>> symbol with the flashing cursor) in the Python shell, and when you press ENTER, you'll see the *result* of the expression, or the answer to the math problem.

Try typing some of the examples listed in Table 3-1 and see what Python says; Figure 3-2 shows some sample output. Feel free to try your own math problems as well.

```
76                     Python Shell         –  ☐   ✕
File  Edit  Shell  Debug  Options  Windows  Help
>>> 4 + 2
6
>>> 4 - 2
2
>>> 4 * 2
8
>>> 4 / 2
2.0
>>> 4 ** 2
16
>>> (4 + 2) * 3
18
>>> |

GUI: OFF (TK)                          Ln: 13 Col: 4
```

Figure 3-2: Type the example math problems (expressions) from Table 3-1, and Python gives the answers!

SYNTAX ERRORS: WHAT DID YOU SAY?

While we're typing in the Python shell, we have a chance to learn about *syntax errors*. Whenever Python, or any programming language, can't understand the command you typed, it may respond with a message like "Syntax Error". This means there was a problem with the *way* you asked the computer to do something, or your syntax.

Syntax is the set of rules we follow in building sentences or *statements* in a language. When we program computers, we call a mistake in a statement a syntax error; when we make a mistake in a sentence in English, we might call it bad grammar. The difference is that, unlike English speakers, computers can't understand bad grammar *at all*. Python, like most programming languages, is very good at performing calculations as long as we follow syntax rules, but it can't understand anything we're saying if we mess up the syntax. Take a look at Figure 3-3 to see some examples of syntax errors, followed by the expressions stated in a way that Python can understand.

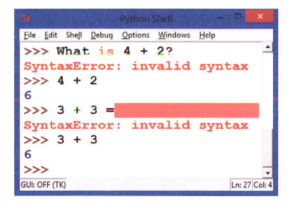

Figure 3-3: Learning to speak Python's language

When we ask Python "What is 4 + 2?" in regular English, Python responds with "SyntaxError: invalid syntax" to let us know that it can't understand what we've asked it to do. When we give Python the correct expression, 4 + 2, Python will answer correctly every time: 6. In the same way, an extra character, like the equal sign at the end of the statement 3 + 3 =, confuses Python because Python sees the equal sign as an assignment operator to assign a value to a variable. When we type 3 + 3 and press ENTER, Python understands and will always give the right answer: 6.

The fact that we can rely on a computer to answer correctly and quickly every time we give it proper input is one of the most powerful aspects of coding. We can count on computers for fast, accurate calculations, as long as we program them correctly in a language they understand. That's what you're learning to do as you learn to code in Python.

VARIABLES IN THE PYTHON SHELL

As we've discussed, the Python shell gives us direct access to the programming power of Python without having to write entire stand-alone programs. We can even use variables, like x and my_age, when we're typing in the Python shell; we just have to assign them values, as you learned to do in this chapter's opening example.

If you type x = 5 at the command prompt (>>>), Python will store the value 5 in memory as the variable x and will remember it until you tell Python to change the value (for example, by entering x = 9 to give x a new value of 9). See the examples in the Python shell in Figure 3-4.

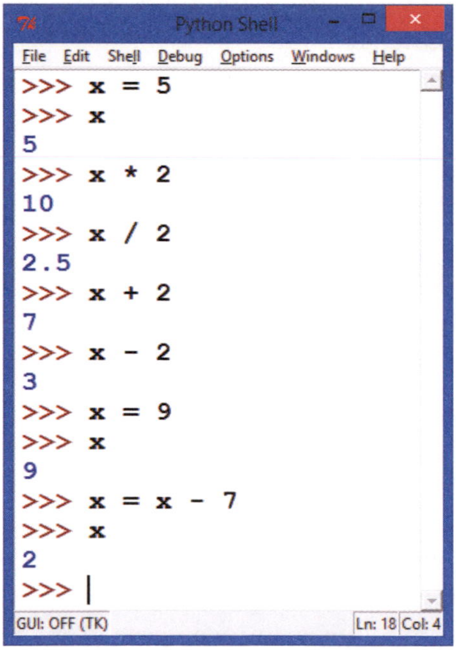

```
>>> x = 5
>>> x
5
>>> x * 2
10
>>> x / 2
2.5
>>> x + 2
7
>>> x - 2
3
>>> x = 9
>>> x
9
>>> x = x - 7
>>> x
2
>>> |
```

Figure 3-4: Python remembers our variable's value for as long as we want.

Notice that in the last assignment statement, we used x on *both sides* of the equal sign: x = x - 7. In an algebra class, this would be an invalid statement, since x can never equal x - 7. But in a program, the computer evaluates the right side of the equation *first*, calculating the value of x - 7 *before* it assigns that value to the x on the left side. Variables on the right side of the equal sign get substituted with their values; here, the value of x is 9, so the computer plugs 9 into x - 7 to get 9 - 7, which is 2. Finally, the variable on the left side of the equal sign, x, is assigned the result of the calculation from the right side. The value of x changes only at the end of the assignment process.

Before we move on to a programming example, let's go over one additional feature of math in Python. In Table 3-1 and in Figures 3-2 and 3-4, we used the division operator—the forward slash (/)—and Python responded with a decimal value. For 4 / 2, Python gave us 2.0, not the 2 that we might expect. This is because Python uses what it calls *true division*, which is meant to be easier to understand and less likely to cause errors.

We see the positive effect of Python's true division in Figure 3-4 when we ask Python to calculate x / 2, with x equal to 5. Python tells us that 5 divided by 2 is equal to 2.5, which *is* the result we expect. This division is like dividing five pizzas equally between two teams: each team gets 2.5 pizzas (the result of 5 / 2). In some programming languages, the division operator returns only the whole number (that would be 2 in this case). Just remember that Python does "pizza division."

PROGRAMMING WITH OPERATORS: A PIZZA CALCULATOR

Speaking of pizza, now let's imagine you own a pizzeria.

Let's write a small program to figure out the total cost of a simple pizza order, including sales tax. Say we're ordering one or more pizzas that all cost the same, and we're ordering in Atlanta, Georgia, in the United States. There's a sales tax that's not included in the menu price but is added at the end of the purchase. The rate is 8 percent, meaning that for every dollar we pay for the pizza, we must also pay eight cents in sales tax. We could model this program in words as follows:

1. Ask the person how many pizzas they want.
2. Ask for the menu cost of each pizza.

3. Calculate the total cost of the pizzas as our subtotal.
4. Calculate the sales tax owed, at 8 percent of the subtotal.
5. Add the sales tax to the subtotal for the final total.
6. Show the user the total amount due, including tax.

We've seen how to ask the user for input. To calculate with numbers we've entered as input, we need one more function: eval(). The eval() function *evaluates*, or figures out the value of, the input that we typed. Keyboard input in Python is always received as a string of text characters, so we use eval() to turn that input into a number. So if we type "20" into our program, eval("20") would give us the number value 20, which we can then use in math formulas to calculate new numbers, like the cost of 20 pizzas. The eval() function is pretty powerful when it comes to working with numbers in Python.

Now that we know how to turn user input into numbers that we can calculate with, we can convert the numbered steps of our program plan into actual code.

NOTE *For each programming example, you can try writing your own program first, before you look at the code in the book. Start by writing comments (#) outlining the steps you'll need to solve the problem. Then fill in the programming steps below each comment, checking the code in the book when you need a hint.*

Type this into a new window and save it as *AtlantaPizza.py*.

AtlantaPizza.py

```python
# AtlantaPizza.py - a simple pizza cost calculator

# Ask the person how many pizzas they want, get the number with eval()
number_of_pizzas = eval(input("How many pizzas do you want? "))

# Ask for the menu cost of each pizza
cost_per_pizza = eval(input("How much does each pizza cost? "))

# Calculate the total cost of the pizzas as our subtotal
subtotal = number_of_pizzas * cost_per_pizza

# Calculate the sales tax owed, at 8% of the subtotal
tax_rate = 0.08   # Store 8% as the decimal value 0.08
sales_tax = subtotal * tax_rate
```

```
# Add the sales tax to the subtotal for the final total
total = subtotal + sales_tax

# Show the user the total amount due, including tax
print("The total cost is $",total)
print("This includes $", subtotal, "for the pizza and")
print("$", sales_tax, "in sales tax.")
```

This program combines what you've learned about variables and operators into a single powerful program. Read through it and make sure you understand how each part works. How would you change the program to make it work for a different rate of sales tax?

Notice that we have included the steps of our program as comments, using the # (hash mark). Remember that comments are there for humans to read; the IDLE editor colors comments red to remind us that Python will ignore those parts. This practice of spelling out our programs step by step in words first, then putting those steps into our program as comments, can be very helpful as we build longer and more complex programs. This is our algorithm, the set of steps to be followed in our program. Algorithms are like recipes: if we follow all the steps in the right order, our program turns out great!

When we write our algorithm in words (as # comments) *and* in code (as programming statements), we're accomplishing two goals. First, we're reducing errors in our program by making sure we don't leave out steps. Second, we're making our program easier for us and others to read and understand later. You should get in the habit of writing clear comments in your programs from the very beginning, and we'll do this often throughout the book. If you don't want to type all of the comments, the program will still run; they're just there to help you understand what the program is doing.

When you've written your program, you can run it and interact with it by going to **Run ▸ Run Module**. Figure 3-5 shows some sample output.

Figure 3-5: A sample run of our AtlantaPizza.py pizza calculator program

STRINGS: THE REAL CHARACTERS IN PYTHON

We've seen that Python is terrific at working with numbers, but what about when we want to communicate with people? People are better at understanding words and sentences, rather than just numbers all by themselves. To write programs that people can use, we need another variable type known as *strings*. Strings are what we call *text*, or keyboard characters, in a programming language; they are groups (or "strings") of letters, numbers, and symbols. Your name is a string, as is your favorite color—even this paragraph (or this whole book) is a long string of letters, spaces, numbers, and symbols all mixed together.

One difference between strings and numbers is that we can't calculate with strings; they're usually names, words, or other information that can't go into a calculator. A common way to use strings is in printing. For example, we asked the user for their name in our program at the beginning of the chapter so that we could print it out later.

Let's do that again with a new program. We'll ask the user for their name, store their name in a variable called name, and then print their name on the screen 100 times. As in our cool spiral drawing examples in Chapters 1 and 2, we're using a *loop* to repeat the printing of the user's name 100 times. Type the following code into a new IDLE window and save it as *SayMyName.py*.

SayMyName.py

```
# SayMyName.py - prints a screen full of the user's name

# Ask the user for their name
name = input("What is your name? ")

# Print their name 100 times
for x in range(100):
    # Print their name followed by a space, not a new line
    print(name, end = " ")
```

There's something new in the `print()` statement in this program's last line: it contains a *keyword argument*. In this case, the *keyword* is end, and we're telling the program to *end* each `print()` statement with a space (there's a space between our quotes: " ") instead of the regular end-of-line character. Print statements in Python usually end with the newline character, which is like pressing ENTER on your keyboard, but with this keyword argument we are telling Python we don't want every printout of our name to be on a new line.

To see this change a little more clearly, modify the last line of the program to the following, and then run the program:

```
print(name, end = " rules! ")
```

If you run this, you'll see "*Your Name* rules!" printed 100 times! The keyword argument end = " rules! " lets us change how the `print()` statement works. The end of every `print()` statement is now " rules! " instead of a RETURN or ENTER newline character.

In programming languages, an *argument* isn't a bad thing; it's simply how we tell a function, like `print()`, to do something. We do so by putting extra values inside the parentheses for that function. Those values inside the `print()` statement's parentheses are the arguments, and the special keyword argument means that we're using the keyword end to change the way `print()` ends each line it prints. When we change the end of the line from the newline character to a simple space character, words are added to the end of the current line without *returning*, or starting a new line, until the current line fills up completely and wraps around to the next one. Take a look at the result in Figure 3-6.

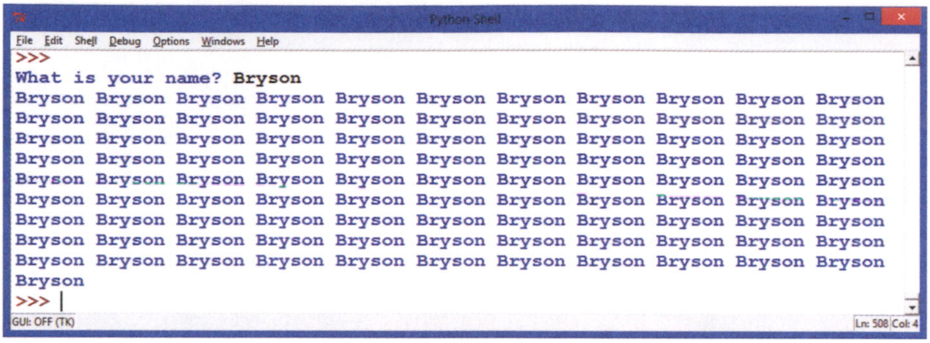

Figure 3-6: Python prints a screen full of my name when I run SayMyName.py.

IMPROVING OUR COLOR SPIRAL WITH STRINGS

Strings are so popular that even turtle graphics in Python have functions for taking strings as input and writing them to the screen. The function to ask a user for a string, or text, in the Turtle library is turtle.textinput(); this opens a pop-up window asking the user for text input and lets us store that as a string value. Figure 3-7 shows the nice graphical window that Turtle pops up for us when we use turtle.textinput("Enter your name", "What is your name?"). There are two arguments in Turtle's textinput() function. The first argument, "Enter your name", is the window title for the pop-up window. The second argument, "What is your name?", is the prompt that asks the user for the information we want.

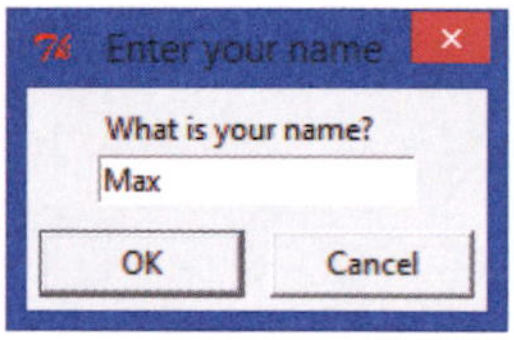

Figure 3-7: A text input window in turtle graphics

The function for writing a string on the turtle screen is write(); it draws text in the turtle's pen color and at the turtle's location on the screen. We can use write() and turtle.textinput() to combine the power of strings with colorful turtle graphics. Let's give it a try! In the following program, we'll set up turtle graphics just like in our earlier spirals, but instead of drawing lines or circles on the screen, we'll ask the user for their name and then draw it on the screen in a colorful spiral. Type this into a new window and save it as *SpiralMyName.py*.

SpiralMyName.py

```
# SpiralMyName.py - prints a colorful spiral of the user's name

import turtle                    # Set up turtle graphics
t = turtle.Pen()
turtle.bgcolor("black")
colors = ["red", "yellow", "blue", "green"]

# Ask the user's name using turtle's textinput pop-up window
❶ your_name = turtle.textinput("Enter your name", "What is your name?")

# Draw a spiral of the name on the screen, written 100 times
for x in range(100):
    t.pencolor(colors[x%4])  # Rotate through the four colors
❷    t.penup()                # Don't draw the regular spiral lines
❸    t.forward(x*4)           # Just move the turtle on the screen
❹    t.pendown()              # Write the user's name, bigger each time
❺    t.write(your_name, font = ("Arial", int( (x + 4) / 4), "bold") )
    t.left(92)                # Turn left, just as in our other spirals
```

Most of the code in *SpiralMyName.py* looks just like our earlier color spirals, but we ask the user their name in a turtle.textinput pop-up window at ❶ and store the user's answer in your_name. We've also changed the drawing loop by lifting the turtle's pen off the screen at ❷ so when we move the turtle forward at ❸, it doesn't leave a trail or draw the normal spiral line. All we want in the spiral is the user's name, so after the turtle moves at ❸, we tell it to start drawing again with t.pendown() at ❹. Then with the write command at ❺, we tell the turtle to write your_name on the screen every time through the loop. The final result is a lovely spiral; my son Max ran the one shown in Figure 3-8.

Figure 3-8: A colorful text spiral

LISTS: KEEPING IT ALL TOGETHER

In addition to strings and number values, variables can also contain lists. A *list* is a group of values, separated by commas, between square brackets, []. We can store any value type in lists, including numbers and strings; we can even have lists of lists.

In our spiral programs, we stored a list of strings—["red", "yellow", "blue", "green"]—in the colors variable. Then, when our program needed to use a color, we just called the t.pencolor() function and told it to use the list colors to find the name of the color it should use next. Let's add some more color names to our list of colors and learn one more input function in the Turtle package: numinput().

To red, yellow, blue, and green, let's add four more named colors: orange, purple, white, and gray. Next, we want to ask the user how many sides their shape should have. Just as the turtle.textinput()

function asked the user for a string, `turtle.numinput()` allows the user to enter a number.

We'll use this `numinput()` function to ask the user for the number of sides (between 1 and 8), and we'll give the user a *default* choice of 4, meaning that if the user doesn't enter a number, the program will automatically use 4 as the number of sides. Type the following code into a new window and save it as *ColorSpiralInput.py*.

ColorSpiralInput.py

```
import turtle                          # Set up turtle graphics
t = turtle.Pen()
turtle.bgcolor("black")
# Set up a list of any 8 valid Python color names
colors = ["red", "yellow", "blue", "green", "orange", "purple", "white", "gray"]
# Ask the user for the number of sides, between 1 and 8, with a default of 4
sides = int(turtle.numinput("Number of sides",
                            "How many sides do you want (1-8)?", 4, 1, 8))
# Draw a colorful spiral with the user-specified number of sides
for x in range(360):
    t.pencolor(colors[x % sides])      # Only use the right number of colors
    t.forward(x * 3 / sides + x)       # Change the size to match number of sides
    t.left(360 / sides + 1)            # Turn 360 degrees / number of sides, plus 1
    t.width(x * sides / 200)           # Make the pen larger as it goes outward
```

❶ `t.pencolor(colors[x % sides])`
❷ `t.forward(x * 3 / sides + x)`
❸ `t.left(360 / sides + 1)`
❹ `t.width(x * sides / 200)`

This program uses the number of sides the user entered to do some calculations every time it draws a new side. Let's look at the four numbered lines inside the for loop.

At ❶, the program changes the turtle's pen color, matching the number of colors to the number of sides (triangles use three colors for the three sides, squares use four colors, and so on). At ❷, we change the lengths of each line based on the number of sides (so that triangles aren't too much smaller than octagons on our screen).

At ❸, we turn the turtle by the correct number of degrees. To get this number, we divide 360 by the number of sides, which gives us the *exterior angle*, or the angle we need to turn to draw a regular shape with that number of sides. For example, a circle is 360 degrees with one "side"; a square is made up of four 90-degree angles (also 360 degrees total); you need six 60-degree turns to go around a hexagon (also 360 degrees total); and so on.

Finally, at ❹, we increase the width or thickness of the pen as we get farther from the center of the screen. Figure 3-9 shows the drawings that result from entering eight sides and three sides.

Figure 3-9: The picture from ColorSpiralInput.py with eight sides (left) and three sides (right)

PYTHON DOES YOUR HOMEWORK

We've seen that Python is a powerful and fun programming language that can handle all sorts of data: numbers, strings, lists, and even complex math expressions. Now you're going to put Python's power to work to do something very practical: your math homework!

We're going to write a short program that combines strings and numbers, using the eval() function to turn math problems into answers. Earlier in the chapter, I said that the eval() function could turn the string "20" into the number 20. As promised, eval() can do even more than that: it can also turn "2 * 10" into the number 20. When the eval() function operates on a string of keyboard characters, it evaluates them just like the Python shell would. So when we enter a math problem as input, running eval() on that input can give us the answer to the problem.

By printing the original problem that the user entered, then outputting eval(*problem*), we can show the original problem and the answer all on one line. Remember the operators in Table 3-1: if you needed the answer to 5 ÷ 2, you'd type 5 / 2, and for 4², you'd type 4 ** 2. Here's what our program, *MathHomework.py*, looks like when we put it together:

MathHomework.py

```python
print("MathHomework.py")
# Ask the user to enter a math problem
problem = input("Enter a math problem, or 'q' to quit: ")
# Keep going until the user enters 'q' to quit
while (problem != "q"):
    # Show the problem, and the answer using eval()
    print("The answer to ", problem, "is:", eval(problem) )
    # Ask for another math problem
    problem = input("Enter another math problem, or 'q' to quit: ")
    # This while loop will keep going until you enter 'q' to quit
```

This while statement will keep asking for problems and printing answers until the user presses the Q key to quit the program.

While this short program can't help us with algebra yet, it can do more than basic math. Remember our discussion about Python's true division? We called it "pizza division," because it let us split pizzas evenly among any number of people. Well, Python can still do integer division (whole-number division); we just need to learn two new operators.

When would you want to do integer division? Let's say your teacher gives you and your three friends 10 cartons of chocolate milk to enjoy, and you want to divide the milk fairly so that each of you gets the same number of cartons. There are four of you (you plus three friends), so 10 ÷ 4 equals 2.5. Unfortunately, you can't just cut a carton of milk in half. If you had cups, you could split a carton between two friends, but let's pretend there are no cups around. If you wanted to be fair, you would have to take two cartons each, and give the teacher back the remaining two cartons. That sounds a lot like long division: the two leftover cartons that you return to the teacher are the *remainder* when you divide 10 by 4. In math, we sometimes note the remainder from long division like this: 10 ÷ 4 = 2 R2. In other words, 10 divided by 4 equals a *quotient* of 2, with a remainder of 2. This means that 4 goes into 10 evenly 2 times, with 2 remaining.

In Python, integer division is performed with the double-forward slash operator, //. So 10 // 4 equals 2, and 7 // 4 equals 1 (because 4 goes into 7 only 1 time, with a remainder of 3). The // operator gives us our quotient, but what about the remainder? To get the remainder, we use the modulo operator, which we represent in Python with the % symbol. Don't confuse % with percent—in Python, you'll write percentages as decimals (5% becomes 0.05), and the % operator is *always* the *modulus*, or remainder resulting from integer division. To get the remainder of long division in Python, type **10 % 4** (gives a remainder of 2) or **7 % 4** (equals a remainder of 3). Figure 3-10 shows the result of several math operations, including integer division and remainders using the // and % operators.

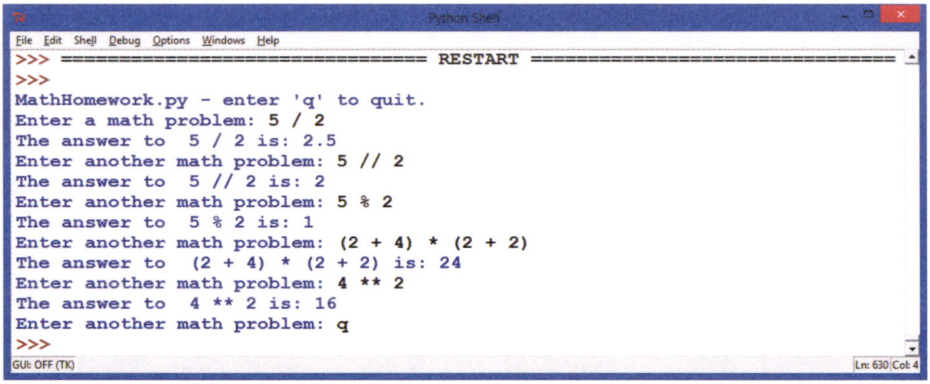

```
>>> ================================ RESTART ================================
>>>
MathHomework.py - enter 'q' to quit.
Enter a math problem: 5 / 2
The answer to  5 / 2 is: 2.5
Enter another math problem: 5 // 2
The answer to  5 // 2 is: 2
Enter another math problem: 5 % 2
The answer to  5 % 2 is: 1
Enter another math problem: (2 + 4) * (2 + 2)
The answer to  (2 + 4) * (2 + 2) is: 24
Enter another math problem: 4 ** 2
The answer to  4 ** 2 is: 16
Enter another math problem: q
>>>
```

Figure 3-10: Python tackles your math homework.

As we continue through the book, we'll be using the % operator in programs like our spiral drawings to keep numbers fixed in a certain range.

WHAT YOU LEARNED

In this chapter, you've seen how to store different types of information, including numbers, lists, and strings, in variables. You learned the rules for naming variables in Python (letters, underscores, numbers; case sensitive; no spaces) and how to assign values to them with the equal sign operator (`my_name = "Alex"` or `my_age = 5`).

You also learned about integers (whole numbers) and floating-point numbers (decimal values). You learned about the various math operators in Python and how they differ from the symbols you might use in a math textbook. You saw how to use strings of words, letters, characters, and symbols, including how to make Python understand and evaluate certain strings, like when we wanted to use a number that the user entered to perform calculations.

You saw a few examples of syntax errors and learned how to avoid some of them when you program. You learned about the list variable type, which you can use to store lists of all kinds of values, such as colors = ["red", "yellow", "blue", "green"]. You even found out how Python can help you with simple calculations, including long division.

You'll build on your understanding of variables and data types as you learn how to use variables to create your own loops in Chapter 4, use the computer to make decisions in Chapter 5, and even program the computer to play games in Chapter 6 and beyond. Variables are the first, crucial programming tools that help us break down the most complex problems, from video games to satellites to medical software, into small chunks that we can solve with code. Work on the samples from this chapter, and create your own examples, until you're familiar enough with variables to dig in to the next chapter.

At this point, you should be able to do the following:

- Create your own variables to store numbers, strings, and lists.

- Discuss the differences between number types in Python.

- Use basic math operators in Python to perform calculations.

- Explain the difference between strings, numbers, and lists.

- Write out short programs as steps in English and then write those steps as comments to help you build your code.

- Ask for user input in a variety of situations and use that input in your programs.

PROGRAMMING CHALLENGES

To practice what you've learned in this chapter, try these challenges. (If you get stuck, go to *http://www.nostarch .com/teachkids/* for sample answers.)

#1: CIRCULAR SPIRALS

Look back at the *ColorCircleSpiral.py* program in Chapter 2 (page 24) that drew circles instead of lines on each side of the spiral. Run that example again and see if you can determine which lines of code you'd need to add to and delete from the *ColorSpiralInput.py* program (page 47) to be able to draw circular spirals with any number of sides between one and eight. Once you get it working, save the new program as *CircleSpiralInput.py*.

#2: CUSTOM NAME SPIRALS

Wouldn't it be cool to ask the user how many sides their spiral should have, ask for their name, and then draw a spiral that writes their name in the correct number of spiral sides and colors? See if you can figure out which parts of *SpiralMyName.py* (page 45) to incorporate into *ColorSpiralInput.py* (page 47) to create this new, impressive design. When you get it right (or come up with something even cooler), save the new program as *ColorMeSpiralled.py*.

LOOPS ARE FUN
(YOU CAN SAY THAT AGAIN)

We've used loops since our very first program to draw repeating shapes. Now it's time to learn how to build our own loops from scratch. Whenever we need to do something over and over again in a program, loops allow us to repeat those steps without having to type each one separately. Figure 4-1 shows a visual example—a rosette made up of four circles.

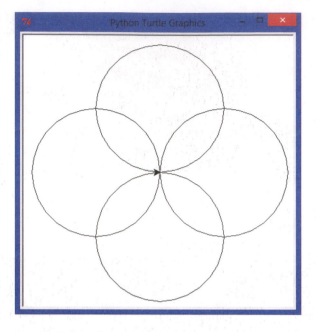

Figure 4-1: A four-circle rosette pattern

Let's think about how we might write a program to draw four circles overlapping as shown. As you saw in Chapter 2, Turtle's circle() command draws a circle with the radius we specify inside its parentheses. Those circles look like they're at the north, south, east, and west of the screen, 90 degrees apart, and we know how to turn left or right 90 degrees. So we could write four pairs of statements to draw a circle, then turn 90 degrees, and then draw another circle, as in the following code. Type this into a new window and save it as *Rosette.py*.

Rosette.py

```python
import turtle
t = turtle.Pen()
t.circle(100) # This makes our first circle (pointing north)
t.left(90)    # Then the turtle turns left 90 degrees
t.circle(100) # This makes our second circle (pointing west)
t.left(90)    # Then the turtle turns left 90 degrees
t.circle(100) # This makes our third circle (pointing south)
t.left(90)    # Then the turtle turns left 90 degrees
t.circle(100) # This makes our fourth circle (pointing east)
```

This code works, but doesn't it feel repetitive? We typed the code to draw a circle four times and the code to turn left three times. We know from our spiral examples that we should be able to write a chunk of code once and reuse that code in a for loop. In this chapter, we're going to learn how to write those loops ourselves. Let's try it now!

BUILDING YOUR OWN FOR LOOPS

To build our own loop, we first need to identify the repeated steps. The instructions that we're repeating in the preceding code are t.circle(100) to draw a turtle circle with a radius of 100 pixels and t.left(90) to turn the turtle left 90 degrees before drawing the next circle. Second, we need to figure out how many times to repeat those steps. We want four circles, so let's start with four.

Now that we know the two repeated instructions and the number of times to draw the circle, it's time to build our for loop.

A for loop in Python *iterates over* a list of items, or repeats once for each item in a list—like the numbers 1 through 100, or 0 through 9. We want our loop to run four times—once for each circle—so we need to set up a list of four numbers.

The built-in function range() allows us to easily create lists of numbers. The simplest command to construct a range of n numbers is range(n); this command will let us build a list of n numbers from 0 to $n - 1$ (from zero to one less than our number n).

For example, range(10) allows us to create a list of the 10 numbers from 0 to 9. Let's enter a few sample range() commands in the IDLE command prompt window to see how this works. To see our lists printed out, we'll need to use the list() function around our range. At the >>> prompt, enter this line of code:

```
>>> list(range(10))
```

IDLE will give you the output [0, 1, 2, 3, 4, 5, 6, 7, 8, 9]: a list of 10 numbers, starting from 0. To get longer or shorter lists of numbers, you can enter different numbers inside the parentheses of the range() function:

```
>>> list(range(3))
[0, 1, 2]
>>> list(range(5))
[0, 1, 2, 3, 4]
```

As you can see, entering list(range(3)) gives you a list of three numbers starting at 0, and entering list(range(5)) gives you a list of five numbers starting at 0.

USING A FOR LOOP TO MAKE A ROSETTE WITH FOUR CIRCLES

For our four-circle rosette shape, we need to repeat drawing a circle four times, and range(4) will help us do that. The syntax, or word order, of our for loop will look like this:

```
for x in range(4):
```

We start with the keyword for and then we give a variable, x, that will be our counter or *iterator* variable. The in keyword tells the for loop to step x through each of the values in the range list, and range(4) gives the loop a list of the numbers from 0 to 3, [0,1,2,3], to step through. Remember that the computer usually starts counting from 0 instead of starting from 1 as we do.

To tell the computer which instructions are supposed to be repeated, we use *indentation*; we indent each command that we want to repeat in the loop by pressing the TAB key in the new file window. Type this new version of our program and save it as *Rosette4.py*.

Rosette4.py

```
import turtle
t = turtle.Pen()
for x in range(4):
    t.circle(100)
    t.left(90)
```

This is a much shorter version of our *Rosette.py* program, thanks to the for loop, yet it produces the same four circles as the version without the loop. This program loops through lines 3,

4, and 5 a total of four times, generating a rosette of four circles on the top, left, bottom, and right sides of our window. Let's take a step-by-step look through the loop as it draws our rosette, one circle at a time.

1. The first time through the loop, our counter x has a starting value of 0, the first value in the range list [0, 1, 2, 3]. We draw our first circle at the top of the window with t.circle(100) and then turn the turtle to the left by 90 degrees with t.left(90).

2. Python goes back to the beginning of the loop and sets x to 1, the second value in [0, 1, 2, 3]. Then it draws the second circle on the left side of the window and turns the turtle left by 90 degrees.

    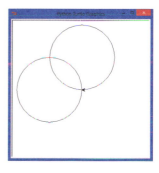

3. Python goes back through the loop again, increasing x to 2. It draws the third circle at the bottom of the window and turns the turtle left.

    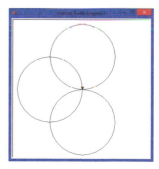

4. On the fourth and final time through the loop, Python increases x to 3, then runs t.circle(100) and t.left(90) to draw our fourth circle on the right side of the window and turn the turtle. The rosette is now complete.

    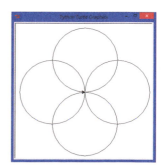

MODIFYING OUR FOR LOOP TO MAKE A ROSETTE WITH SIX CIRCLES

Now that we've built our own for loop together from scratch, could you modify the program on your own to draw something new? What if we wanted to draw a rosette with six circles instead of four? What might we need to change in our program? Take a moment to think about how you might solve this problem.

*   *   *

Did you come up with some ideas? Let's walk through the problem together. First, we know that we need six circles this time instead of four, so our range will need to change to range(6) in our for loop. But if we just change that, we're not going to see any difference in our drawing, because we'll continue to draw over the same four circles separated by 90 degrees. If we want six circles around the rosette, we'll need to divide the rosette into six left turns instead of four. There are 360 degrees around the center of our drawing: four 90-degree turns took us 4 × 90 = 360 degrees all the way around. If we divide 360 by 6 instead of 4, we get 360 ÷ 6 = 60 degrees for each turn. So in our t.left() command, we need to turn left 60 degrees each time through the loop, or t.left(60).

Modify your rosette program and save it as *Rosette6.py*.

Rosette6.py

```
import turtle
t = turtle.Pen()
❶ for x in range(6):
❷     t.circle(100)
❸     t.left(60)
```

This time, the for loop statement in ❶ will step x through the list of six values from 0 to 5, so we'll repeat the indented steps ❷ and ❸ six times each. At ❷, we're still drawing a circle with a radius of 100. At ❸, though, we're turning only 60 degrees each turn, or one-sixth of 360 degrees, so we get six circles around the center of the screen this time, as shown in Figure 4-2.

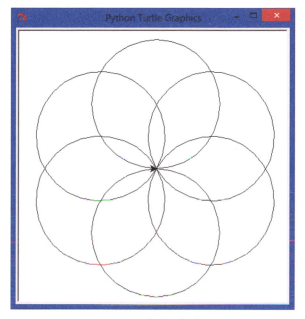

Figure 4-2: A rosette of six circles

The rosette with six circles is even prettier than the one with four circles, and thanks to our for loop, we didn't have to write any more lines of code to get six circles than we did to get four—we just changed two numbers! Because we varied those two numbers, you may be tempted to replace them with a variable. Let's give in to that temptation. Let's give the user the power to draw a rosette with *any* number of circles.

IMPROVING OUR ROSETTE PROGRAM WITH USER INPUT

In this section, we'll use the turtle.numinput() function that we saw in Chapter 3 (see *ColorSpiralInput.py* on page 47) to write a program that asks the user to enter a number and then draws a rosette with that number of circles. We'll set the user's number as the size of our range() constructor. Then, all we have to do is divide

360 degrees by that number, and we'll find the number of degrees to turn left each pass through the loop. Type and run the following code as *RosetteGoneWild.py*:

RosetteGoneWild.py

```
import turtle
t = turtle.Pen()
# Ask the user for the number of circles in their rosette, default to 6
❶ number_of_circles = int(turtle.numinput("Number of circles",
                                  "How many circles in your rosette?", 6))
❷ for x in range(number_of_circles):
❸     t.circle(100)
❹     t.left(360/number_of_circles)
```

At ❶, we assign a variable called `number_of_circles` using a couple of functions together. We're using Turtle's `numinput()` function to ask the user how many circles to draw. The first value, `Number of circles`, is the pop-up window's title; the second, `How many circles in your rosette?`, is the text that will appear in the box; and the last, `6`, is a default value in case the user doesn't enter anything. The `int()` function outside `numinput()` turns the user's number into an integer we can use in our `range()` function. We store the user's number as `number_of_circles` to use as the size of the `range()` in our drawing loop.

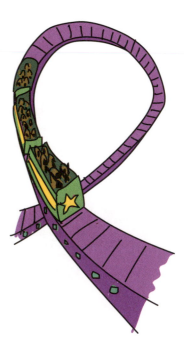

The `for` statement at ❷ is our loop. It uses the `number_of_circles` variable to loop x through a list of that many numbers. The command to draw a circle is still the same at ❸ and will draw circles with a radius of 100 pixels. At ❹, we're dividing a full turn of 360 degrees by the number of circles so we can draw the circles evenly spaced around the center of the screen. For example, if the user enters 30 as the number of circles, 360 ÷ 30 would give us a 12-degree turn between each of the 30 circles around our center point, as shown in Figure 4-3.

Run the program and try your own numbers. You can even make a rosette of 90 circles, or 200 (but you'll be waiting a while as Python draws that many circles!). Customize the program to make it your own: change the background color or the rosette color, make the circles bigger or smaller, or make them bigger *and* smaller! Play with your programs as you create them and as you think of fun things you'd like them to do. Figure 4-4 shows what my five-year-old son, Alex, dreamed up by adding just three extra lines of code to *RosetteGoneWild.py*. Go to *http://www.nostarch .com/teachkids/* for the source code.

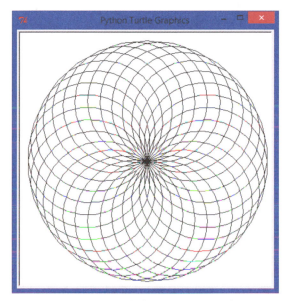

Figure 4-3: A user-defined rosette of 30 circles

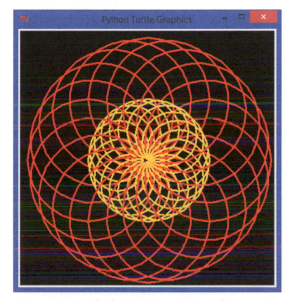

Figure 4-4: A little imagination and a touch of code can turn our rosette program into a lot of colorful fun!

GAME LOOPS AND WHILE LOOPS

The for loop is powerful, but there are limits to its power. For instance, what if we wanted to stop our loop when some event occurred, instead of going all the way through a long list of numbers? Or what if we weren't sure how many times to run our loop?

For example, consider a *game loop*—when we write a program, especially a game, where the user gets to choose whether to keep playing or to quit. We, as programmers, can't know in advance how many times users will choose to play our game or run our program, but we need to give them the ability to play again without having to reload and run the program every time. Can you imagine if you had to restart an Xbox or PlayStation every time you wanted to play a game again, or if you always had to play a game exactly 10 times before moving on to a different one? That might make it less fun.

One way we solve the game loop problem is by using another type of loop, the while loop. Instead of iterating over a predefined list of values, as the for loop does, a while loop can check for a *condition* or situation and decide whether to loop again or end the loop. The syntax of the while statement looks like this:

```
while condition:
    indented statement(s)
```

The condition is usually a *Boolean* expression, or true/false test. One everyday example of a while loop is eating and drinking. While you are hungry, you eat. When the answer to the question "Am I hungry?" is no longer yes, that means the condition "I am hungry" is no longer true, and you stop eating. While you are thirsty, you take another drink of water. When you stop feeling thirsty, you quit drinking. Hunger and thirst are conditions, and when those conditions become false, you exit the eating and drinking "loops." A while loop continues repeating the statements in the loop (the indented statements) as long as the condition is true.

The true/false conditions in while loops often involve comparing values. We might say, "Is the value of x bigger than 10? As long as it is, run this code. When x isn't bigger than 10 anymore, stop running the code." In other words, we run the code *while* the condition x > 10 evaluates to True. The greater-than symbol (>) is a *comparison operator*, a different kind of operator from arithmetic operators like + (plus) and - (minus). Comparison operators—such as > (greater than), < (less than), == (equal to), or != (not equal to)— let you compare two values to see

if one of them is greater or less than the other, or if they are equal or not equal. Is x less than 7? Yes or no? `True` or `False`? Based on the result, `True` or `False`, you can tell your program to run different pieces of code.

The `while` loop shares some features with the `for` loop. First, like the `for` loop, it repeats a set of statements over and over as needed. Second, with both `while` loops and `for` loops, we tell Python which statements to repeat by indenting them to the right with the TAB key.

Let's try a program with a `while` loop to see it in action. Type the following code (or download it from *http://www.nostarch.com/teachkids/*), and run it:

SayOurNames.py

```
  # Ask the user for their name
❶ name = input("What is your name? ")
  # Keep printing names until we want to quit
❷ while name != "":
      # Print their name 100 times
❸     for x in range(100):
          # Print their name followed by a space, not a new line
❹         print(name, end = " ")
❺     print()   # After the for loop, skip down to the next line
      # Ask for another name, or quit
❻     name = input("Type another name, or just hit [ENTER] to quit: ")
❼ print("Thanks for playing!")
```

We begin the program by asking the user their name at ❶ and storing their answer in the variable `name`. We need a name to test as the condition of our `while` loop, so we have to ask once *before* the loop starts. Then, at ❷, we start our `while` loop, which will run as long as the name the user enters is not an empty string (represented by two double quotes with nothing between them: `""`). The empty string is what Python sees as the input when the user presses ENTER to quit.

At ❸, we start our `for` loop, which will print the name 100 times, and at ❹, we tell the `print()` statement to print a space after the name each time. We'll keep going back to ❸ and checking to see if x has reached 100, then printing at ❹ until the name fills a few lines of the screen. When our `for` loop has finished printing the name 100 times, we print a blank line without a space ❺, moving the printout down to the next clear line. Then, it's time to ask for another name ❻.

Because ❻ is the last line indented under the while loop ❷, the new name that the user enters is passed back up to ❷ so the while loop can check whether it's an empty string. If it's not empty, our program will start the for loop to print the new name 100 times. If the name is an empty string, that means the user pressed ENTER to end the program, so the while loop at ❷ skips down to ❼, and we thank the user for playing. Figure 4-5 shows the output of the program when my sons ran it.

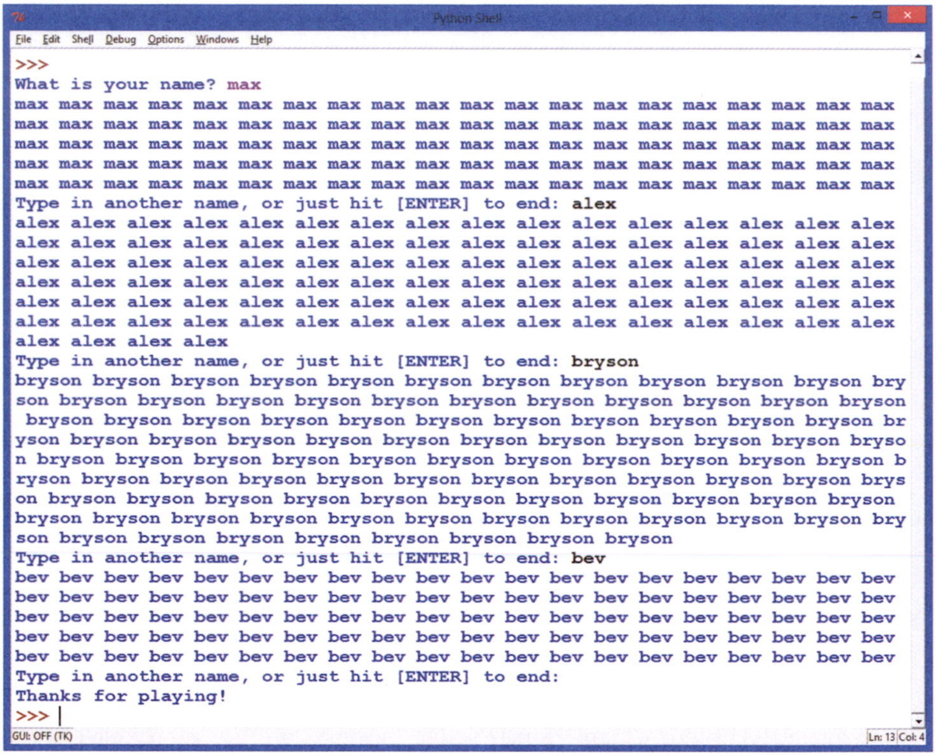

Figure 4-5: My sons ran SayOurNames.py and put in the names of everyone in our family!

THE FAMILY SPIRAL

Now that we can ask for a list of names and print them to the screen, let's combine the name printer loop with one of our programs from Chapter 3, *SpiralMyName.py* on page 45, to create a colorful spiral of our family's or friends' names.

Our new, combined program will be different from the name repeater in *SayOurNames.py* in a few ways, but the most important difference is that we can't just print each name one by one; to draw our spiral, we need to have all the names at once so that we can draw each name in sequence as we wind around our spiral.

In *SayOurNames.py*, we were able to ask for one name at a time, but for our graphical spiral name program, we'll need to keep all of the names in a list, just as we do with our colors. Then, as we go around the loop, we can change the names and colors together at each corner of the spiral. To do this, we'll set up an empty list:

```
family = []    # Set up an empty list for family names
```

Whenever we've made a list of colors in our programs, we've known the color names that we wanted to use, like red, yellow, blue, and so on. In our family list, though, we have to wait until the user enters the names. We use an empty list—a pair of square brackets, []—to let Python know that we're going to use a list called family but that we don't know what will be in the list until the program runs.

Once we have an empty list, we can ask for names in a while loop like we did in *SayOurNames.py*, and we will append those names to the list. To *append* means to add items to the end of the list. In this program, the first name the user enters will be added to the empty list, the second name will be appended after the first, and so on. When the user has entered all the names they want in their spiral, they will press ENTER to tell the program that they've finished entering names. Then we'll use a for loop to draw the names on the screen in a colorful spiral shape.

Type and run the following code to see a while loop and a for loop do some beautiful work together:

SpiralFamily.py

```
import turtle     # Set up turtle graphics
t = turtle.Pen()
turtle.bgcolor("black")
colors = ["red", "yellow", "blue", "green", "orange",
        "purple", "white", "brown", "gray", "pink" ]
❶ family = []        # Set up an empty list for family names
```

```python
    # Ask for the first name
❷  name = turtle.textinput("My family",
                            "Enter a name, or just hit [ENTER] to end:")
    # Keep asking for names
❸  while name != "":
        # Add their name to the family list
❹      family.append(name)
        # Ask for another name, or end
        name = turtle.textinput("My family",
                            "Enter a name, or just hit [ENTER] to end:")

    # Draw a spiral of the names on the screen
    for x in range(100):
❺      t.pencolor(colors[x%len(family)]) # Rotate through the colors
❻      t.penup()                          # Don't draw the regular spiral lines
❼      t.forward(x*4)                     # Just move the turtle on the screen
❽      t.pendown()                        # Draw the next family member's name
❾      t.write(family[x%len(family)], font = ("Arial", int((x+4)/4), "bold") )
❿      t.left(360/len(family) + 2)        # Turn left for our spiral
```

At ❶, we set up an empty list [] called family that will hold the names the user enters. At ❷, we ask for the first name in a turtle.textinput window and start the while loop to gather all the names in the family at ❸. The command to add a value to the end of a list is append(), shown at ❹. This takes the name the user entered and appends it to the list called family. We then ask for another name and keep repeating the while loop ❸ until the user presses ENTER to let us know they're finished.

Our for loop starts out like previous spirals, but we use a new command at ❺ to set our pen color. The len() command is short for *length* and tells us the length of the list of names stored in family. For example, if you entered four names for your family, len(family) would return 4. We use the modulo operator, %, with this value to rotate through four colors, one for each name in family. Larger families would rotate through more colors (up to the 10 colors in our list), while smaller families would need fewer colors.

At ❻, we use the penup() command to "lift" the turtle's pen off the screen so that when we move forward at ❼, the turtle won't draw anything; we'll be drawing names at the corners of the spiral, with no lines in between. At ❽, we put the turtle's pen down again so that our names will be drawn.

At ❾, we're doing a lot. First, we tell the turtle which name to draw. Notice that family[x%len(family)] uses the modulo operator, %, to rotate through the names the user entered in the `family` list. The program will start with the first name entered, `family[0]`, and continue with `family[1]`, `family[2]`, and so on until it reaches the final name in the list. The `font =` portion of this statement tells the computer we want to use the Arial font, in bold style, for our names. It also sets the font size to grow as x grows; our font size of (x+4)/4 means that when the loop finishes with x = 100, the font size will be (100 + 4) / 4 = 26-point font—a nice size. You can make the fonts bigger or smaller by changing this equation.

Finally, at ❿, we turn the turtle left by `360/len(family)` degrees plus 2. For a family with four members, we would turn 90 degrees plus 2 for a nice square spiral; a family of six would get 60-degree turns plus 2 for a six-sided spiral, and so on. The extra 2 degrees make the spiral spin to the left a bit for the swirl effect we've seen in our other spirals. In Figure 4-6, we ran this program and entered our family's names, including our two cats, Leo and Rocky, to get a wonderful family spiral picture.

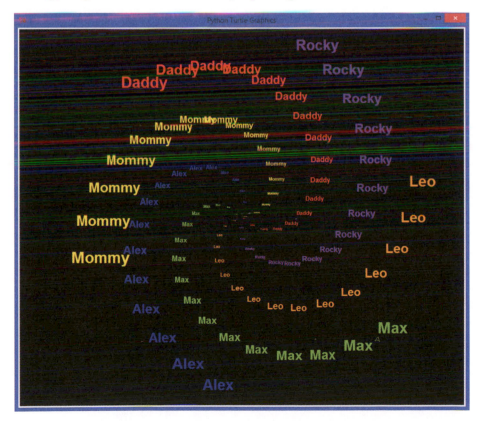

Figure 4-6: The Payne family spiral, including our two cats, Leo and Rocky

PUTTING IT ALL TOGETHER: SPIRAL GOES VIRAL

We've seen the power of loops: they take pieces of code and repeat them over and over to do repetitive work that we wouldn't want to do by hand, like typing a name 100 times. Let's take loops one step further and build our own *nested loop*, which is a loop inside another loop (like Russian nesting dolls—look inside one doll, and there's another doll).

To explore nested loops, let's draw a spiral not of names or lines but *of spirals*! Instead of drawing a name at every corner of our spiral like we did in Figure 4-6, we could draw a smaller spiral. To accomplish that, we need a big loop to draw a big spiral on the screen and a little loop inside to draw small spirals around the big spiral.

Before we write a program to do that, let's learn how to nest a loop inside another loop. First, start a loop as usual. Then, inside that loop, press TAB once and start a second loop:

```
# This is our first loop, called the outer loop
for x in range(10):
    # Things indented once will be done 10 times
    # Next is our inner loop, or the nested loop
    for y in range(10):
        # Things indented twice will be done 100 (10*10) times!
```

The first loop is called the *outer* loop, because it surrounds our nested loop. The nested loop is called the *inner* loop, because it sits inside the other loop. Notice that in our nested loop, any lines of code that are indented twice (so they're inside the second loop) will be repeated 10 times for y and 10 times for x, or 100 times total.

Let's start writing our program, *ViralSpiral.py*. We'll write it step by step—the finished program is shown on page 72.

```
import turtle
t = turtle.Pen()
❶ t.penup()
turtle.bgcolor("black")
```

The first few lines of our program look like the other spirals we've programmed, except that we won't be drawing lines for the big spiral. We plan to replace those with smaller spirals, so we have a t.penup() at ❶ to lift the turtle's pen off the screen right from the beginning. We then set the background color to black.

Keep typing: we're not done! Next we'll ask the user for the number of sides they want using turtle.numinput(), with a default of 4 if the user doesn't choose something different, and we'll restrict the range of allowable sides to between 2 and 6.

```
sides = int(turtle.numinput("Number of sides",
            "How many sides in your spiral of spirals (2-6)?", 4,2,6))
colors = ["red", "yellow", "blue", "green", "purple", "orange"]
```

The turtle.numinput() function allows us to specify a title for our input dialog; a prompt question; and default, minimum, and maximum values, in that order: turtle.numinput(*title, prompt, default, minimum, maximum*). Here, we specify a default value of 4, a minimum of 2, and a maximum of 6. (If the user tries to enter 1 or 7, for example, they'll get a warning that the minimum allowed value is 2 and the maximum allowed value is 6.) We also set up our colors list with six colors.

Next we'll write our outer spiral loop. The outer loop will position the turtle at each corner of the big spiral.

```
❷ for m in range(100):
      t.forward(m*4)
❸     position = t.position() # Remember this corner of the spiral
❹     heading = t.heading()   # Remember the direction we were heading
```

Our outer loop takes m from 0 to 99 for 100 total passes ❷. In our outer loop, we move forward just like in our other spiral programs, but when we reach each corner of our big spiral, we stop to remember our position ❸ and heading ❹. The *position* is the turtle's (x, y) coordinate location on the screen, and the *heading* is the direction the turtle is moving in.

Our turtle is taking a bit of a detour at every spot along the large spiral in order to draw the smaller spirals, so it must return to this position and heading after finishing each small spiral in order to maintain the shape of the big spiral. If we didn't remember the location and direction of the turtle before starting to draw the small spirals, our turtle would wander all over the screen, starting each small spiral relative to where it left off with the last small spiral.

The two commands that will tell us the turtle's location and direction are t.position() and t.heading(). The turtle's position is accessed through t.position(), and it consists of both the x (horizontal) and y (vertical) coordinates of the turtle's location on the screen, just like on a coordinate graph. The direction the turtle is heading is available through the command t.heading() and is measured from 0.0 degrees to 360.0 degrees, with 0.0 degrees pointing up toward the top of the screen. We will store these pieces of information in the variables position and heading before we start each small spiral so that we can pick up where we left off on the big spiral each time.

It's time for the inner loop. We're indented even farther here. This inner loop will draw a small spiral at each corner of the bigger spiral.

```
❺      for n in range(int(m/2)):
           t.pendown()
           t.pencolor(colors[n%sides])
           t.forward(2*n)
           t.right(360/sides - 2)
           t.penup()
❻      t.setx(position[0])      # Go back to the big spiral's x location
❼      t.sety(position[1])      # Go back to the big spiral's y location
❽      t.setheading(heading)    # Point in the big spiral's heading
❾      t.left(360/sides + 2)    # Aim at the next point on the big spiral
```

Our inner loop ❺ begins with n = 0 and stops when n = m/2, or one-half of m, to keep the inner spirals smaller than the outer spiral. The inner spirals look like our previous spirals, except that we put the pen down before drawing each line and lift it after each line is drawn so that our big spiral stays clean.

After we draw our inner spiral from ❺, we pick back up at ❻ by setting the horizontal position of the turtle to the one we stored at ❸. The horizontal axis is commonly called the *x-axis*, so when we set the horizontal location, we use t.setx(), or set the x-axis position of our turtle's location on the screen. At ❼, we set the y-axis location, or vertical position, that we stored at ❸. At ❽, we turn the turtle to the heading we stored at ❹ before going on to the next part of the big spiral at ❾.

When our big loop ends after m has gone from 0 to 99, we will have drawn 100 small spirals in a big spiral pattern for a nice kaleidoscope effect, as shown in Figure 4-7.

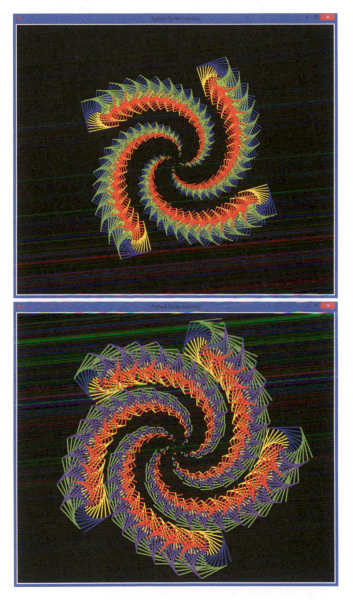

Figure 4-7: A square spiral with square spirals at every corner (top) and a five-sided (pentagonal) spiral of spirals (bottom) from our ViralSpiral.py program

You'll notice the one drawback to nested loops while you're waiting for this program to run: the shapes shown in Figure 4-7 take longer to draw than our simple spirals did. That's because we're performing so many more steps than we did with our simple spirals. In fact, when we draw the six-sided version of our *ViralSpiral.py*, the final drawing consists of 2,352 separate lines! All those drawing commands, plus the turning and setting the pen color, add up to a lot of work, even for a fast computer. Nested loops are useful, but remember that the extra steps can slow our programs down, so we use nested loops only when the effect is worth the wait.

Here's the completed code for *ViralSpiral.py*.

ViralSpiral.py

```python
import turtle
t = turtle.Pen()
t.penup()
turtle.bgcolor("black")
# Ask the user for the number of sides, default to 4, min 2, max 6
sides = int(turtle.numinput("Number of sides",
            "How many sides in your spiral of spirals? (2-6)", 4,2,6))
colors = ["red", "yellow", "blue", "green", "purple", "orange"]
# Our outer spiral loop
for m in range(100):
    t.forward(m*4)
    position = t.position() # Remember this corner of the spiral
    heading = t.heading()   # Remember the direction we were heading
    print(position, heading)
    # Our "inner" spiral loop
    # Draws a little spiral at each corner of the big spiral
    for n in range(int(m/2)):
        t.pendown()
        t.pencolor(colors[n%sides])
        t.forward(2*n)
        t.right(360/sides - 2)
        t.penup()
    t.setx(position[0])      # Go back to the big spiral's x location
    t.sety(position[1])      # Go back to the big spiral's y location
    t.setheading(heading)    # Point in the big spiral's heading
    t.left(360/sides + 2)    # Aim at the next point on the big spiral
```

WHAT YOU LEARNED

In this chapter, you learned to build your own loops by identifying repeated steps in a program and moving those repeated steps inside the right kind of loop. With a `for` loop, you can run your code a set number of times, like looping 10 times with `for x in range(10)`. With a `while` loop, you can run your code until a condition or event occurs, like the user entering nothing at an input prompt with `while name != ""`.

You learned that the flow of a program is changed by the loops that you create. We used the `range()` function to generate lists of values that allow us to control the number of times our `for` loops repeat, and we used the modulo operator, `%`, to loop through the values in a list to change colors in a list of colors, pick names out of a list of names, and more.

We used an empty list, `[]`, and the `append()` function to add information from the user into a list that we then used in a program. You learned that the `len()` function can tell you the length of a list—that is, how many values the list contains.

You learned how to remember the turtle's current position and the direction it's heading with the `t.position()` and `t.heading()` functions, and you learned how to get the turtle back to this location and heading with `t.setx()`, `t.sety()`, and `t.setheading()`.

Finally, you saw how you can use nested loops to repeat one set of instructions inside another set, first to print a list of names on a screen and then to create spirals of spirals in a kaleidoscope pattern. Along the way, we've drawn lines, circles, and strings of words or names on the screen.

At this point, you should be able to do the following:

- Create your own `for` loops to repeat a set of instructions a certain number of times.

- Use the `range()` function to generate lists of values to control your `for` loops.

- Create empty lists and add to lists using the `append()` function.

- Create your own `while` loops to repeat while a condition is `True` or until the condition is `False`.

- Explain how each type of loop works and how you code it in Python.

- Give examples of situations in which you would use each type of loop.

- Design and modify programs that use nested loops.

PROGRAMMING CHALLENGES

Try these challenges to practice what you've learned in this chapter. (If you get stuck, go to *http://www.nostarch.com/ teachkids/* for sample answers.)

#1: SPIRAL ROSETTES

Think about how you might modify the *ViralSpiral.py* program to replace the small spirals with rosettes like those in *Rosette6.py* (page 58) and *RosetteGoneWild.py* (page 60). Hint: first replace the inner loop with an inner loop that will draw a rosette. Then, add the code to change the colors and sizes of the circles in each rosette. As an added touch, change the width of the pen slightly as your circles get bigger. When you finish, save the new program as *SpiralRosettes.py*. Figure 4-8 shows a drawing produced by one solution to this challenge.

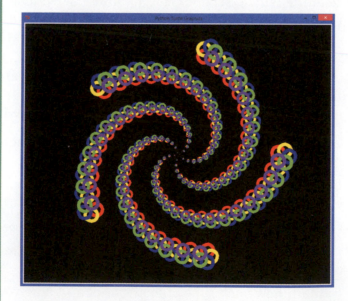

Figure 4-8: A spiral of rosettes from one solution to Programming Challenge #1

#2: A SPIRAL OF FAMILY SPIRALS

Wouldn't it be cool to draw a spiral of spirals of your family's names? Take a look at *SpiralFamily.py* (page 65) and then refer back to the code for *ViralSpiral.py*. Create an inner loop inside the for loop in *SpiralFamily.py* that draws the smaller spiral. Then, modify your outer loop to remember the position and heading of the turtle before drawing each small spiral, and set it back before continuing to the next big spiral location. When you get it right, save the new program as *ViralFamilySpiral.py*.

5
CONDITIONS (WHAT IF?)

In addition to speed and accuracy, one quality that makes computers powerful is their ability to evaluate information and make small decisions quickly: a thermostat checks the temperature continuously and turns on heating or cooling as soon as the temperature goes below or above a certain number; sensors on new cars react and apply brakes more quickly than we can when another car suddenly stops ahead; spam filters turn away dozens of emails to keep our inboxes clean.

In each of these cases, the computer checks a set of conditions: Is the temperature too cold? Is there something in the path of the car? Does the email look like spam?

In Chapter 4, we saw a statement that uses a condition to make a decision: the while statement. In those examples, the condition told the while loop how many times to run. What if we wanted to make decisions about *whether* to run a set of statements at all? Imagine if we could write one program and let the user decide whether they wanted circles or other shapes on their spiral. Or what if we wanted circles *and* other shapes, like in Figure 5-1?

Figure 5-1: A spiral of rosettes and smaller spirals, courtesy of an if statement

The statement that makes all this possible is the if statement. It asks *if* something is true, and based on the answer, it decides whether to perform a set of actions or skip over them. If the temperature in a building is fine, the heating and cooling system doesn't run, but if it's too hot or too cold, the system turns on. If it's raining outside, you

bring an umbrella; otherwise, you don't. In this chapter, we'll learn how to program the computer to make decisions based on whether a condition is true or false.

IF STATEMENTS

The `if` statement is an important programming tool. It allows us to tell the computer whether to run a group of instructions, based on a condition or set of conditions. With an `if` statement, we can tell the computer to make a choice.

The syntax of the `if` statement—that is, the way we code an `if` statement so the computer understands it—looks like this:

```
if condition:
    indented statement(s)
```

The condition we're testing in an `if` statement is usually a Boolean expression, or a true/false test. A Boolean expression evaluates to either True or False. When you use a Boolean expression with an `if` statement, you specify an action or set of actions that you want performed if the expression is true. If the expression is true, the program will run the indented statement(s), but if it's false, the program will skip them and continue with the rest of the program at the next unindented line.

IfSpiral.py shows an example of an `if` statement in code:

IfSpiral.py

```
❶ answer = input("Do you want to see a spiral? y/n:")
❷ if answer == 'y':
❸     print("Working...")
       import turtle
       t = turtle.Pen()
       t.width(2)
❹     for x in range(100):
❺         t.forward(x*2)
❻         t.left(89)
❼ print("Okay, we're done!")
```

The first line of our *IfSpiral.py* program ❶ asks the user to enter y or n for whether they would like to see a spiral and stores the user's response in answer. At ❷, the if statement checks to see if answer is equal to 'y'. Notice that the operator to test "is equal to" uses two equal signs together, ==, to distinguish it from the assignment operator, which is a single equal sign like at ❶. The == operator checks to see if answer and 'y' are equal. If they are, the condition in our if statement is true. We use a pair of single quotation marks (') around a letter or other character when we're testing a variable to see if it contains a single character entered by the user.

If our condition at ❷ is true, we print Working... on the screen at ❸, then draw a spiral on the screen. Notice that the print statement at ❸ and the statements that draw the spiral all the way down to ❻ are indented. These indented statements will be executed only if the condition at ❷ is true. Otherwise, the program will skip all the way to ❼ and just print Okay, we're done!.

The statements after our for loop at ❹ are indented farther (❺ and ❻). This is because they belong to the for statement. Just as we added a loop inside another loop in Chapter 4 by indenting the nested loop, we can put a loop inside an if statement by indenting the whole loop.

Once the spiral is complete, our program picks back up at ❼ and tells the user we're done. This is also the line our program jumps to if the user typed n or anything other than y at ❶. Remember, the whole if block from ❸ through ❻ is skipped if the condition at ❷ is False.

Type *IfSpiral.py* in a new IDLE window or download it from *http://www.nostarch.com/teachkids/*, and run it a few times, testing different answers. If you enter the letter y when prompted, you'll see a spiral like the one in Figure 5-2.

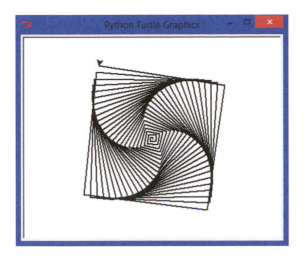

Figure 5-2: If you answer y to the question in IfSpiral.py, you'll see a spiral like this one.

If you enter a character other than a lowercase y—or more than one character—the program prints `Okay, we're done!` and ends.

MEET THE BOOLEANS

Boolean expressions, or *conditional expressions*, are important programming tools: the computer's ability to make decisions depends on its ability to evaluate Boolean expressions to `True` or `False`.

We have to use the computer's language to tell it the condition we'd like to test. The syntax of a conditional expression in Python is this:

```
expression1 conditional_operator expression2
```

Each expression can be a variable, a value, or another expression. In *IfSpiral.py*, `answer == 'y'` was a conditional expression, with `answer` as the first expression and `'y'` as the second. The conditional operator was `==`, to check if `answer` was equal to `'y'`. There are many other conditional operators in Python besides `==`. Let's learn about some of them.

COMPARISON OPERATORS

The most common conditional operators are *comparison operators*, which let you test two values to see how they compare to each other. Is one of the values bigger or smaller than the other? Are they equal? Each comparison you make using a comparison operator is a condition that will evaluate to True or False. One real-world example of a comparison is when you enter a passcode to access a building. The Boolean expression takes the passcode you entered and compares it to the correct passcode; if the input matches (is equal to) the correct passcode, the expression evaluates to True, and the door opens.

The comparison operators are shown in Table 5-1.

Table 5-1: Python Comparison Operators

Math symbol	Python operator	Meaning	Example	Result
<	<	Less than	1 < 2	True
>	>	Greater than	1 > 2	False
≤	<=	Less than or equal to	1 <= 2	True
≥	>=	Greater than or equal to	1 >= 2	False
=	==	Equal to	1 == 2	False
≠	!=	Not equal to	1 != 2	True

As we saw with math operators in Chapter 3, some of the operators in Python are different from math symbols to make them easier to type on a standard keyboard. *Less than* and *greater than* use the symbols we're used to, < and >.

For *less than or equal to*, Python uses the less than sign and equal sign together, <=, with no space in between. The same goes for *greater than or equal to*, >=. Remember *not* to put a space between the two signs, as that will cause an error in your program.

The operator to see if two values are equal is the double equal sign, ==, because the single equal sign is already used as the assignment operator. The expression x = 5 assigns the value 5 to the variable x, but x == 5 tests to see if x *is equal to* 5. It's helpful to read the double equal sign out loud as "is equal to" so you can avoid the common mistake of writing the incorrect statement if x = 5 instead of the correct if x == 5 ("if x *is equal to* five") in your programs.

The operator that tests to see if two values are *not equal* is !=, an exclamation point followed by the equal sign. This combination may be easier to remember if you say "not equal to" when you see != in a statement. For example, you might read if x != 5 aloud as "if x *is not equal to* five."

The result of a test involving a conditional operator is one of the Boolean values, True or False. Go to the Python shell and try entering some of the expressions shown in Figure 5-3. Python will respond with either True or False.

```
>>> x = 5
>>> x
5
>>> x > 2
True
>>> x < 2
False
>>> x <= 7
True
>>> x >= 7
False
>>> x == 5
True
>>> x != 3
True
>>>
```

Figure 5-3: Testing conditional expressions in the Python shell

We start by going to the shell and entering **x = 5** to create a variable called x that holds the value 5. On the second line, we check the value of x by typing it by itself, and the shell responds with its value, 5. Our first conditional expression is x > 2, or "x is greater than two." Python responds with True because 5 is greater than 2. Our next expression, x < 2 ("x is less than two"), is false when x is equal to 5, so Python returns False. The remaining conditionals use the <= (less than or equal to), >= (greater than or equal to), == (is equal to), and != (not equal to) operators.

Every conditional expression will evaluate to either True or False in Python. Those are the only two Boolean values, and the capital *T* in True and capital *F* in False are required. True and False are built-in constant values in Python. Python will not understand if you type True as true without the capital *T*, and the same goes for False.

YOU'RE NOT OLD ENOUGH!

Let's write a program that uses Boolean conditional expressions to see if you're old enough to drive a car. Type the following in a new window and save it as *OldEnough.py*.

OldEnough.py

```
❶ driving_age = eval(input("What is the legal driving age where you live? "))
❷ your_age = eval(input("How old are you? "))
❸ if your_age >= driving_age:
❹     print("You're old enough to drive!")
❺ if your_age < driving_age:
❻     print("Sorry, you can drive in", driving_age - your_age, "years.")
```

At ❶, we ask the user for the legal driving age in their area, evaluate the number they enter, and store that value in the variable driving_age. At ❷, we ask for the user's current age and store that number in your_age.

The if statement at ❸ checks to see if the user's current age is *greater than or equal to* the driving age. If ❸ evaluates to True, the program runs the code at ❹ and prints, "You're old enough to drive!". If the condition at ❸ evaluates to False, the program skips ❹ and goes to ❺. At ❺, we check if the user's age is *less than* the driving age. If so, the program runs the code at ❻ and tells the user how many years it'll be until they can drive by subtracting driving_age from your_age and printing the result. Figure 5-4 shows the results of this program for my son and me.

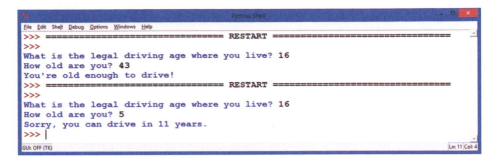

Figure 5-4: I'm old enough to drive in the United States, but my five-year-old son isn't.

The only catch is that the last if statement at ❺ feels redundant. If the user is old enough at ❸, we shouldn't need to test to see if they're too young, because we already know they're not. And if the user *isn't* old enough at ❸, we shouldn't need to test to see if they're too young at ❺, because we already know they are. If only Python had a way of getting rid of that unnecessary code . . . well, it just so happens that Python *does* have a shorter, faster way to handle situations like this one.

ELSE STATEMENTS

Often we want our program to do one thing if a condition evaluates to True and something else if the condition evaluates to False. This is so common, in fact, that we have a shortcut, the else statement, that allows us to test if the condition is true without having to perform another test to see if it's false. The else statement can only be used after an if statement, not by itself, so we sometimes refer to the two together as an if-else. The syntax looks like this:

```
if condition:
    indented statement(s)
else:
    other indented statement(s)
```

If the condition in an if statement is true, the indented statements under the if are executed, and the else and all its statements are skipped. If the condition in the if statement is false, the program skips directly to the else's other indented statements and runs those.

We can rewrite *OldEnough.py* with an else statement to remove the extra conditional test (your_age < driving_age). This not only makes the code shorter and easier to read, but it also helps prevent coding errors in the two conditions. For example, if we test your_age > driving_age in the first if statement and your_age < driving_age in the second if statement, we might accidentally leave out the case where your_age == driving_age. By using the if-else statement pair, we can just test if your_age >= driving_age to see if you're old enough to drive and inform you if you are, and otherwise go to the else statement and print how many years you must wait to drive.

Here's *OldEnoughOrElse.py*, a revised version of *OldEnough.py* with an if-else instead of two if statements:

OldEnoughOrElse.py

```
driving_age = eval(input("What is the legal driving age where you live? "))
your_age = eval(input("How old are you? "))
if your_age >= driving_age:
    print("You're old enough to drive!")
else:
    print("Sorry, you can drive in", driving_age - your_age, "years.")
```

The only difference between the two programs is that we replaced the second if statement and condition with a shorter, simpler else statement.

POLYGONS OR ROSETTES

As a visual example, we can ask the user to input whether they'd like to draw a polygon (triangle, square, pentagon, and so on) or a rosette with a certain number of sides or circles. Depending on the user's choice (p for polygon or r for rosette), we can draw exactly the right shape.

Let's type and run this example, *PolygonOrRosette.py*, which has an if-else statement pair.

PolygonOrRosette.py

```
import turtle
t = turtle.Pen()
# Ask the user for the number of sides or circles, default to 6
❶ number = int(turtle.numinput("Number of sides or circles",
                "How many sides or circles in your shape?", 6))
# Ask the user whether they want a polygon or rosette
❷ shape = turtle.textinput("Which shape do you want?",
                    "Enter 'p' for polygon or 'r' for rosette:")
```

```
❸  for x in range(number):
❹      if shape == 'r':          # User selected rosette
❺          t.circle(100)
❻      else:                     # Default to polygon
❼          t.forward (150)
❽      t.left(360/number)
```

At ❶, we ask the user for a number of sides (for a polygon) or circles (for a rosette). At ❷, we give the user a choice between p for polygon or r for rosette. Run the program a few times, trying each option with different numbers of sides/circles, and see how the for loop at ❸ works.

Notice that ❹ through ❽ are indented, so they are part of the for loop at ❸ and are executed the number of times the user entered as the number of lines or circles at ❶. The if statement at ❹ checks to see if the user entered r to draw a rosette, and if that's true, ❺ is executed and draws a circle at this location as part of the rosette. If the user entered p or anything other than r, the else statement at ❻ is selected and draws a line at ❼ by default, to make one side of a polygon. Finally, at ❽ we turn left by the correct number of degrees (360 degrees divided by the number of sides or rosettes) and keep looping from ❸ to ❽ until the shape is finished. See Figure 5-5 for an example.

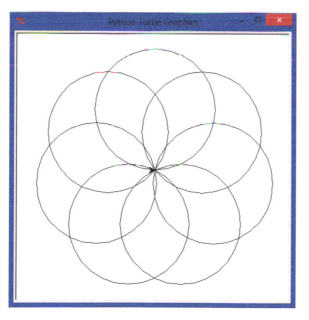

Figure 5-5: Our PolygonOrRosette.py program with user input of 7 sides and r for rosette

EVEN OR ODD?

The `if-else` statement can test more than user input. We can use it to alternate shapes, like in Figure 5-1, by using an `if` statement to test our loop variable each time it changes to see if it's even or odd. On every even pass through the loop—when our variable is equal to 0, 2, 4, and so on—we can draw a rosette, and on every odd pass through the loop, we can draw a polygon.

To do this, we need to know how to check if a number is odd or even. Think about how we decide if a number is even; that means the number is divisible by two. Is there a way to see if a number is evenly divisible by two? "Evenly divisible" means there's no remainder. For example, four is *even*, or evenly divisible by two, because $4 \div 2 = 2$ with no remainder. Five is *odd* because $5 \div 2 = 2$ with a remainder of 1. So even numbers have a remainder of zero when they're divided by two, and odd numbers have a remainder of one. Remember the remainder operator? That's right: it's our old friend the modulo operator, %.

In Python code, we can set up a loop variable `m` and check to see if `m` is even by testing `m % 2 == 0`—that is, checking to see if the remainder when we divide `m` by two is equal to zero:

```python
for m in range(number):
    if (m % 2 == 0):  # Tests to see if m is even
        # Do even stuff
    else:             # Otherwise, m must be odd
        # Do odd stuff
```

Let's modify a spiral program to draw rosettes at even corners and polygons at odd corners of a big spiral. We'll use a big `for` loop for the big spiral, an `if-else` statement to check whether to draw a rosette or a polygon, and two small inner loops to draw either a rosette or a polygon. This will be longer than most of our programs so far, but comments will help explain what the program is doing. Type and run the following program, *RosettesAndPolygons.py*, and be sure to check that your indentation is correct for the loops and `if` statements.

RosettesAndPolygons.py

```python
# RosettesAndPolygons.py - a spiral of polygons AND rosettes!
import turtle
t = turtle.Pen()
```

```
# Ask the user for the number of sides, default to 4
sides = int(turtle.numinput("Number of sides",
          "How many sides in your spiral?", 4))
# Our outer spiral loop for polygons and rosettes, from size 5 to 75
```
❶ `for m in range(5,75):`
```
    t.left(360/sides + 5)
```
❷ `    t.width(m//25+1)`
❸ `    t.penup()          # Don't draw lines on spiral`
```
    t.forward(m*4)    # Move to next corner
```
❹ `    t.pendown()        # Get ready to draw`
```
    # Draw a little rosette at each EVEN corner of the spiral
```
❺ `    if (m % 2 == 0):`
❻ `        for n in range(sides):`
```
            t.circle(m/3)
            t.right(360/sides)
    # OR, draw a little polygon at each ODD corner of the spiral
```
❼ `    else:`
❽ `        for n in range(sides):`
```
            t.forward(m)
            t.right(360/sides)
```

Let's look at how this program works. At ❶, we set up a for
loop over the range 5 to 75; we're skipping 0 to 4 because it's hard
to see shapes that are 4 pixels across or smaller. We turn for our
spiral; then, at ❷ we use integer division to make the pen wider
(thicker) after every 25th shape. Figure 5-6 shows the lines getting
thicker as the shapes get bigger.

At ❸, we lift our turtle's pen off the screen and move forward
so we don't draw lines between rosettes and polygons. At ❹, we put
the pen back down and get ready to draw a shape at the corner
of the big spiral. At ❺, we test our loop variable m to see if we're
drawing at an even corner. If m is even (m % 2 == 0), we draw the
rosette with the for loop at ❻. Otherwise, the else at ❼ tells us to
draw a polygon using the for loop beginning at ❽.

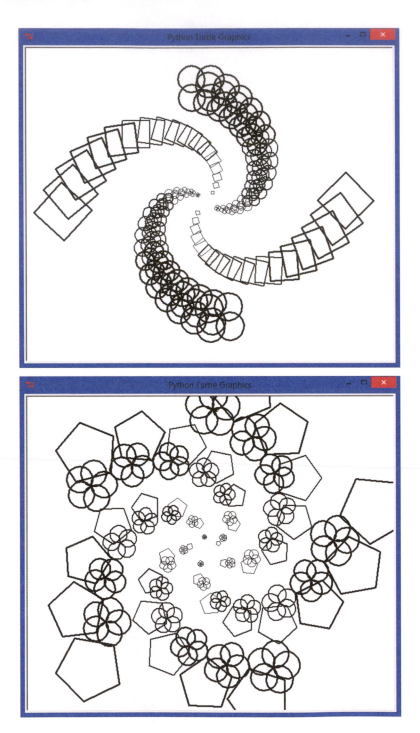

Figure 5-6: Two runs of our RosettesAndPolygons.py program with user inputs of 4 sides (top) and 5 sides (bottom)

Notice that when we use an even number of sides, the alternating shapes form separate legs of the spiral, as shown at the top in Figure 5-6. But when the number of sides is odd, each leg of the spiral alternates with the even (rosette) shape and the odd (polygon) shape. With color and some thought, you can make this program draw a design like the one in Figure 5-1. The if-else statements add another dimension to our programming toolkit.

ELIF STATEMENTS

There's one more useful add-on to an if statement: the elif clause. No, that's not one of Santa's helpers! An elif is a way to string together if-else statements when you need to check for more than two possible outcomes. The keyword elif is short for "else if." Think about letter grades in school: if you score 98 percent on an exam, the teacher might assign a grade of A or A+ depending on the grading scale. But if you score lower, there's not just one grade (there are more options than A or F, thank goodness). Instead, there are several possible grades your teacher might use: A, B, C, D, or F.

This is a case where an elif statement or a set of elif statements can help. Let's take the example of a 10-point grading scale, where 90 or above is an A, 80–89 is a B, and so on. If your score is 95, we can print the letter grade A and skip all other options. Similarly, if you earned an 85, we don't need to test further than a B. The if-elif-else construct helps us do this in a straightforward way. Try running the following program, *WhatsMyGrade.py*, and entering different values between 0 and 100.

WhatsMyGrade.py

```
❶ grade = eval(input("Enter your number grade (0-100): "))
❷ if grade >= 90:
      print("You got an A! :) ")
❸ elif grade >= 80:
      print("You got a B!")
❹ elif grade >= 70:
      print("You got a C.")
❺ elif grade >= 60:
      print("You got a D...")
❻ else:
      print("You got an F. :( ")
```

At ❶, we ask the user for a numeric grade from 0 to 100 with an input() prompt, convert it to a number with the eval() function, and store it in the variable grade. At ❷, we compare the user's grade to the value 90, the cutoff for a letter grade of A. If the user entered a score of 90 or greater, Python will print You got an A! :), skip the other elif and else statements, and continue with the rest of the program. If the score is not 90 or greater, we proceed to ❸ to check for a grade of B. Again, if the score is 80 or greater, the program prints the correct grade and skips past the else statement. Otherwise, the elif statement at ❹ checks for a C, the elif statement at ❺ checks for a D, and, finally, any score less than 60 makes it all the way to ❻ and results in the else statement's You got an F. :(.

We can use if-elif-else statements to test a variable across multiple ranges of values. Sometimes, though, we need to test multiple variables. For example, when deciding what to wear for the day, we want to know the temperature (warm or cold) and the weather (sun or rain). To combine conditional statements, we need to learn a few new tricks.

COMPLEX CONDITIONS: IF, AND, OR, NOT

There are times when a single conditional statement isn't enough. What if we want to know if it's warm *and* sunny or cold *and* rainy?

Think back to our first program in this chapter, in which we answered y if we wanted to draw a spiral. The first two lines asked for input and checked to see if that input was y:

```
answer = input("Do you want to see a spiral? y/n:")
if answer == 'y':
```

To see a spiral, the user has to enter y exactly; only this one answer is accepted. Even something similar, like capital Y or the word yes, doesn't work because our if statement checks only for y.

One easy way to solve the Y versus y problem is to use the lower() function, which makes strings all lowercase. You can try it in IDLE:

```
>>> 'Yes, Sir'.lower()
'yes, sir'
```

The `lower()` function changed the capital Y and capital S in Yes, Sir to lowercase, leaving the rest of the string unchanged.

We can use `lower()` on the user's input so that no matter which they enter, Y or y, the condition in our `if` statement will be True:

```
if answer.lower() == 'y':
```

Now, if a user enters either Y or y, our program checks to see if the lowercase version of their answer is y. But if we want to check for the full word Yes, we need a *compound if statement.*

Compound `if` statements are like compound sentences: "I'm going to the store, *and* I'm going to buy some groceries." Compound `if` statements are useful when we want to do a bit more than just test whether one condition is true. We might want to test if this condition *and* another condition are both true. We might test if this condition *or* another condition is true. And we might want to see if the condition is *not* true. We do this in everyday life, too. We say, "If it's cold *and* raining, I'll wear my heavy raincoat," "If it's windy *or* cold, I'll wear a jacket," or "If it's *not* raining, I'll wear my favorite shoes."

When we build a compound `if` statement, we use one of the *logical operators* shown in Table 5-2.

Table 5-2: Logical Operators

Logical operator	Usage	Result
and	if(*condition1* and *condition2*):	True only if both *condition1* and *condition2* are True
or	if(*condition1* or *condition2*):	True if either of *condition1* or *condition2* are True
not	if not(*condition*):	True only if the *condition* is False

We can use the or operator to check if the user entered y *or* yes; either one will do.

```
answer = input("Do you want to see a spiral? y/n:").lower()
if answer == 'y' or answer == 'yes': # Checks for either 'y' or 'yes'
```

Now we're testing if either of two conditions is True. If either is True, the user gets to see the spiral. Notice that we write the full conditional on either side of the or keyword: answer == 'y' or answer == 'yes'. One common error for new programmers is trying to shorten or conditions by leaving out the second answer ==. To remember the right way to use an or statement, think about each condition separately. If any of the conditions joined by an or evaluates to True, the whole statement is true, but each condition has to be complete for the statement to work.

A compound condition using and looks similar, but and requires *every* condition in the statement to be true for the overall statement to evaluate to True. For an example, let's write a program to decide what to wear based on the weather. Type *WhatToWear.py* in a new window or download it from *http://www.nostarch.com/teachkids/*, and run it:

WhatToWear.py

```
❶ rainy = input("How's the weather? Is it raining? (y/n)").lower()
❷ cold = input("Is it cold outside? (y/n)").lower()
❸ if (rainy == 'y' and cold == 'y'):       # Rainy and cold, yuck!
      print("You'd better wear a raincoat.")
❹ elif (rainy == 'y' and cold != 'y'):     # Rainy, but warm
      print("Carry an umbrella with you.")
❺ elif (rainy != 'y' and cold == 'y'):     # Dry, but cold
      print("Put on a jacket, it's cold out!")
❻ elif (rainy != 'y' and cold != 'y'):     # Warm and sunny, yay!
      print("Wear whatever you want, it's beautiful outside!")
```

At ❶, we ask the user whether it's raining outside, and at ❷, we ask if it's cold or not. We also make sure the answers stored in rainy and cold are lowercase by adding the lower() function to the end of the input() functions on both lines. With these two conditions (whether it's rainy and whether it's cold), we can help the user decide what to wear. At ❸, the compound if statement checks to see if it's both rainy and cold; if it is, the program suggests a raincoat. At ❹, the program checks to see if it's both rainy and not cold. For rainy but not cold weather, the program recommends an umbrella. At ❺, we check to see if it's *not* raining (rainy *not equal to* 'y') but still cold, requiring a jacket. Finally, at ❻, if it's not raining *and* it's not cold, wear whatever you want!

SECRET MESSAGES

Now that we understand how to use conditions, we're going to learn to encode and decode secret messages using a Caesar cipher. A *cipher* is a secret code, or a way of changing messages to make them harder to read. The *Caesar cipher* is named after Julius Caesar, who is said to have liked sending private messages by shifting letters in the alphabet:

SECRET MESSAGES ARE SO COOL! -> FRPERG ZRFFNTRF NER FB PBBY!

We can create a simple Caesar cipher by using an encoder ring like the one shown in Figure 5-7. To create the encoded message, decide on the *key*, or the number of letters you want to shift each letter by. In the coded message and in Figure 5-7, each letter is being shifted by a key value of 13, meaning we take the letter we want to encode and count 13 letters past it in the alphabet to get our encoded letter. An *A* becomes an *N*, a *B* becomes an *O*, and so on.

We sometimes call this shift a *rotation* because by the time we get to *M* (which becomes *Z*), we're at the end of the alphabet. To be able to encode an *N*, we wrap around to *A* again. *O* wraps around to *B*, all the way to *Z*, which becomes an *M*. Here's an example of a Caesar cipher lookup table for the key value of 13, where each letter is shifted by 13 letters for encoding or decoding:

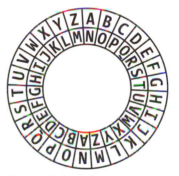

Figure 5-7: A Caesar cipher

A	B	C	D	E	F	G	H	I	J	K	L	M	N	O	P	Q	R	S	T	U	V	W	X	Y	Z
N	O	P	Q	R	S	T	U	V	W	X	Y	Z->A	B	C	D	E	F	G	H	I	J	K	L	M	

Notice a pattern? The letter *A* is encoded as an *N*, and *N* is encoded as an *A*. We call this a *symmetric cipher* or *symmetric code* because it has *symmetry*—it's the same in both directions. We can encode and decode messages using the same key of 13 because the English alphabet has 26 letters, and the key value of 13 means that we shift every letter exactly halfway around. You can try it with a message of your own: HELLO -> URYYB -> HELLO.

If we can write a program that looks at each letter in a secret message, then encodes that letter by shifting it 13 letters to the right, we can send encoded messages to anyone who has the same program (or who can figure out the pattern in the cipher). To write a program that manipulates individual letters in a string, we need to pick up more skills for working with strings in Python.

MESSIN' WITH STRINGS

Python comes with powerful functions for working with strings. There are built-in functions that can change a string of characters to all uppercase, functions that can change single characters into their number equivalents, and functions that can tell us whether a single character is a letter, number, or other symbol.

Let's start with a function to change a string to uppercase letters. To make our encoder/decoder program easier to understand, we're going to change the message to all uppercase so that we're encoding only one set of 26 letters (*A* to *Z*) instead of two (*A* to *Z* and *a* to *z*). The function that converts a string to all uppercase letters is upper(). Any string followed by the dot (.) and the function name upper() will return the same string with letters in uppercase and other characters unchanged. In the Python shell, try typing your name or any other string in quotes, followed by .upper(), to see this function in action:

```
>>> 'Bryson'.upper()
'BRYSON'
>>> 'Wow, this is cool!'.upper()
'WOW, THIS IS COOL!'
```

As we saw earlier, the lower() function does the opposite:

```
>>> 'Bryson'.lower()
'bryson'
```

You can check to see whether a single character is an uppercase letter with the isupper() function:

```
>>> 'B'.isupper()
True
>>> 'b'.isupper()
False
>>> '3'.isupper()
False
```

And you can check whether a character is a lowercase letter with the `islower()` function:

```
>>> 'P'.islower()
False
>>> 'p'.islower()
True
```

A string is a collection of characters, so looping through a string in Python with a for loop will break the string into individual characters. Here, `letter` will loop through each character in the string variable `message`:

```
for letter in message:
```

Finally, we can use the regular addition operator + (plus) to add strings together or add letters onto a string:

```
>>> 'Bry' + 'son'
'Bryson'
>>> 'Payn' + 'e'
'Payne'
```

Here, we add the second string onto the end of the first. Adding strings together is called *appending*. You may also see string addition referred to as *concatenation*; just remember that's a fancy word for adding two or more strings together.

THE VALUE OF CHARACTER(S)

The final tool we need to build our encoder/decoder program is the ability to perform math on individual letters, like adding 13 to the value of the letter *A* to get the letter *N*. Python has a function or two that can help.

Every letter, number, and symbol is turned into a number value when stored on a computer. One of the most popular numbering systems is *ASCII (American Standard Code for Information Interchange)*. Table 5-3 shows the ASCII values of some keyboard characters.

Table 5-3: Numeric Values for Standard ASCII Characters

Value	Symbol	Description	Value	Symbol	Description
32		Space	65	A	Uppercase A
33	!	Exclamation mark	66	B	Uppercase B
34	"	Double quote	67	C	Uppercase C
35	#	Hash mark	68	D	Uppercase D
36	$	Dollar sign	69	E	Uppercase E
37	%	Percent	70	F	Uppercase F
38	&	Ampersand	71	G	Uppercase G
39	'	Single quote, apostrophe	72	H	Uppercase H
40	(	Opening parenthesis	73	I	Uppercase I
41	)	Closing parenthesis	74	J	Uppercase J
42	*	Asterisk	75	K	Uppercase K
43	+	Plus	76	L	Uppercase L
44	,	Comma	77	M	Uppercase M
45	-	Hyphen	78	N	Uppercase N
46	.	Period, dot, full stop	79	O	Uppercase O
47	/	Slash or divide	80	P	Uppercase P
48	0	Zero	81	Q	Uppercase Q
49	1	One	82	R	Uppercase R
50	2	Two	83	S	Uppercase S
51	3	Three	84	T	Uppercase T
52	4	Four	85	U	Uppercase U
53	5	Five	86	V	Uppercase V
54	6	Six	87	W	Uppercase W
55	7	Seven	88	X	Uppercase X
56	8	Eight	89	Y	Uppercase Y
57	9	Nine	90	Z	Uppercase Z
58	:	Colon	91	[	Opening bracket
59	;	Semicolon	92	\	Backslash
60	<	Less than	93	]	Closing bracket
61	=	Equals	94	^	Caret, circumflex
62	>	Greater than	95	_	Underscore
63	?	Question mark	96	`	Grave accent
64	@	At symbol	97	a	Lowercase a

The Python function to turn a character into its ASCII number value is `ord()`:

```
>>> ord('A')
65
>>> ord('Z')
90
```

The reverse function is `chr()`:

```
>>> chr(65)
'A'
>>> chr(90)
'Z'
```

This function turns a numeric value into the corresponding character.

OUR ENCODER/DECODER PROGRAM

With all these pieces, we can put together a program that takes in a message and makes it all uppercase. It then loops through each character in the message and, if the character is a letter, shifts it by 13 to encode or decode it, adds the letter to an output message, and prints the output message.

EncoderDecoder.py

```
  message = input("Enter a message to encode or decode: ") # Get a message
❶ message = message.upper()           # Make it all UPPERCASE :)
❷ output = ""                         # Create an empty string to hold output
❸ for letter in message:             # Loop through each letter of the message
❹     if letter.isupper():           # If the letter is in the alphabet (A-Z),
❺         value = ord(letter) + 13   # shift the letter value up by 13,
❻         letter = chr(value)        # turn the value back into a letter,
❼         if not letter.isupper():   # and check to see if we shifted too far
❽             value -= 26            # If we did, wrap it back around Z->A
❾             letter = chr(value)    # by subtracting 26 from the letter value
❿     output += letter               # Add the letter to our output string
  print("Output message: ", output)  # Output our coded/decoded message
```

The first line prompts the user for an input message to encode or decode. At ❶, the `upper()` function makes the message all uppercase to make the letters easier for the program to read and to make the encoding simpler to write. At ❷, we create an empty string (nothing between the double quotes, "") named output, in which we'll store our encoded message, letter by letter. The `for` loop at ❸ makes use of the fact that Python treats strings like collections of characters; the variable `letter` will iterate over, or loop through, the string `message` one character at a time.

At ❹, the `isupper()` function checks each character in the message to see if it's an uppercase letter (A to Z). If it is, then at ❺ we get the numeric value of the letter in ASCII using `ord()` and add 13 to that value to encode it. At ❻, we turn the new, encoded value back into a character with `chr()`, and at ❼, we check to see if it's still a letter from A to Z. If not, we wrap the letter back around to the front of the alphabet at ❽ by subtracting 26 from the encoded value (that's how Z becomes an M), and we turn the new value into its letter equivalent in ❾.

At ❿, we add the letter to the end of the `output` string (appending the character onto the end of the string) using the `+=` operator. The `+=` operator is one of a handful of shortcut operators that combine math (+) and assignment (=), and `output += letter` means `output` gets `letter` added to it. This is the last line in our `for` loop, so the whole process is repeated for each character in the input message until `output` has been built up one letter at a time to hold the encoded version of the entire message. When the loop is finished, the last line of the program prints the output message.

You can use this program to send coded messages for fun, but you should know that it's not as secure as modern ways of encoding messages—anyone who can solve a puzzle in the Sunday paper can read the encoded messages you've sent—so use it only for fun with friends.

Do a web search for *encryption* or *cryptography* to learn about the science of making secret messages secure.

WHAT YOU LEARNED

In this chapter, you learned how to program a computer to make decisions based on conditions in code. We saw that the if statement lets a program execute a set of statements only if a condition is true (like age >= 16). We used Boolean (true/false) expressions to represent the conditions we wanted to check for, and we built expressions using conditional operators like <, >, <=, and more.

We combined if and else statements to run one piece of code or the other, so that if our if statement is not executed, the else statement runs. We extended this further by selecting among multiple options using if-elif-else statements, like in our letter grade program that gave out grades of A, B, C, D, or F depending on the numeric score entered.

We learned how to test multiple conditions at the same time using the and and or logical operators to combine conditions (like rainy == 'y' and cold == 'y'). We used the not operator to check whether a variable or expression is False.

In our secret message program at the end of the chapter, you learned that all letters and characters are converted into numeric values when stored on a computer and that ASCII is one method of storing text as number values. We used the chr() and ord() functions to convert characters into their ASCII values and back again. We changed strings of letters to all uppercase or lowercase with upper() and lower(), and we checked whether a string was uppercase or lowercase with isupper() and islower(). We built a string by adding letters one at a time onto the end of the string using the + operator, and we learned that adding strings together is sometimes called *appending* or *concatenating*.

At this point you should be able to do the following:

- Use if statements to make decisions using conditionals.
- Use conditionals and Boolean expressions to control program flow.
- Describe how a Boolean expression evaluates to True or False.
- Write conditional expressions using comparison operators (<, >, ==, !=, <=, >=).
- Use if-else statement combinations to choose between two alternative program paths.

- Test a variable to see if it is odd or even using the modulo operator, %.

- Write if-elif-else statements that select from among a number of options.

- Use and and or to test multiple conditions at once.

- Use the not operator to check whether a value or variable is False.

- Explain how letters and other characters are stored as numeric values in computers.

- Use ord() and chr() to convert characters into their ASCII equivalents and vice versa.

- Manipulate strings using various string functions like lower(), upper(), and isupper().

- Add strings and characters together using the + operator.

PROGRAMMING CHALLENGES

To practice what you've learned in this chapter, try these challenges. (If you get stuck, go to *http://www.nostarch .com/teachkids/* for sample answers.)

#1: COLORFUL ROSETTES AND SPIRALS

For a more visual challenge, look back at the colorful spiral and rosette image in Figure 5-1 on page 78. You should be able to modify *RosettesAndPolygons.py* on page 88 to make it more colorful and, if you like, replace the polygons with small spirals to match the illustration in Figure 5-1.

#2: USER-DEFINED KEYS

For a more text-based challenge, create an advanced version of our *EncoderDecoder.py* program by allowing the user to input their own key value, from 1 to 25, to determine how many letters to shift the message by. Then, at the line marked ❺ in *EncoderDecoder.py* (page 99), instead of shifting by 13 every time, shift by the user's key value.

To decode a message sent with a different key (let's use 5 as a key value, so *A* becomes *F*, *B* becomes *G*, and so on), the person receiving the message needs to know the key. They retrieve the message by encoding again with the reverse key (26 minus the key value, $26 - 5 = 21$) so that *F* wraps around to *A*, *G* becomes *B*, and so on.

If you'd like to make this program easier to use, start by asking the user whether they'd like to encode or decode (e or d) and then ask them for a key value that you store as key (the number of letters to shift by). If the user chooses to encode, add the key value to each letter at ❺, but if they choose to decode, add 26 - key to each letter. Send this program to a friend and message away!

6

RANDOM FUN AND GAMES: GO AHEAD, TAKE A CHANCE!

In Chapter 5, we programmed the computer to make decisions based on conditions. In this chapter, we'll program the computer to pick a number between 1 and 10, to play Rock-Paper-Scissors, and even to roll dice or pick a card!

The common element in these games is the idea of *randomness*. We want the computer to pick a number at random between 1 and 10, and we guess what that number is. We want the computer to randomly pick rock, paper, or scissors, and then we choose what to play and see who wins. These examples—plus dice games, card games, and so on—are called *games of chance*. When we roll five dice to play Yahtzee, we usually get a different result every time we roll. That element of chance is what makes these games fun.

We can program the computer to behave randomly. Python has a module called random that allows us to simulate random choices. We can use the random module to draw random shapes on the screen and program games of chance. Let's start with a guessing game.

A GUESSING GAME

We can use random numbers in the classic Hi-Lo guessing game. One player picks a number between 1 and 10 (or 1 and 100), and the other tries to guess the number. If the guess is too high, the guesser tries a lower number. If they guessed too low, they try a higher number. When they guess the right number, they win!

We already know how to compare numbers with the if statement, and we know how to keep guessing using input() and a while loop. The only new skill we need to learn is how to generate a random number. We can do this with the random module.

First, we have to import the random module with the command import random. You can try this in the Python shell by typing **import random** and pressing ENTER. The module has a few different functions for generating a random number. We'll use randint(), short for *random integer*. The randint() function expects us to give it two arguments—that is, two pieces of information—between its parentheses: the lowest and highest numbers we want. Specifying a lowest number and a highest number in the parentheses will tell `randint()` what range to choose randomly from. Type the following in IDLE:

```
>>> import random
>>> random.randint(1, 10)
```

Python will respond with a random number between 1 and 10, *inclusive* (which means the random number can include 1 and 10). Try the `random.randint(1, 10)` command a few times and see the different numbers you get back. (Tip: you can use ALT-P, or CONTROL-P on a Mac, to repeat the most recently entered line without having to type it all again.)

If you run that line enough (at least 10 times), you'll notice that numbers sometimes repeat, but there's no pattern in the numbers as far as you can tell. We call these *pseudorandom* numbers because they're not *actually* random (the `randint` command tells the computer what number to "pick" next based on a complex mathematical pattern), but they *seem* random.

Let's put the `random` module to work in a program called *GuessingGame.py*. Type the following in a new IDLE window or download the program from *http://www.nostarch.com/teachkids/*:

GuessingGame.py

```
❶ import random
❷ the_number = random.randint(1, 10)
❸ guess = int(input("Guess a number between 1 and 10: "))
❹ while guess != the_number:
❺     if guess > the_number:
           print(guess, "was too high. Try again.")
❻     if guess < the_number:
           print(guess, "was too low. Try again.")
❼     guess = int(input("Guess again: "))
❽ print(guess, "was the number! You win!")
```

At ❶, we import the `random` module, which gives us access to all functions defined in `random`, including `randint()`. At ❷, we write the module name, `random`, followed by a dot and the name of the function we want to use, `randint()`. We pass `randint()` the arguments 1 and 10 so it generates a pseudorandom number between 1 and 10, and we store the number in the variable `the_number`. This will be the secret number the user is trying to guess.

At ❸, we ask the user for a guess between 1 and 10, evaluate the number, and store it in the variable guess. Our game loop starts with the while statement at ❹. We're using the != (not equal to) operator to see if the guess is not equal to the secret number. If the user guesses the number on the first try, guess != the_number evaluates to False and the while loop doesn't run.

As long as the user's guess is not equal to the secret number, we check with two if statements at ❺ and ❻ to see if the guess was too high (guess > the_number) or too low (guess < the_number) and then print a message to the user asking for another guess. At ❼, we accept another guess from the user and start the loop again, until the user guesses correctly.

At ❽, the user has guessed the number, so we tell them it was the right number, and our program ends. See Figure 6-1 for a few sample runs of the program.

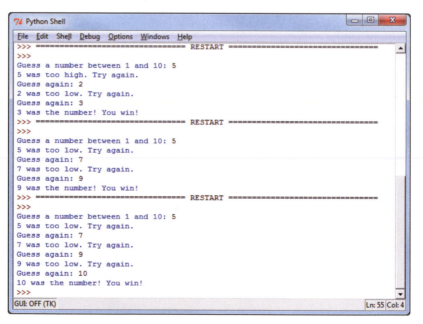

```
7/4 Python Shell                                                    _ □ X
File  Edit  Shell  Debug  Options  Windows  Help
>>> ============================== RESTART ==============================
>>>
Guess a number between 1 and 10: 5
5 was too high. Try again.
Guess again: 2
2 was too low. Try again.
Guess again: 3
3 was the number! You win!
>>> ============================== RESTART ==============================
>>>
Guess a number between 1 and 10: 5
5 was too low. Try again.
Guess again: 7
7 was too low. Try again.
Guess again: 9
9 was the number! You win!
>>> ============================== RESTART ==============================
>>>
Guess a number between 1 and 10: 5
5 was too low. Try again.
Guess again: 7
7 was too low. Try again.
Guess again: 9
9 was too low. Try again.
Guess again: 10
10 was the number! You win!
>>>
GUI: OFF (TK)                                               Ln: 55 Col: 4
```

Figure 6-1: Our GuessingGame.py *program, asking the user to guess higher or lower for three random numbers*

In the first run of the program in Figure 6-1, the user guessed 5, and the computer responded that 5 was too high. The user guessed lower with 2, but 2 was too low. Then the user gave 3 a shot, and that was right! Guessing halfway between the lowest and highest possible numbers each time, as in the examples in Figure 6-1, is a strategy called a *binary search*.

If players learn to use this strategy, they can guess a number between 1 and 10 in four tries or less, every time! Give it a shot!

To make the program more interesting, you could change the arguments you pass to the randint() function to generate a number between 1 and 100 or an even higher number (be sure to change the input() prompts as well). You could also make a variable called number_of_tries and add 1 to it every time the user guesses, to keep track of the user's number of tries. Print the number of tries at the end of the program to let the user know how well they did. For an additional challenge, you could add an outer loop that asks the user if they want to play again after they guess the number correctly. Try these on your own, and go to *http://www.nostarch.com/teachkids/* for sample solutions.

COLORFUL RANDOM SPIRALS

The random module has other handy functions besides randint(). Let's use them to help us create an interesting visual: a screen full of spirals of random sizes and colors like the one in Figure 6-2.

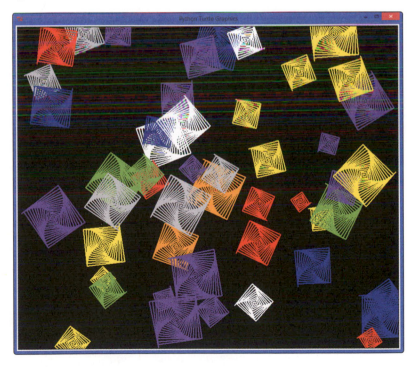

Figure 6-2: Spirals of random sizes and colors at random locations on the screen, from RandomSpirals.py

Think about how you could write a program like the one that created Figure 6-2. You know *almost* all of the tricks needed to draw random spirals like these. First, you can draw spirals of various colors using loops. You can generate random numbers and use one to control how many times each spiral's for loop runs. This changes its size: more iterations create a bigger spiral, while fewer iterations create a smaller spiral. Let's look at what else we'll need and build the program step by step. (The final version is *RandomSpirals.py* on page 115.)

PICK A COLOR, ANY COLOR

One new tool we'll need is the ability to choose a random color. We can easily do this with another method in the random module, random.choice(). The random.choice() function takes a list or other collection as the argument (the part inside the parentheses), and it returns a randomly selected element from that collection. In our case, we could create a list of colors, and then pass that list to the random.choice() method to get a random color for each spiral.

You can try this in the command line shell in IDLE:

```
>>> # Getting a random color
>>> colors = ["red", "yellow", "blue", "green", "orange", "purple", "white", "gray"]
>>> random.choice(colors)
'orange'
>>> random.choice(colors)
'blue'
>>> random.choice(colors)
'white'
>>> random.choice(colors)
'purple'
>>>
```

In this code, we created our old friend colors and set it equal to a list of color names. Then we used the random.choice() function, passing it colors as its argument. The function chooses a color at random from the list. The first time, we got orange, the second time blue, the third time white, and so on. This function can give us a random color to set as our turtle's pen color before it draws each new spiral.

GETTING COORDINATED

One remaining problem is how to get the spirals to spread out all over the screen, including the upper-right and lower-left corners. To place spirals randomly on the turtle screen, we need to understand the x- and y-coordinate system used in our Turtle environment.

CARTESIAN COORDINATES

If you've taken a geometry course, you've seen (x, y) coordinates drawn on graph paper as in Figure 6-3. These are *Cartesian* coordinates, named after French mathematician René Descartes, who labeled points on a grid with a pair of numbers we call the x- and y-coordinates.

In the graph in Figure 6-3, the dark horizontal line is called the *x-axis*, and it runs from left to right. The dark vertical line is the *y-axis*, running from bottom to top. We call the point where these lines meet, (0, 0), the *origin* because all other points on the grid are labeled with coordinates measured from, or *originating* from, that point. Think of the origin, (0, 0), as the center of your screen. Every other point you want to find can be labeled with an x- and y-coordinate by starting at the origin and moving left or right, down or up.

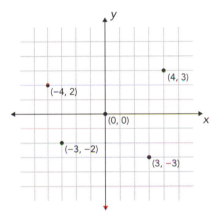

Figure 6-3: A graph with four points and their Cartesian (x, y) coordinates

We label points on a graph with this pair of coordinates inside parentheses, separated by a comma: (x, y). The first number, the x-coordinate, tells us how far to move left or right, while the second number, the y-coordinate, tells us how far to move up or down. Positive x-values tell us to move right from the origin; negative x-values tell us to move left. Positive y-values tell us to move up from the origin, and negative y-values tell us to move down.

Look at the points labeled in Figure 6-3. The point in the upper right is labeled with the x- and y-coordinates (4, 3). To find the location of this point, we start at the origin (0, 0) and move 4 spaces to the right (because the x-coordinate, 4, is positive) and then 3 spaces up (because the y-coordinate, 3, is positive).

To get to the point in the lower right, (3, −3), we go back to the origin and then move right 3 spaces or units. This time, the y-coordinate is −3, so we move *down* 3 units. Moving right 3 and down 3 puts us at (3, −3). For (−4, 2), we move *left* 4 units from the origin and then up 2 units to the point in the upper left. Finally, for (−3, −2), we move left 3 units and then down 2 units to the lower-left point.

SETTING A RANDOM TURTLE POSITION

In turtle graphics, we can move the turtle from the origin (0, 0) to any other location by telling the computer the x- and y-coordinates of the new location with the `turtle.setpos(x,y)` command. The function name `setpos()` is short for *set position*. It sets the position of the turtle to the x- and y-coordinates we give it. For example, `turtle.setpos(10,10)` would move the turtle right 10 units and up 10 units from the center of the screen.

On the computer, the unit we usually use is our old friend the *pixel*. So `turtle.setpos(10,10)` would move the turtle right 10 pixels and up 10 pixels from the center of the screen. Because pixels are so tiny—about 1/70 of an inch (0.3 millimeters) or smaller on most displays—we might want to move 100 pixels or more at a time. `setpos()` can handle any coordinates we give it.

To move the turtle to a random location on the screen, we'll generate a random pair of numbers, x and y, then use `turtle.setpos(x,y)` to move the turtle to those coordinates. Before we move the turtle, though, we'll need to lift the turtle's pen with `turtle.penup()`. After we've set the new position, we'll call `turtle.pendown()` to put the pen back down and enable the turtle to draw again. If we forget to lift the pen, the turtle will draw a line as it moves to wherever we tell it to go with `setpos()`. As you can see in Figure 6-2, we don't want extra lines between our spirals. Our code will look like this:

```
t.penup()
t.setpos(x,y)
t.pendown()
```

The `setpos()` function combined with a couple of random numbers as (*x*, *y*) coordinates will let us place spirals in different locations, but how do we know what range to use for our random numbers? That question brings us to the last issue we have to resolve in our quest for random spirals.

HOW BIG IS OUR CANVAS?

Now that we know how to position spirals at random locations on the window, or canvas, we have one problem remaining: how do we know how big our canvas is? We can generate a random number for the x- and y-coordinates of a location and draw a spiral at that location, but how can we make sure that the location we choose is on the visible window—not off the window to the right, left, top, or bottom? Then, how can we make sure we cover the entire drawing window, from left to right, top to bottom?

To answer the question about canvas size, we need to use two more functions, `turtle.window_width()` and `turtle.window_height()`. First, `window_width()` tells us how wide our turtle window is, in pixels. The same goes for `window_height()`; we get the number of pixels from the bottom of our turtle window to the top. For example, our turtle window in Figure 6-2 is 960 pixels wide and 810 pixels tall.

`turtle.window_width()` and `turtle.window_height()` will help us with random x- and y-coordinates, but we have one more obstacle. Remember that in turtle graphics, the center of the window is the origin, or (0, 0). If we just generate random numbers between 0 and `turtle.window_width()`, the first problem is that we will never draw anything in the lower left of the window: the coordinates there are negative in both the x- and y-directions (left and down), but a random number between 0 and our `window_width()` value is always positive. The second problem is that if we start from the center and go `window_width()` to the right, we'll end up off the right-hand edge of the window.

We have to figure out not just how wide and tall the window is but also what the range of the coordinates is. For example, if our window is 960 pixels wide and the origin (0, 0) is at the center of our window, we need to know how many pixels we can move to the right and left without leaving the visible window. Because (0, 0) is in the middle of our window, halfway across, we just divide the width in half. If the origin is in the middle of a window that is 960 pixels across, there are 480 pixels to the right of the origin and 480 pixels to the left of the origin. The range of x-coordinate values would be from −480 (left 480 pixels from the origin) to +480 (480 pixels right of the origin) or, in other words, from −960/2 to +960/2.

To make our range work for any size window, we would say the x-coordinates go from -turtle.window_width()//2 to +turtle.window_width()//2. Our origin is also in the middle of the window from bottom to top, so there are turtle.window_height()//2 pixels above and below the origin. We use integer division, the // operator, in these calculations to make sure we'll get an integer result when we divide by 2; a window could measure an odd number of pixels wide, and we want to keep all our pixel measurements in whole numbers.

Now that we know how to calculate the size of our canvas, we can use these expressions to limit the range of our random coordinates. Then we can be sure that any random coordinates we generate will be visible in our window. The random module in Python has a function that lets us generate a random number within a specified range: randrange(). We just tell the randrange() function to use negative one-half the window width as the start value for the range and positive one-half the window width as the end value for the range (we'll have to import both turtle and random in our program to make these lines work):

```
x = random.randrange(-turtle.window_width()//2,
                      turtle.window_width()//2)
y = random.randrange(-turtle.window_height()//2,
                      turtle.window_height()//2)
```

These lines of code will use the randrange() function to generate a pair of (x, y) coordinate values that are always on the viewing window and cover the full area of the viewing window from left to right, bottom to top.

PUTTING IT ALL TOGETHER

Now we have all the pieces—we just have to put them together to build a program that will draw random spirals in different colors, sizes, and locations. Here's our finished *RandomSpirals.py* program; in just about 20 lines, it creates the kaleidoscope-like picture in Figure 6-2.

RandomSpirals.py

```python
import random
import turtle
t = turtle.Pen()
turtle.bgcolor("black")
colors = ["red", "yellow", "blue", "green", "orange", "purple",
          "white", "gray"]
for n in range(50):
    # Generate spirals of random sizes/colors at random locations
    t.pencolor(random.choice(colors))    # Pick a random color
    size = random.randint(10,40)         # Pick a random spiral size
    # Generate a random (x,y) location on the screen
    x = random.randrange(-turtle.window_width()//2,
                         turtle.window_width()//2)
    y = random.randrange(-turtle.window_height()//2,
                         turtle.window_height()//2)

    t.penup()
    t.setpos(x,y)
    t.pendown()
    for m in range(size):
        t.forward(m*2)
        t.left(91)
```

❶ `t.pencolor(random.choice(colors))`
❷ `size = random.randint(10,40)`
❸ `x = random.randrange(...)`
❹ `y = random.randrange(...)`
❺ `t.penup()`
❻ `t.setpos(x,y)`
❼ `t.pendown()`
❽ `for m in range(size):`

First we import the `random` and `turtle` modules and set up our turtle window and a list of colors. At our `for` loop (n will go from 0 to 49 to give us 50 spirals total), things get interesting. At ❶, we pass `colors` to `random.choice()` to have the function choose a random color from the list. We pass the random color choice to `t.pencolor()` to set the turtle's pen color to that random color. At ❷, `random.randint(10,40)` picks a random number from 10 to 40. We store that number in the variable `size`, which we'll use at ❽ to tell Python how many lines to draw in a spiral. The lines at ❸ and ❹ are exactly the ones we built earlier to generate a random pair of coordinate values (*x*, *y*) that give us a random location on our viewing window.

At ❺, we lift the turtle's pen off the virtual paper before we move the turtle to its new random location. At ❻, we move the turtle to its new location by setting its position to x and y, the random coordinates chosen by `randrange()` earlier. Now that the turtle is in position, we put the pen back down at ❼ so we'll be able to see the spiral we're about to draw. At ❽, we have a for loop to draw each line of the spiral. For `m` in `range(size)`, the turtle will move forward a distance of `m*2`, drawing a line segment of length `m*2` (`m` is 0, 1, 2, 3, and so on, so the length of the segment is 0, 2, 4, 6, and so on). The turtle will then rotate left 91 degrees and get ready to draw the next segment.

The turtle starts in the center of the spiral, draws a segment (length 0), and rotates left; that's the first time through the loop. The next time through, `m` is 1, so the turtle draws a segment of length 2, then rotates. As Python iterates through the loop, the turtle will move outward from the center of the spiral, drawing longer and longer line segments. We use the randomly generated size, an integer between 10 and 40, as the number of lines we draw in our spiral.

After we finish drawing the current spiral, we go back to the top of our outer `for` loop. We pick a new random color, size, and location; lift the pen; move it to the new location; put down the pen; and go through the inner `for` loop to draw a new spiral of some new random size. After drawing this spiral, we go back to the outer loop and repeat the entire process. We do this 50 times, giving us 50 spirals of assorted colors and shapes spread randomly across the screen.

ROCK-PAPER-SCISSORS

One game that we have the skills to program now is Rock-Paper-Scissors. Two players (or one player and the computer) each pick one of three possible items (rock, paper, or scissors); both show their choice; and the winner is decided by three rules: rock crushes scissors, scissors cut paper, paper covers rock.

To simulate this game, we'll create a list of choices (like our colors list in *RandomSpirals.py*) and we'll use `random.choice()` to pick one of the three items from the list as the computer's choice. Then, we'll ask the user for their choice and use a series of `if` statements to determine the winner. The user will be playing against the computer!

Let's jump into the code. Type *RockPaperScissors.py* into a new window in IDLE or download it from *http://www.nostarch.com/teachkids/*.

RockPaperScissors.py

```python
❶ import random
❷ choices = ["rock", "paper", "scissors"]
   print("Rock crushes scissors. Scissors cut paper. Paper covers rock.")
❸ player = input("Do you want to be rock, paper, or scissors (or quit)? ")
❹ while player != "quit":                    # Keep playing until the user quits
       player = player.lower()               # Change user entry to lowercase
❺      computer = random.choice(choices)     # Pick one of the items in choices
       print("You chose " +player+ ", and the computer chose " +computer+ ".")
❻      if player == computer:
           print("It's a tie!")
❼      elif player == "rock":
           if computer == "scissors":
               print("You win!")
           else:
               print("Computer wins!")
❽      elif player == "paper":
           if computer == "rock":
               print("You win!")
           else:
               print("Computer wins!")
❾      elif player == "scissors":
           if computer == "paper":
               print("You win!")
           else:
               print("Computer wins!")
       else:
           print("I think there was some sort of error...")
       print()                               # Skip a line
❿      player = input("Do you want to be rock, paper, or scissors (or quit)? ")
```

At ❶, we import the random module to get access to the functions that help us make random choices. At ❷, we set up the list of the three items—rock, paper, and scissors—and call the list choices. We print the simple rules of the game to make sure the user knows them. At ❸, we prompt the user to input their choice of rock, paper, scissors, or quit and store their choice in the variable player. At ❹, we begin the game loop by checking whether the user chose quit at the input prompt; if they did, the game ends.

As long as the user has not entered quit, the game begins. After changing the player's input to lowercase for easy comparison in our if statements, we tell the computer to pick an item. At ❺, we tell the computer to pick at random one of the items in the list choices and store the item in the variable computer. Once the computer's choice is stored, it's time to begin testing to see who won. At ❻, we check whether the player and the computer picked the same item; if so, we tell the user that the outcome was a tie. Otherwise, we check at ❼ whether the user selected rock. Inside the `elif` statement at ❼, we nest an `if` statement to see whether the computer picked scissors. If our player picks rock and the computer chooses scissors, rock crushes scissors, and the player wins! If it's not rock and rock, and if the computer didn't pick scissors, then the computer must have picked paper, and we print that the computer wins.

At the remaining two `elif` statements, ❽ and ❾, we do the same testing to check for wins when the user picks paper or scissors. If none of those statements was true, we let the user know they've entered something that did not compute: either they made a choice that doesn't exist, or they misspelled their choice. Finally, at ❿, we ask the user for their next choice before beginning the game loop all over again (a new round). See Figure 6-4 for a sample run of the program.

```
7% Python Shell                                          [ - ] [ □ ] [ X ]
File  Edit  Shell  Debug  Options  Windows  Help
Do you want to be rock, paper, or scissors (or quit)? rock
You chose rock, and the computer chose scissors.
You win!

Do you want to be rock, paper, or scissors (or quit)? paper
You chose paper, and the computer chose scissors.
Computer wins!

Do you want to be rock, paper, or scissors (or quit)? lizard
You chose lizard, and the computer chose rock.
I think there was some sort of error...

Do you want to be rock, paper, or scissors (or quit)? spock
You chose spock, and the computer chose scissors.
I think there was some sort of error...

Do you want to be rock, paper, or scissors (or quit)? rock
You chose rock, and the computer chose rock.
It's a tie!

Do you want to be rock, paper, or scissors (or quit)? scissors
You chose scissors, and the computer chose rock.
Computer wins!

Do you want to be rock, paper, or scissors (or quit)? quit
>>> |
GUI: OFF (TK)                                          Ln: 85  Col: 4
```

Figure 6-4: Thanks to random choices by the computer, RockPaperScissors.py *is a fun game!*

Sometimes the user wins, sometimes the computer wins, and sometimes they tie. Because the outcome is somewhat random, the game is fun enough to play to pass a little time. Now that we have a sense of how a game with two players can use the computer's random choices, let's try creating a card game.

PICK A CARD, ANY CARD

One thing that makes card games fun is randomness. No two rounds turn out exactly the same (unless you're bad at shuffling), so you can play again and again without getting bored.

We can program a simple card game with the skills we've learned. Our first try at this won't show graphical playing cards (we need to learn more tricks to make that possible), but we can generate a random card name ("two of diamonds" or "king of spades," for example) just by using an *array*, or list, of strings, like we did with color names in our spiral programs. We could program a game like War in which two players each pull a random card from the deck, and the player with the higher card wins; we just need some way of comparing cards to see which is higher. Let's see how that might work, step by step. (The final program is *HighCard.py* on page 125.)

STACKING THE DECK

First, we need to think about how to build a virtual deck of cards in our program. As I mentioned, we won't draw the cards yet, but we at least need the card names to simulate a deck. Fortunately, card names are just strings ("two of diamonds", "king of spades"), and we know how to build an array of strings—we've done it with color names since the very first chapter!

An *array* is an ordered or numbered collection of similar things. In many programming languages, arrays are a special type of collection. In Python, though, lists can be used like arrays. We'll see how to treat a list like an array in this section, accessing individual elements in the array one at a time.

We could build a list of all the card names by creating an array name (cards) and setting it equal to a list of all 52 card names:

```
cards = ["two of diamonds",
        "three of diamonds",
        "four of diamonds",
        # This is going to take forever...
```

But ouch—we're going to have to type 52 long strings of card names! Our code will be 52 lines long before we even program the game part, and we'll be so tired from typing that we won't have energy left to play the game. There's got to be a better way. Let's think like a programmer! All of that typing is repetitive, and we want to let the computer do the repetitive work. The suit names (*diamonds*, *hearts*, *clubs*, *spades*) are going to be repeated 13 times each, for the 13 cards in each suit. The face values (*two* through *ace*) are going to be repeated 4 times each, because there are 4 suits. Worse, we're typing the word *of* 52 times!

When we ran into repetition before, we used loops to make the problem easier. If we wanted to generate the whole deck of cards, a loop would do the job nicely. But we don't need the whole deck to play a single hand of War: we just need two cards, the computer's card and the player's. If a loop won't help us avoid repeating all those suits and face values, we need to break the problem down further.

In War, each player shows one card, and the higher card wins. So as we've discussed, we need just 2 cards, not 52. Let's start with one card. A card name consists of a face value (two through ace) and a suit name (clubs through spades). Those look like good possibilities for lists of strings: one list for faces and one for suits. Instead of using a list of 52 repeated entries for each separate card, we pick a face value at random from the list of 13 possibilities, then pick a suit name at random from the 4 possible choices. This approach should let us generate any single card in the deck.

We replace our long array cards with two much shorter arrays, suits and faces:

```
suits = ["clubs", "diamonds", "hearts", "spades"]
faces = ["two", "three", "four", "five", "six", "seven", "eight", "nine",
         "ten", "jack", "queen", "king", "ace"]
```

We reduced 52 lines of code to about 3! That's smart programming. Now let's see how to use these two arrays to deal a card.

DEALING CARDS

We already know how to use the random.choice() function to pick an item at random from a list. So to deal a card, we simply use random.choice() to pick a face value from a list of faces and a suit name from a list of suits. Once

we have a random face and a random suit, all we do to complete a card name is add the word *of* between them (*two of diamonds*, for example).

Notice that we might deal the same card twice or more in a row using `random.choice()` this way. We're not forcing the program to check whether a card has already been dealt, so you might get two aces of spades in a row, for example. The computer's not cheating; we're just not telling it to deal from a single deck. It's like this program is dealing cards from an *infinite deck*, so it can keep dealing forever without running out.

```python
import random
suits = ["clubs", "diamonds", "hearts", "spades"]
faces = ["two", "three", "four", "five", "six", "seven", "eight", "nine",
         "ten", "jack", "queen", "king", "ace"]
my_face = random.choice(faces)
my_suit = random.choice(suits)
print("I have the", my_face, "of", my_suit)
```

If you try running this code, you'll get a new, random card every time. To deal a second card, you'd use similar code, but you'd store the random choices in variables called `your_face` and `your_suit`. You'd change the `print` statement so it printed the name of this new card. Now we're getting closer to our game of War, but we need some way to compare the computer's card and the user's card to see who wins.

COUNTING CARDS

There's a reason we listed face card values in ascending order, from two through ace. We want the cards' `faces` list to be ordered by value from lowest to highest so that we can compare cards against each other and see which card in any pair has the higher value. It's important to determine which of two cards is higher, since in War the higher card wins each hand.

FINDING AN ITEM IN A LIST

Fortunately, because of the way lists and arrays work in Python, we can determine where a value occurs in a list, and we can use that information to decide whether one card is higher than another. The position number of an item in a list or array is called the *index* of that item. We usually refer to each item in an array by its index.

For a visual representation of the suits array and the index of each suit, see Table 6-1.

Table 6-1: The suits Array

value	"clubs"	"diamonds"	"hearts"	"spades"
index	0	1	2	3

When we create our list suits, Python automatically assigns an index to each value in the list. The computer starts counting at zero, so the index of "clubs" is 0, "diamonds" is at index 1, and so on. The function to find the index of an item in a list is .index(), and it can be used on any list or array in Python.

To find the index of the suit name "clubs" in the list suits, we call the function suits.index("clubs"). It's like we're asking the suits array which index corresponds to the value "clubs". Let's try that in our Python shell. Enter the following lines:

```
>>> suits = ["clubs", "diamonds", "hearts", "spades"]
>>> suits.index("clubs")
0
>>> suits.index("spades")
3
>>>
```

After we create the array of suit values, suits, we ask Python what the index of the value "clubs" is, and it responds with the correct index, 0. In the same way, the index of "spades" is 3, and diamonds and hearts are at index locations 1 and 2, respectively.

WHICH CARD IS HIGHER?

We created our faces array with values in order from two to ace, so the value two, the first item in faces, would get the index 0, all the way through the ace at index 12 (the 13th location, starting from 0). We can use the index to test which card value is higher—in other words, which face value's index is larger. Our lowest card is two, and its index is the smallest, 0; the ace is our highest card, and its index is the largest, 12.

If we generate two random face card values (my_face and your_face), we can compare the index of my_face with the index of your_face to see which card is higher, as follows.

```
import random
faces = ["two", "three", "four", "five", "six", "seven", "eight", "nine",
         "ten", "jack", "queen", "king", "ace"]
my_face = random.choice(faces)
your_face = random.choice(faces)
if faces.index(my_face) > faces.index(your_face):
    print("I win!")
elif faces.index(my_face) < faces.index(your_face):
    print("You win!")
```

We use `random.choice()` twice to pull two random values out of the `faces` array, and then we store the values in `my_face` and `your_face`. We use `faces.index(my_face)` to find the index of `my_face` in `faces`, and we use `faces.index(your_face)` to get the index of `your_face`. If the index of `my_face` is higher, my card has a higher face value, and the program prints `I win!`. Otherwise, if the index of `my_face` is lower than the index of `your_face`, your card's face value is higher, and the program prints `You win!`. Because of the way we ordered our list, a higher card will always correspond to a higher index. With this handy tool, we've got almost everything we need to build a "high card" game like War. (We haven't added the ability to test for a tie game yet, but we'll add that as part of the complete program in "Putting It All Together" on page 125.)

KEEPING IT GOING

The final tool we need is a loop so the user can keep playing as long as they want. We're going to build this loop a little differently so that we can reuse it in other games.

First, we need to decide which kind of loop to use. Remember that a `for` loop usually means we know exactly the number of times we want to do something. Because we can't always predict how many times someone will want to play our game, a `for` loop is not the right fit. A `while` loop can keep going until some condition becomes false—for example, when the user presses a key to end the program. The `while` loop is what we'll use for our game loop.

The `while` loop needs a condition to check, so we're going to create a variable that we'll use as our *flag*, or signal, to end the program. Let's call our flag variable `keep_going` and set it equal to `True` to start:

```
keep_going = True
```

Because we start with keep_going = True, the program will enter the loop at least the first time.

Next we'll ask the user if they want to keep going. Rather than make the user enter Y or yes every time they want to play, let's make it easier by just asking them to press ENTER.

```
answer = input("Hit [Enter] to keep going, any other keys to exit: ")
if answer == "":
    keep_going = True
else:
    keep_going = False
```

Here we set a variable answer equal to an input function. Then we use an if statement to check whether answer == "" to see if the user pressed ENTER only or if they pressed other keys before ENTER. (The empty string "" tells us the user didn't type any other characters before pressing ENTER.) If the user wants to exit, all they have to do is make answer equal anything other than the empty string, "". In other words, they just have to press any key or keys before pressing ENTER, and the Boolean expression answer == "" will evaluate to False.

Our if statement checks whether answer == "" is True, and if so, it stores True in our flag variable keep_going. But do you notice some repetition there? If answer == "" is True, we assign the value True to keep_going; if answer == "" evaluates to False, we need to assign the value False to keep_going.

It would be simpler if we just set keep_going equal to whatever answer == "" evaluates to. We can replace our code with the following, more concise code:

```
answer = input("Hit [Enter] to keep going, any other keys to exit: ")
keep_going = (answer == "")
```

The first line hasn't changed. The second line sets keep_going equal to the result of the Boolean expression answer == "". If that's True, keep_going will be True, and our loop will continue. If that's False, keep_going will be False, and our loop will end.

Let's see the whole loop together:

```
keep_going = True
while keep_going:
    answer = input("Hit [Enter] to keep going, any key to exit: ")
    keep_going = (answer == "")
```

Here we add the `while` statement, so our loop will continue as long as `keep_going` evaluates to `True`. In the final program, we will "wrap" this `while` loop around the code to play a single hand. We'll do this by putting the `while` statement before the code that chooses the cards, and by putting the prompt to hit a key after the code that tells who wins. Remember to indent the code inside the loop!

PUTTING IT ALL TOGETHER

Putting all those components together, we can build a War-like game that we'll call *HighCard.py*. The computer draws a card for itself and a card for the player, checks to see which card is higher, and declares the winner. Type the code for *HighCard.py* into a new IDLE window or go to *http://www.nostarch.com/teachkids/* to download it and play.

HighCard.py

```
import random
suits = ["clubs", "diamonds", "hearts", "spades"]
faces = ["two", "three", "four", "five", "six", "seven", "eight", "nine",
         "ten", "jack", "queen", "king", "ace"]
keep_going = True
while keep_going:
    my_face = random.choice(faces)
    my_suit = random.choice(suits)
    your_face = random.choice(faces)
    your_suit = random.choice(suits)
    print("I have the", my_face, "of", my_suit)
    print("You have the", your_face, "of", your_suit)
    if faces.index(my_face) > faces.index(your_face):
        print("I win!")
    elif faces.index(my_face) < faces.index(your_face):
        print("You win!")
    else:
        print("It's a tie!")
    answer = input("Hit [Enter] to keep going, any key to exit: ")
    keep_going = (answer == "")
```

Run the game, and it'll print the computer's card and your card, followed by an announcement of who won and a prompt that offers you the opportunity to play again or exit. Play a few rounds and you'll notice that the cards are random enough to make the outcome fun—sometimes the computer wins, sometimes you win, but it's a fun game thanks to the element of chance.

ROLL THE DICE: CREATING A YAHTZEE-STYLE GAME

We used arrays in our card game to help simplify the code needed to deal a card, and to test which card was higher in value based on its position in the list of cards. In this section, we'll use the array concept to generate five random dice and check to see if we roll three of a kind, four of a kind, or five of a kind, like a simplified version of the dice game Yahtzee.

In Yahtzee, you have five dice. Each die has six sides, with each side showing a number of dots from one to six. In the full game, the user rolls all five dice, trying to get points by rolling three dice of the same value (which we call *three of a kind*) and other various "hands," similar to the card game poker. Rolling five of the same value (say, all five dice land with the six-dot side facing up) is called a Yahtzee and scores the highest points possible. In our simplified version of the game, we're just going to simulate the roll of five dice and check whether the user rolled three of a kind, four of a kind, or Yahtzee and let them know the outcome.

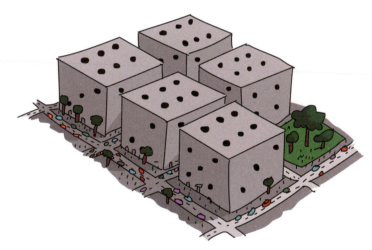

SETTING UP THE GAME

Now that we understand the game's objective, let's talk about how we'll code the game. First, we'll need to set up a game loop so that the user can keep rolling until they want to quit. Second, we'll need to set up a hand of five simulated dice as an array that can hold five random values, from 1 to 6, representing the value of each of the rolled dice. Third, we'll simulate the roll of the dice by assigning a random value from 1 to 6 in each of the five array slots. Finally, we need to compare the five rolled dice to each other to see whether we have three, four, or five of the same value and let the user know the outcome.

That last part is perhaps the most challenging. We could check for a Yahtzee by seeing if all five dice are a 1, or if all five dice are a 2, and so on, but that would mean a long list of complex if statement conditions. Since we don't care whether we have five 1s, five 2s, or five 6s—we just care that we have five of a kind—we could simplify this process by checking to see if the first die's value equals the second die's value and the second die's value equals the third die's value, all the way to the fifth die. Then, no matter what the value of the five of a kind, we know all five dice are the same, and we have a Yahtzee.

Five of a kind seems easy enough to test for, but let's try to figure out how we might test for four of a kind. A possible hand for four of a kind might be an array of values like [1, 1, 1, 1, 2] (here we rolled four 1s and a 2). However, the array [2, 1, 1, 1, 1] would also be a four of a kind with four 1s, as would [1, 1, 2, 1, 1], [1, 2, 1, 1, 1], and [1, 1, 1, 2, 1]. That's five possible configurations just to test for four 1s! That sounds like it's going to take a long set of if conditions. . . .

Fortunately, as a skilled programmer, you know that there's usually an easier way to do things. What all five arrays in the previous paragraph have in common is that there are four 1s in the list of values; the problem is that the fifth value, the 2, can be in any of the five different array positions. We could test for four of a kind much more easily if the four 1s were side by side, with the other value (the 2) off by itself. If we could sort the array in order from lowest to highest or highest to lowest, for example, all of the 1s would be grouped together, reducing the five different cases to just two: [1, 1, 1, 1, 2] or [2, 1, 1, 1, 1].

SORTING THE DICE

Lists, collections, and arrays in Python have a built-in sort function, sort(), that allows us to sort the elements in the array by value in order from smallest to largest or vice versa. For example, if our dice array were called dice, we could sort the values with dice.sort(). By default, sort() will order the elements in dice from smallest to largest, or in *ascending* order.

For our test to see if the array of dice contains four of a kind, sorting the array means we only have to test for two cases: four matching low values and a high value (as in [1, 1, 1, 1, 2]), or a low value and four matching high values (like [1, 3, 3, 3, 3]). In the first case, we know that if the dice are sorted and the first and fourth dice are equal in value, we have four of a kind or better. In the second case, again with sorted dice, if the second and fifth dice are equal in value, we have four of a kind or better.

We say four of a kind *or better*, because the first and fourth dice are also the same in a five of a kind. This brings us to our first logic challenge: if a user rolls five of a kind, they have also rolled four of a kind, and we only want to give them credit for the larger score. We'll handle this with an if-elif chain so that if a user gets Yahtzee, they don't also get four of a kind and three of a kind; only the highest hand wins. Combining this if-elif sequence with what we learned about sorting the dice to check for four of a kind, the code would look like this:

```
if dice[0] == dice[4]:
    print("Yahtzee!")
elif (dice[0] == dice[3]) or (dice[1] == dice[4]):
    print("Four of a kind!")
```

First, if we have already sorted the dice array, we notice a shortcut: if the first and last dice have the same value (if dice[0] == dice[4]), we know we have a Yahtzee! Remember that we number our array positions from 0 through 4 for the first through fifth dice. If we don't have five of a kind, we check for both cases of four of a kind (the first four dice are the same, dice[0] == dice[3], or the last four dice are the same, dice[1] == dice[4]). We use the Boolean operator or here to recognize four of a kind if *either* of the two cases evaluates to True (the first four *or* the last four).

TESTING THE DICE

We're referring to each die in the array individually by its index, or position: dice[0] refers to the first item in the dice array, and dice[4] refers to the fifth item because we start counting from zero. This is the way we can check the value of any of the dice individually or compare them to one another. Just as in our suits[] array back in Table 6-1, each entry in the dice[] array is an individual value. When we call on dice[0] to see if it's equal to dice[3], we're looking at the value in the first `dice` element and comparing it to the value in the fourth `dice` element. If the array is sorted, and these are the same, we have four of a kind.

To test for three of a kind, we add another `elif` statement, and we put the three-of-a-kind test after the four-of-a-kind test so that we test for three of a kind only if there's no five of a kind and no four of a kind; we want the highest hand to be reported. There are three possible cases of three of a kind if we're working with sorted dice: the first three dice match, the middle three, or the last three. In code, that would be:

```
elif (dice[0] == dice[2]) or (dice[1] == dice[3]) or (dice[2] == dice[4]):
    print("Three of a kind")
```

Now that we can test for various winning hands in our dice game, let's add the game loop and the `dice` array.

PUTTING IT ALL TOGETHER

Here's the complete *FiveDice.py* program. Type the code in a new window or download it from *http://www.nostarch.com/teachkids/*.

FiveDice.py

```
import random
# Game loop
keep_going = True
while keep_going:
    # "Roll" five random dice
➊   dice = [0,0,0,0,0]          # Set up an array for five values dice[0]-dice[4]
➋   for i in range(5):          # "Roll" a random number from 1-6 for all 5 dice
➌       dice[i] = random.randint(1,6)
➍   print("You rolled:", dice)  # Print out the dice values
    # Sort them
➎   dice.sort()
    # Check for five of a kind, four of a kind, three of a kind
    # Yahtzee - all five dice are the same
    if dice[0] == dice[4]:
        print("Yahtzee!")
    # FourOfAKind - first four are the same, or last four are the same
    elif (dice[0] == dice[3]) or (dice[1] == dice[4]):
        print("Four of a kind!")
    # ThreeOfAKind - first three, middle three, or last three are the same
    elif (dice[0] == dice[2]) or (dice[1] == dice[3]) or (dice[2] == dice[4]):
        print("Three of a kind")
    keep_going = (input("Hit [Enter] to keep going, any key to exit: ") == "")
```

After we import the `random` module and start the game loop with a `while` statement, the next few lines deserve a little explanation. At ❶, we set up an array called `dice` that holds five values, and we initialize all those values to zero. The square brackets, [and], are the same ones we used for our very first lists of colors, as well as for the arrays of card face values and suit names earlier in this chapter. At ❷, we set up a `for` loop to run five times for the five dice, using the range from 0 to 4; these will be the array positions, or index numbers, of the five dice.

At ❸, we set each individual die, from `dice[0]` to `dice[4]`, equal to a random integer from 1 to 6 to represent our five dice and their randomly rolled values. At ❹, we show the user what dice they rolled by printing the contents of the `dice` array; the result of this print statement is shown in Figure 6-5.

```
7% *Python Shell*                                        [-] [□] [X]
File  Edit  Shell  Debug  Options  Windows  Help
You rolled: [3, 6, 3, 5, 3]
Three of a kind
Hit [Enter] to keep going, any key to exit:
You rolled: [4, 3, 5, 1, 2]
Hit [Enter] to keep going, any key to exit:
You rolled: [1, 4, 2, 3, 6]
Hit [Enter] to keep going, any key to exit:
You rolled: [5, 6, 3, 2, 6]
Hit [Enter] to keep going, any key to exit:
You rolled: [5, 4, 5, 1, 5]
Three of a kind
Hit [Enter] to keep going, any key to exit:
You rolled: [4, 3, 6, 5, 6]
Hit [Enter] to keep going, any key to exit:
You rolled: [4, 2, 3, 2, 6]
Hit [Enter] to keep going, any key to exit:
You rolled: [5, 1, 5, 5, 2]
Three of a kind
Hit [Enter] to keep going, any key to exit:
You rolled: [3, 3, 3, 3, 1]
Four of a kind!
Hit [Enter] to keep going, any key to exit:
You rolled: [6, 1, 4, 6, 2]
Hit [Enter] to keep going, any key to exit:
You rolled: [5, 3, 1, 1, 4]
Hit [Enter] to keep going, any key to exit:
You rolled: [3, 1, 4, 6, 3]
Hit [Enter] to keep going, any key to exit:
You rolled: [2, 1, 1, 5, 6]
Hit [Enter] to keep going, any key to exit:
You rolled: [1, 5, 1, 3, 3]
Hit [Enter] to keep going, any key to exit:
You rolled: [6, 6, 4, 4, 4]
Three of a kind
Hit [Enter] to keep going, any key to exit:
You rolled: [2, 2, 2, 5, 5]
Three of a kind
Hit [Enter] to keep going, any key to exit:
You rolled: [2, 5, 3, 4, 1]
Hit [Enter] to keep going, any key to exit: |
GUI: OFF (TK)                                         Ln: 138 Col: 44
```

Figure 6-5: A sample run of our dice program. Notice that we rolled several three of a kinds and one four of a kind.

At ❺, we call the .sort() function on the dice array. This makes it easy to test for various hands—like five of a kind, four of a kind, and so on—by arranging the rolled dice values from smallest to largest, grouping like values. So, for example, if we roll [3, 6, 3, 5, 3], the dice.sort() function turns that into [3, 3, 3, 5, 6]. The if statement checks if the first value is equal to the fifth value; in this case, since the first and fifth values (3 and 6) aren't equal, we know not all the dice landed on the same value and it's not five of a kind. The first elif checks for four of a kind by comparing the first and fourth values (3 and 5) and second and fifth values (3 and 6); again, there are no matches here, so it's not four of a kind. The second elif checks for three of a kind; since the first and third values, 3 and 3, are equal, we know the first three values are equal. We inform the user that they got three of a kind and then prompt them to press keys depending on whether they want to continue playing or exit, as shown in Figure 6-5.

Run the program and press ENTER several times to see what you roll.

You'll notice that you roll three of a kind fairly often, as much as once every five or six rolls. Four of a kind is rarer, occurring about once every 50 rolls. We rolled four of a kind only once in a screen full of attempts in Figure 6-5. The Yahtzee is even rarer: you could roll several hundred times before getting a Yahtzee, but because of the random-number generator, you might roll one the first few times you try. Even though it's not as complex as the real game, our simplified version of Yahtzee is interesting enough to play because of its random nature.

We've seen how randomness can make a game interesting and fun by adding the element of chance to dice and card games, Rock-Paper-Scissors, and a guessing game. We also enjoyed the kaleidoscope-like graphics we created using a random number generator to place colorful spirals all over the screen. In the next section, we'll combine what you've learned about random numbers and loops with a bit of geometry to turn the random spirals program into a true virtual kaleidoscope that generates a different set of reflected images every time you run it!

KALEIDOSCOPE

The random spiral color graphic from Figure 6-2 looked a bit like a kaleidoscope. To make it look more like a real kaleidoscope, let's add an important feature that our spiral program was missing: reflections.

In a kaleidoscope, it's the positioning of the mirrors that makes random colors and shapes into a lovely pattern. In this closing example, we're going to mimic the mirror effect by modifying our *RandomSpiral.py* program to "reflect" the spirals four times on the screen.

To understand how to achieve this mirror effect, we need to talk more about Cartesian coordinates. Let's take a look at four points, (4, 2), (−4, 2), (−4, −2), and (4, −2), as shown in Figure 6-6.

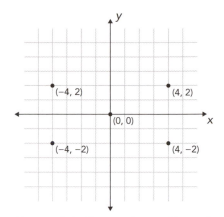

Compare (4, 2) and (−4, 2), the top two points. If the vertical y-axis were a mirror, these two points would be mirror images of each other; we call (4, 2) a reflection of (−4, 2) *about* the y-axis. Something similar occurs with (4, 2) and (4, −2), the two points on the right, but with the horizontal x-axis as the imaginary mirror: (4, −2) is the reflection of (4, 2) about the x-axis.

Figure 6-6: Four points reflected about the x- and y-axes starting with (4, 2)

If you look at each pair of (x, y) coordinates in Figure 6-6, you'll notice something: all four (x, y) coordinates use the same numbers, 4 and 2, just with different signs, + or −, depending on their location. We can create any four reflected points around the x- and y-axes by changing the signs on the two coordinates as follows: (x, y), (−x, y), (−x, −y), (x, −y). If you'd like, you can try drawing this on a piece of graph paper with any pair of (x, y) coordinates. Try (2, 3), for example: (2, 3), (−2, 3), (−2, −3), and (2, −3) are four reflected points above and below the x-axis and on either side of the y-axis.

With this knowledge, we can build the outline of a kaleidoscope program as follows:

1. Pick a random location (x, y) in the upper right of the screen and draw a spiral there.
2. Draw the same spiral at (−x, y) in the upper left of the screen.
3. Draw the same spiral at (−x, −y) in the lower left of the screen.
4. Draw the same spiral at (x, −y) in the lower right of the screen.

If we repeat these steps over and over, we'll have a lovely kaleidoscope effect with our random spirals.

Let's step through the full code for *Kaleidoscope.py* and see this in action.

Kaleidoscope.py

```python
import random
import turtle
t = turtle.Pen()
❶ t.speed(0)
turtle.bgcolor("black")
colors = ["red", "yellow", "blue", "green", "orange", "purple", "white", "gray"]
for n in range(50):
    # Generate spirals of random sizes/colors at random locations on the screen
    t.pencolor(random.choice(colors))   # Pick a random color from colors[]
    size = random.randint(10,40)        # Pick a random spiral size from 10 to 40
    # Generate a random (x,y) location on the screen
❷   x = random.randrange(0,turtle.window_width()//2)
❸   y = random.randrange(0,turtle.window_height()//2)
    # First spiral
    t.penup()
❹   t.setpos(x,y)
    t.pendown()
    for m in range(size):
        t.forward(m*2)
        t.left(91)
    # Second spiral
    t.penup()
❺   t.setpos(-x,y)
    t.pendown()
    for m in range(size):
        t.forward(m*2)
        t.left(91)
    # Third spiral
    t.penup()
❻   t.setpos(-x,-y)
    t.pendown()
    for m in range(size):
        t.forward(m*2)
        t.left(91)
    # Fourth spiral
    t.penup()
❼   t.setpos(x,-y)
    t.pendown()
    for m in range(size):
        t.forward(m*2)
        t.left(91)
```

Our program begins with the turtle and random modules imported as usual, but at ❶ we do something new: we change the speed of the turtle to the fastest value possible with t.speed(0). The speed() function in turtle graphics takes an argument from 0 to 10, with 1 as the slow animation setting, 10 as the fast animation setting, and 0 meaning no animation (draw as fast as the computer can go). It's an odd scale from 1 to 10, then 0, but just remember that if you want the fastest turtle possible, set the speed to 0. You'll notice when you run the program that the spirals appear almost instantly. You can make this change to any of our previous drawing programs if you'd like the turtle to move faster.

Our for loop looks just like the one from our *RandomSpirals.py* program, until we get to ❷ and ❸. At ❷, we cut the horizontal range for our random number in half, to just the positive x-coordinate values (the right side of the screen, from x = 0 to x = turtle.window_width()//2), and at ❸, we restrict the vertical range to the upper half of the screen, from y = 0 to y = turtle.window_height()//2. Remember that we're doing integer division with the // operator to keep our pixel measurements in whole numbers.

These two lines of code give us a random (*x*, *y*) coordinate pair in the upper right of the screen every time. We set the turtle pen's position to that point at ❹, and we draw the first spiral with the for loop immediately after. Then, we change the signs of each of the coordinate values, like we did in Figure 6-6, to create the three reflections of this point in the upper left (–*x*, *y*) at ❺, lower left (–*x*, –*y*) at ❻, and lower right (*x*, –*y*) at ❼. See Figure 6-7 for an example of the patterns *Kaleidoscope.py* can produce.

You can find the three reflections for each spiral by looking in the other three corners of the screen. These are not true mirror images: we don't start at the same angle for each spiral, and we don't turn right in our reflected spirals and left in the originals. However, these are tweaks you can make to the program if you'd like. See this chapter's Programming Challenges for ideas to make this kaleidoscope program even cooler.

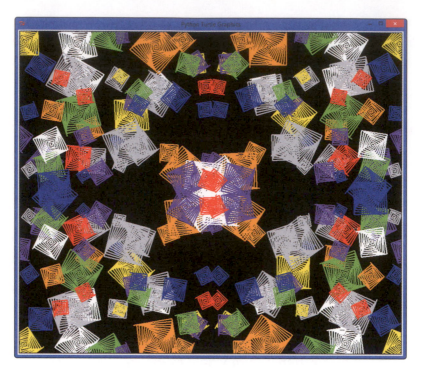

Figure 6-7: The mirrored/repeated effect in Kaleidoscope.py.

WHAT YOU LEARNED

Before this chapter, we had no way of making a computer behave randomly. Now we can make a computer roll dice; draw random cards from a deck; draw spirals of random color, shape, size, and location; and even beat us now and then at Rock-Paper-Scissors.

The tool that made these programs possible was the `random` module. We used `random.randint(1, 10)` to generate a random number between 1 and 10 in our guessing game. We added the `random.choice()` function to pick a random color out of a list in our random spirals program. You learned how to use the functions `turtle.window_width()` and `turtle.window_height()` to find the width and height of our turtle screen.

You also learned how to use Cartesian coordinates to find an (*x, y*) location on the screen, and you used the `random.randrange()` function to generate a number in the range between our left and right x-coordinate values and top and bottom y-coordinate values. We then used `turtle.setpos(x,y)` to move the turtle to any position on the drawing screen.

We combined our ability to choose an item from a list at random using `random.choice()` with our ability to test and compare variables using `if-elif` statements to build a "user versus computer" version of Rock-Paper-Scissors.

You learned the concept of an array, and we made our card game easier to code by building one array of suit names and one array of face values. We used `random.choice()` on each array to simulate dealing a card. We ordered the face values from least to greatest and used the `.index()` function to find the location of an element in an array. We used the index of each of two card face values to see which card had a higher index value and which player won a hand of the card game War. We built a reusable game loop with user input, a flag variable `keep_going`, and a `while` statement; we can put the loop into any game or app that a user might want to play or run multiple times in a row.

We extended our understanding of arrays by building a simplified version of Yahtzee. We created an array of five values from 1 to 6 to simulate five dice, used `randint()` to simulate rolling the dice, and used `sort()` on the dice array to make it easier to check for winning hands. We saw that, in a sorted array, if the first and last values are the same, all elements in the array are the same. In our game, this meant we had five of a kind. We used compound `if` statements joined by the or operator to test for two cases of four of a kind and three cases of three of a kind. We used `if-elif` statements to control the logic of our program so that five of a kind wasn't also counted as four of a kind, and so on.

We worked more with Cartesian coordinates in the kaleidoscope program and simulated the effect of reflections by changing the signs of (x, y) coordinate values. We repeated each spiral of random size, color, and location four times on the screen to create our kaleidoscope effect. You learned how to increase the turtle's drawing speed with `t.speed(0)`.

Random numbers and choices add an element of chance to make a game more interesting. Just about every game you've played has an element of chance. Now that you can build randomness into programs, you can code games people love to play.

At this point, you should be able to do the following:

- Import the `random` module into your programs.
- Use `random.randint()` to generate a random integer number in a given range.

- Use `random.choice()` to pick a value at random out of a list or array.

- Use `random.choice()` to generate 52 card values from two arrays of strings containing only the faces and suits.

- Determine the size of your drawing window with `turtle.window_width()` and `turtle.window_height()`.

- Move the turtle to any position on the drawing screen with `turtle.setpos(x,y)`.

- Use the `random.randrange()` function to generate a random number in any range.

- Find the index of an element in a list or array with the `.index()` function.

- Build a `while` game loop using a Boolean flag variable like `keep_going`.

- Construct an array of similar types of values, assign values to elements in the array by their index (as in `dice[0] = 2`), and use array elements like regular variables.

- Sort lists or arrays with the `.sort()` function.

- Reflect points about the x- and y-axes by changing the signs of the points' (*x*, *y*) coordinate values.

- Change the turtle's drawing speed with the `.speed()` function.

PROGRAMMING CHALLENGES

For this chapter's challenge problems, we'll extend the *Kaleidoscope.py* and *HighCard.py* programs. (If you get stuck, go to *http://www.nostarch.com/teachkids/* for sample answers.)

#1: RANDOM SIDES AND THICKNESS

Add more randomness to *Kaleidoscope.py* by adding two more random variables. Add a variable `sides` for the number of sides and then use that variable to change the angle we turn each time in the spiral loop (and therefore, the number of sides in the spiral) by using `360/sides + 1` as your angle instead of `91`. Next, create a variable called `thick` that will store a random number between 1 and 6 for the turtle pen's thickness. Add the line `t.width(thick)` in the right place to change the thickness of the lines of each spiral in our random kaleidoscope.

#2: REALISTIC MIRRORED SPIRALS

If you know some geometry, two more tweaks make this kaleidoscope even more realistic. First, keep track of the direction (between 0 and 360 degrees) the turtle is pointing before drawing the first spiral by getting the result of `t.heading()` and storing it in a variable called angle. Then, before drawing each mirrored spiral, change the angle to the correct mirrored direction by pointing the turtle with `t.setheading()`. Hint: the second angle will be 180 - angle, the third spiral's angle will be angle - 180, and the fourth will be 360 - angle.

Then, try turning left after each drawn line for the first and third spirals and turning right each time for the second and fourth spirals. If you implement these improvements, your spirals should really look like mirror images of each other in size, shape, color, thickness, and orientation. If you like, you can even keep the shapes from overlapping so much by changing the range of the x- and y-coordinate values to `random.randrange(size,turtle.window_width()//2)` and `random.randrange(size,turtle.window_height()//2)`.

#3: WAR

Turn *HighCard.py* into the full game of War by making three changes. First, keep score: create two variables to keep track of how many hands the computer has won and how many the user has won. Second, simulate playing one full deck of cards by dealing 26 hands (perhaps by using a for loop instead of our while loop or by keeping track of the number of hands played so far) and then declare a winner based on which player has more points. Third, handle ties by remembering how many ties have happened in a row; then, the next time one of the players wins, add the number of recent ties to that winner's score and set the number of ties back to zero for the next round.

7

FUNCTIONS:
THERE'S A NAME FOR THAT

We've made use of a number of *functions* so far—
everything from print() to input() to turtle.forward().
But all of these functions have been either built-in or
imported from Python modules and libraries. In this
chapter, we'll write our *own* functions to do anything
we want, including responding to user actions like
mouse-clicking and keypresses.

Functions are helpful because they give us the ability to organize pieces of reusable code, then refer to those pieces later in our programs by a single short name or command. Take input() as an example: it prints a text prompt to ask a user for input, collects what the user types, and passes it to our program as a string that we can store in a variable. We reuse the input() function anytime we want to know something more from the user. If we didn't have this function, we might have to do all that work ourselves every time we wanted to ask the user for information.

The turtle.forward() function is another great visual example: every time we move the turtle forward to draw one of the sides of our spirals, Python draws one pixel at a time in the direction our turtle is currently heading on the screen, to the exact length we ask for. If we didn't have the turtle.forward() function, we would have to figure out how to color pixels on the screen, keep track of locations and angles, and do some fairly complex math to draw a certain distance every time.

Without these functions, our programs would be longer, harder to read, and harder to write. Functions let us take advantage of the previous programming work of lots of fellow coders. The good news is that we can also write our own functions to make our code shorter, easier to read, and more reusable.

In Chapter 6, we built programs that drew random spirals and a kaleidoscope pattern. We can use functions to make the code in these programs easier to read and to make parts of the code more reusable.

PUTTING THINGS TOGETHER WITH FUNCTIONS

Look back at *RandomSpirals.py* on page 115. Everything in the first for loop is the code to create just one random spiral. The for loop uses that code to draw 50 spirals of random color, size, and location.

Say we want to use that random spiral code in another program, like a game or a screensaver app. In *RandomSpirals.py*, it's not easy to tell where the actual spiral drawing starts or stops, and we just wrote that code a few pages ago. Imagine coming back to this program in three months! We would have a hard time figuring out what the app is supposed to do and which lines we need to copy over into a new program if we want to draw random spirals again.

To make a piece of code reusable later, or just easier to read now, we can *define a function* and give it an easy-to-understand name, just like input() or turtle.forward(). Defining a function is also called *declaring* the function, and it just means that we're telling the computer what we want the function to do. Let's create a function to draw a random spiral on the screen; we'll call it random_spiral(). We can reuse this function anytime we want to draw random spirals, in any program.

DEFINING RANDOM_SPIRAL()

Open *RandomSpirals.py* (Chapter 6), save it as a new file called *RandomSpiralsFunction.py*, and begin this function definition *after* setting up the turtle's pen, speed, and colors but *before* the for loop. (You can refer to the final program on page 145 to see how this should look.) Our definition of random_spiral() should go after the turtle setup because the function will need to use the turtle pen t and the list of colors. The definition should go before the for loop because we'll be using random_spiral() in the for loop, and you have to define a function before you can use it. Now that we've found the right place in our program, let's start defining the random_spiral() function.

We define a function in Python using the keyword def (short for *definition*), followed by the name of the function, parentheses (), and a colon (:). Here's the first line of the random_spiral() function we'll build:

```
def random_spiral():
```

The rest of the function definition will be one or more statements, indented from the left, just like when we grouped statements in our for loops. To draw a random spiral, we need to set a random color, a random size, and a random (*x*, *y*) location on the screen, and then move the pen there and draw the spiral. Here's the code to complete our random_spiral() function:

```python
def random_spiral():
    t.pencolor(random.choice(colors))
    size = random.randint(10,40)
    x = random.randrange(-turtle.window_width()//2,
                          turtle.window_width()//2)
    y = random.randrange(-turtle.window_height()//2,
                          turtle.window_height()//2)
    t.penup()
    t.setpos(x,y)
    t.pendown()
    for m in range(size):
        t.forward(m*2)
        t.left(91)
```

Note that the computer doesn't actually *run* the code when the function is being defined. If we type the function definition into IDLE, we won't get a spiral—yet. To actually draw a spiral, we need to call the random_spiral() function.

CALLING RANDOM_SPIRAL()

A function definition tells the computer what we want to do when someone actually calls the function. After defining a function, we *call* it in our program using the function's name followed by parentheses:

```python
random_spiral()
```

You've got to remember the parentheses, because that tells the computer you want to run the function. Now that we've defined random_spiral() as a function, when we call random_spiral() like this in our program, we'll get a random spiral drawn on a turtle screen.

Now, to draw 50 random spirals, instead of using all the code in *RandomSpirals.py*, we can shorten our for loop to this:

```python
for n in range(50):
    random_spiral()
```

This loop is easier to read, thanks to our use of a function that we built all by ourselves. We've made our code easier to understand, and we can easily move the random spiral code over into another program by copying and pasting the function definition.

Here's the whole program together; type this into IDLE and save it as *RandomSpiralsFunction.py* or download it from *http://www.nostarch.com/teachkids/*.

RandomSpiralsFunction.py

```python
import random
import turtle
t = turtle.Pen()
t.speed(0)
turtle.bgcolor("black")
colors = ["red", "yellow", "blue", "green", "orange", "purple",
          "white", "gray"]
def random_spiral():
    t.pencolor(random.choice(colors))
    size = random.randint(10,40)
    x = random.randrange(-turtle.window_width()//2,
                          turtle.window_width()//2)
    y = random.randrange(-turtle.window_height()//2,
                          turtle.window_height()//2)
    t.penup()
    t.setpos(x,y)
    t.pendown()
    for m in range(size):
        t.forward(m*2)
        t.left(91)

for n in range(50):
    random_spiral()
```

In addition to a more readable program, we also get a reusable random_spiral() function that we can copy, modify, and easily use in other programs.

If you find yourself reusing a chunk of code again and again, convert it into a function like we did with random_spiral() using def, and you'll find it much easier to *port* the code—that is, carry it over and reuse it—into new applications.

NOTE   *You can even create your own module full of functions and import your module just like we've imported turtle and random in our programs (see Appendix C on how to create a module in Python). That way you can share your code with friends.*

PARAMETERS: FEEDING YOUR FUNCTION

When creating a function, we can define *parameters* for that function. Parameters allow us to send information to the function by passing values to it as *arguments* inside its parentheses. We've been passing arguments to functions since our first `print()` statement. When we code `print("Hello")`, `"Hello"` is an argument representing the string value that we want printed to the screen. When we call the turtle function `t.left(90)`, we're passing the value 90 as the number of degrees we want our turtle to turn left.

The `random_spiral()` function didn't need parameters. All the information it needed was in the code inside the function. But if we want, functions that we build can take information in the form of parameters. Let's define a function, `draw_smiley()`, to draw a smiley face at a random location on the screen. This function will take a pair of random coordinates and draw the smiley face at those coordinates. We'll define and call `draw_smiley()` in a program called *RandomSmileys.py*. The complete program is shown on page 151— but let's build it step by step.

SMILEYS AT RANDOM LOCATIONS

We want to write a program that, rather than drawing random spirals, draws smiley faces. It'll take a bit more planning to draw a smiley face than it did to randomly pick a color and size and draw a spiral. Let's go back to our friend from Chapter 6, a piece of graph paper. Because we haven't drawn something as complicated as a smiley face in our programs before, it's best to draw this on paper first and then translate it into code, one part at a time. Figure 7-1 shows a smiley face on a graph-paper grid that we can use to plan our drawing.

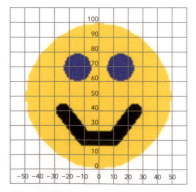

Our program will draw smileys like this one all over the screen at random (*x*, *y*) coordinates. The function definition for `draw_smiley()` will take two parameters, x and y, for the location where the smiley is to be drawn. As shown in Figure 7-1, we will draw the smiley face as if it were

Figure 7-1: We're planning our program by drawing a smiley face on graph paper first.

sitting on the (x, y) location, so picture moving this smiley face template around by placing its origin $(0, 0)$ over any other point (x, y) on the screen. Let's figure out how to draw each smiley face starting from a given point.

DRAWING A HEAD

Each smiley face has a yellow circle for the head, two small blue circles for eyes, and some black lines for the mouth. Given a point on the screen, our draw_smiley() function will need to draw a head, eyes, and a mouth at the correct positions relative to the given point. To figure out the code that will go in our function definition, let's plan the head, eyes, and mouth separately, starting with the head. We'll draw the head first so that it doesn't cover the eyes and mouth we'll draw next.

We'll count each grid line in Figure 7-1 as 10 pixels, so the smiley we've drawn would measure 100 pixels tall; that will equal around an inch, give or take, on most computer screens. Since the *diameter*, or height and width, of the circle is 100 pixels, that means it has a *radius* (one-half the diameter) of 50 pixels. We need the radius because the turtle module's circle() command takes the radius as its parameter. The command to draw a circle with a radius of 50 (which makes a diameter of 100) is t.circle(50). The circle() function draws a circle directly above the turtle's current (x, y) location. We'll need to know this to correctly place the eyes and mouth, so I've drawn my smiley face with the bottom edge resting on the origin, $(0, 0)$. We can figure out where we need to draw everything else by adding the coordinates of each part to that starting (x, y) location of $(0, 0)$.

To draw the big yellow head, we'll make the pen color yellow, make the fill color yellow, turn on the paint fill for our shape, draw the circle (which gets filled with yellow because we turned on the paint fill), and turn off the paint fill when we're done. Assuming we have a turtle pen named t defined earlier in the program, the code to draw the yellow circle as the head of our smiley face at the current (x, y) location looks like this:

```
# Head
t.pencolor("yellow")
t.fillcolor("yellow")
t.begin_fill()
t.circle(50)
t.end_fill()
```

To fill the circle with yellow, we add four lines of code around our t.circle(50) command. First, we set the pen color to yellow with t.pencolor("yellow"). Second, we set the fill color with t.fillcolor("yellow"). Third, before we call the t.circle(50) command to draw the face of our smiley, we tell the computer that we want to fill the circle we're drawing. We do this with the t.begin_fill() function. Finally, after we draw our circle, we call the t.end_fill() function to tell the computer that we're done with the shape that we want to fill with color.

DRAWING EYES

First, we need to figure out where to position the turtle to draw the left eye in the correct place, then set the fill color to blue, and finally draw a circle of the correct size. The eyes are about 20 pixels (two grid lines) tall, and we know that a diameter of 20 means that we need a radius of half that amount, or 10, so we'll use the t.circle(10) command to draw each eye. The tricky part is deciding where to draw them.

Our (x, y) starting point will be the local origin of each smiley face, and you can locate the left eye in Figure 7-1. It looks like it starts about 6 grid lines above the origin (60 pixels up, in the positive y-direction), and it's sitting about 1.5 grid lines to the left of the y-axis (or about 15 pixels left, in the negative x-direction).

To tell our program how to get to the right place to draw the left eye, starting from the bottom of the big yellow circle at a given (x, y) passed to our function as a pair of arguments, we need to start at x and move left 15 pixels, start at y and move up 60 pixels, or move to (x-15, y+60). So, calling t.setpos(x-15, y+60) should put the turtle where we need to start drawing our left eye. Here's the code for the left eye:

```
# Left eye
t.setpos(x-15, y+60)
t.fillcolor("blue")
t.begin_fill()
t.circle(10)
t.end_fill()
```

An easy mistake might be writing the setpos command with just (−15, 60) as arguments, but remember that we want to draw lots of smiley faces at various (x, y) positions on the screen; not all the faces will begin at (0, 0). The command t.setpos(x-15, y+60) will make sure that wherever our yellow face is being drawn, our left eye will be in the upper left of that face.

The code to draw the right eye is almost identical to the code for drawing the left eye. We can see that the right eye is 15 pixels (1.5 grid lines) to the right of our (*x*, *y*) location, and still 60 pixels up. The command t.setpos(x+15, y+60) should place the eye symmetrically. Here's the code for the right eye:

```
# Right eye
t.setpos(x+15, y+60)
t.begin_fill()
t.circle(10)
t.end_fill()
```

The fill color is still blue from the left eye, so we just have to set the turtle to the correct position (x+15, y+60), turn the fill on, draw the eye, and finish filling it.

DRAWING A MOUTH

Now let's plan the most important part of the smiley face: the smile. To make the smile simpler, we're going to draw the mouth with just three thick, black lines. The left side of the mouth looks like it starts about 2.5 grid lines to the left of and 4 grid lines above our point (*x*, *y*), so we'll position the turtle at (x-25, y+40) to start drawing the smile. We'll set the pen color to black and the width to 10 so that the smile is thick and easy to see. From the upper-left corner of the smile, we need to go to (x-10, y+20), then to (x+10, y+20), and finally to the upper-right corner of the smile at (x+25, y+40). Notice that these pairs of points are mirror images of one another across the y-axis; this makes our smiley face nice and even.

Here's the code for the mouth:

```
# Mouth
t.setpos(x-25, y+40)
t.pencolor("black")
t.width(10)
t.goto(x-10, y+20)
t.goto(x+10, y+20)
t.goto(x+25, y+40)
❶ t.width(1)
```

After we set the turtle at the upper-left corner of the mouth, we change the pen color to black and the width to 10. We start drawing by telling the turtle to go to each of the other three points of the smile. The turtle module's goto() function does the same thing as setpos(): it moves the turtle to a given point. I'm using it here just so you can see there's an alternative to setpos(). Finally, at ❶, t.width(1) sets the pen width back down to 1 so that our shapes aren't too thick when the next face is drawn.

DEFINING AND CALLING DRAW_SMILEY()

All that remains is to define the draw_smiley() function with all the code to draw a smiley face, set up a loop to generate 50 random (x, y) locations on the screen, and call the draw_smiley(x,y) function to draw smileys at all 50 locations.

The function definition for draw_smiley() will need to take two parameters, x and y, for the location where the smiley is to be drawn, and it will need to lift the turtle's pen, move the turtle to that (x, y) position, and then put the pen back down to get ready to draw. After that, we just need to add our code snippets for drawing the big yellow face, the left and right eyes, and the mouth.

```
def draw_smiley(x,y):
    t.penup()
    t.setpos(x,y)
    t.pendown()
    # All of your drawing code goes here...
```

The final piece will be our for loop to generate 50 random locations for the smiley faces and call the draw_smiley() function to draw each face. It will look like this:

```
for n in range(50):
    x = random.randrange(-turtle.window_width()//2,
                         turtle.window_width()//2)
    y = random.randrange(-turtle.window_height()//2,
                         turtle.window_height()//2)
    draw_smiley(x,y)
```

Our random x- and y-coordinate values are just like those we saw in Chapter 6, generating random points from the left half to the right half of the screen, and from the bottom half to the top half. With draw_smiley(x,y), we're passing these random coordinates as arguments to the draw_smiley() function, which will draw a smiley at that random spot.

PUTTING IT ALL TOGETHER

Put the program together, and it looks something like this:

RandomSmileys.py

```
import random
import turtle
t = turtle.Pen()
t.speed(0)
t.hideturtle()
turtle.bgcolor("black")
❶ def draw_smiley(x,y):
    t.penup()
    t.setpos(x,y)
    t.pendown()
    # Head
    t.pencolor("yellow")
    t.fillcolor("yellow")
    t.begin_fill()
    t.circle(50)
    t.end_fill()
    # Left eye
    t.setpos(x-15, y+60)
    t.fillcolor("blue")
    t.begin_fill()
    t.circle(10)
    t.end_fill()
```

```
            # Right eye
            t.setpos(x+15, y+60)
            t.begin_fill()
            t.circle(10)
            t.end_fill()
            # Mouth
            t.setpos(x-25, y+40)
            t.pencolor("black")
            t.width(10)
            t.goto(x-10, y+20)
            t.goto(x+10, y+20)
            t.goto(x+25, y+40)
            t.width(1)
❷   for n in range(50):
            x = random.randrange(-turtle.window_width()//2,
                                  turtle.window_width()//2)
            y = random.randrange(-turtle.window_height()//2,
                                  turtle.window_height()//2)
            draw_smiley(x,y)
```

As usual, we import the modules we need and set up our turtle, setting its speed to 0 (the fastest). We use hideturtle() so the turtle itself doesn't show up on the screen; this speeds up drawing too.

At ❶, we define our draw_smiley() function so that its job is to draw the smiley's face, left eye, right eye, and smile, using all that code we wrote before. All it needs to do its job is an x-coordinate and a y-coordinate.

In our for loop at ❷, a random x and y are chosen and passed to draw_smiley(), which then draws a smiley with all features in the correct locations relative to that random point.

The *RandomSmileys.py* program will draw 50 smiley faces at random positions on the drawing screen, as shown in Figure 7-2.

You can customize the program to draw just about any shape you want, as long as you design a function to draw that shape starting from any (x, y) location. Start with graph paper like we did in this example to make it easier to find the important points. If it bothers you that some of the smiley faces are halfway off the screen on the left and right, or almost all the way off the screen at the top, you can use a bit of math in the x and y randrange() statements to keep your smileys completely on the screen. Go to *http://www.nostarch.com/teachkids/* for a sample answer to this challenge.

Figure 7-2: The RandomSmileys.py *program produces a happy result.*

RETURN: IT'S WHAT YOU GIVE BACK THAT COUNTS

We can send information to a function using arguments, but what if we want to *receive* information back *from* a function? For example, what if we build a function to convert inches to centimeters, and we want to store the converted number to use in further calculations, rather than just printing it directly to the screen? To pass information from a function back to the rest of our program, we use a return statement.

RETURNING A VALUE FROM A FUNCTION

There are lots of times when we want to get information back from a function. For example, let's actually build the function to convert inches to centimeters and call it `convert_in2cm()`. We can imagine the parameter that we might want to accept in the function: a measurement in inches. But this function is a perfect candidate for giving information back to the rest of our program—namely, the converted measurement in centimeters.

To convert a length in inches to its equivalent in centimeters, we multiply the number of inches by 2.54—the approximate number of centimeters in an inch. To pass that calculation back to the rest of the program, we would use a return statement. The value after the keyword return will be passed back to the program as the function's *return value*, or result. Let's define our function:

```
def convert_in2cm(inches):
    return inches * 2.54
```

If you type these two lines into the Python shell and then type convert_in2cm(72) and press ENTER, Python will respond with 182.88. There are about 182.88 centimeters in 72 inches (or 6 feet—my height). The value 182.88 is returned by the function, and in the command line shell, we see the return value printed on the next line after we call a function.

We could also perform another useful conversion: pounds to kilograms. To convert pounds to kilograms, we divide the weight in pounds by 2.2, the approximate number of pounds in 1 kilogram. Let's create a function called convert_lb2kg() that will take a value in pounds as its parameter and return the converted value in kilograms:

```
def convert_lb2kg(pounds):
    return pounds / 2.2
```

The return statement is sort of like using parameters in reverse, except that we can return only *one* value, not a set of values like the parameters we take in. (That one value can be a list, however, so with some work you can pass multiple values back in a single return variable.)

USING RETURN VALUES IN A PROGRAM

Using these two conversion functions, let's build a silly application: a Ping-Pong-ball height and weight calculator. This program will answer the questions "How many Ping-Pong balls tall am I?" and "What is my weight in Ping-Pong balls?"

An official Ping-Pong ball weighs 2.7 grams (0.095 ounces) and measures 40 millimeters (4 centimeters, or 1.57 inches) in diameter. To calculate how many Ping-Pong balls it would take to match our height and weight, we need to divide our height in centimeters by 4 and divide our weight in grams by 2.7. But not everyone knows their weight in grams or height in centimeters: in the United States, we usually measure our weight in pounds and our height in feet and inches. Fortunately, the two conversion functions we just developed will help us convert those measurements to their equivalents in the metric system. We can then use these numbers to perform the conversion to Ping-Pong-ball units.

Our program will define the two conversion functions convert_in2cm() and convert_lb2kg(). Then it will ask the user for their height and weight, calculate the user's height and weight in Ping-Pong balls, and display the calculations on the screen. Type and run the following code:

PingPongCalculator.py

```
❶ def convert_in2cm(inches):
      return inches * 2.54

  def convert_lb2kg(pounds):
      return pounds / 2.2

❷ height_in = int(input("Enter your height in inches: "))
  weight_lb = int(input("Enter your weight in pounds: "))

❸ height_cm = convert_in2cm(height_in)
❹ weight_kg = convert_lb2kg(weight_lb)

❺ ping_pong_tall = round(height_cm / 4)
❻ ping_pong_heavy = round(weight_kg * 1000 / 2.7)

❼ feet = height_in // 12
❽ inch = height_in % 12

❾ print("At", feet, "feet", inch, "inches tall, and", weight_lb,
        "pounds,")
  print("you measure", ping_pong_tall, "Ping-Pong balls tall, and ")
  print("you weigh the same as", ping_pong_heavy, "Ping-Pong balls!")
```

At ❶, we enter the two conversion formulas we developed. Both functions take an input parameter (inches and pounds), and each function returns a value. At ❷, we ask the user for a height and weight and store those values in height_in and weight_lb. At ❸, we call the convert_in2cm() function, passing height_in as the value we want to convert, and we store the converted answer in the variable height_cm. We perform another conversion calculation at ❹ using the convert_lb2kg() function to convert the person's weight in pounds (abbreviated as *lbs*) into the equivalent in kilograms (*kg*).

The equation at ❺ does two things: first, it divides the user's height in centimeters by 4 to find their height in Ping-Pong balls; then, it rounds that answer to the nearest whole number with the round() function and stores the result in the variable ping_pong_tall. At ❻, we do something similar by converting the user's weight in kilograms to grams by multiplying by 1,000 and then dividing that amount by 2.7—the mass in grams of a standard Ping-Pong ball. That number is rounded to the nearest whole number and stored in the variable ping_pong_heavy.

At ❼ and ❽, we do just a little more math by figuring out the person's height in feet and inches. As I mentioned previously, this is normally how we express our height in the United States, and it will be a nice finishing touch as well as a way for the person to check that they entered the correct information. The // operator does integer division, so 66 inches, or 5.5 feet, would result in just 5 being stored in the variable feet, and the % operator (modulo) would store the remainder, 6 inches. The print statements at ❾ print out the user's height and weight, both in standard units and in Ping-Pong balls.

Here are the results from a few sample runs of the Ping-Pong calculator program, with Ping-Pong-ball measurements for my sons, Max and Alex, and me. (The only downside is that now my kids want to get 31,000 Ping-Pong balls.)

```
>>> ================================ RESTART ================================
>>>
Enter your height in inches: 42
Enter your weight in pounds: 45
At 3 feet 6 inches tall, and 45 pounds,
you measure 27 Ping-Pong balls tall, and
you weigh the same as 7576 Ping-Pong balls!
```

```
>>> ============================== RESTART ==============================
>>>
Enter your height in inches: 47
Enter your weight in pounds: 55
At 3 feet 11 inches tall, and 55 pounds,
you measure 30 Ping-Pong balls tall, and
you weigh the same as 9259 Ping-Pong balls!
>>> ============================== RESTART ==============================
>>>
Enter your height in inches: 72
Enter your weight in pounds: 185
At 6 feet 0 inches tall, and 185 pounds,
you measure 46 Ping-Pong balls tall, and
you weigh the same as 31145 Ping-Pong balls!
>>>
```

Any function we create can return a value, just like any function that we define can take parameters as input. Depending on what you want your function to do, use one or both of these features to write exactly the code for the function you need.

A TOUCH OF INTERACTION

We've coded some nice-looking graphical apps, but we're still a step or two away from building the next video game or mobile app. One of the remaining skills we need to learn is coding for user interaction: making our programs respond to mouse clicks, keypresses, and so on.

Most apps are *interactive*—they allow the user to touch, click, drag, press buttons, and feel in control of the program. We call these *event-driven* apps because they wait for the user to perform an action, or *event*. The code that responds to a user event, like opening a window when the user clicks an icon or starting a game when they touch a button, is referred to as an *event handler* because it handles or responds to an event from the user. It's also called an event *listener* because it's as if the computer is sitting patiently, listening

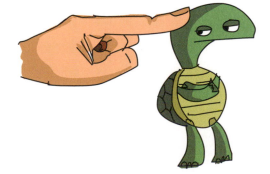

for the user to tell it what to do. We're going to learn to handle user events and make our programs even more engaging and interactive.

HANDLING EVENTS: TURTLEDRAW

There are lots of ways to make apps handle user events. Python's turtle module includes some functions for handling user events, including mouse clicks and keypresses. The first one we'll try is the turtle.onscreenclick() function. As the name suggests, this function allows us to handle events created by the user clicking on the turtle's screen.

There's a difference between this function and the ones we've used and built before: the argument that we send to turtle .onscreenclick() isn't a value—it's the name of another function:

```
turtle.onscreenclick(t.setpos)
```

Remember the setpos() function that we've used to move the mouse to a certain (*x*, *y*) location on the screen? Now we're telling the computer that when the turtle screen gets a mouse click, it should set the turtle to the position of that click on the screen. A function we pass as an argument to another function is sometimes called a *callback* function (because it gets *called back* by the other function). Notice that when we send a function as an argument to another function, the inside function doesn't need the parentheses after its name.

By sending the function name t.setpos to turtle.onscreenclick(), we're telling the computer what we want screen clicks to do: we want to set the position of the turtle to wherever the user clicked. Let's try it in a short program:

TurtleDraw.py

```
import turtle
t = turtle.Pen()
t.speed(0)
turtle.onscreenclick(t.setpos)
```

Type these four lines into IDLE, run the program, and then click different places around the screen. You just created a drawing program in four lines of code! Figure 7-3 shows a sample sketch I drew.

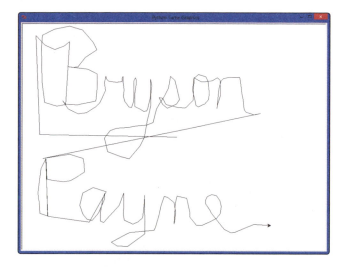

Figure 7-3: A TurtleDraw.py *sketch (there's a reason I'm an author and not an artist)*

The reason this works is that we've told the computer to do something when the user clicks the mouse on the screen: set the position of the turtle to that location. The turtle's pen is down by default, so when the user clicks on the drawing window, the turtle moves there and draws a line from its old location to the location where the user clicked.

You can customize *TurtleDraw.py* by changing the background color of the screen, the turtle's pen color, the width of the pen, and more. Check out the version my four-year-old son created (with some help from his dad):

TurtleDrawMax.py

```
import turtle
t = turtle.Pen()
t.speed(0)
turtle.onscreenclick(t.setpos)
turtle.bgcolor("blue")
t.pencolor("green")
t.width(99)
```

Max liked the drawing program (a lot), but he wanted the screen to be blue and the pen to be green and really thick, so we set the `bgcolor()`, `pencolor()`, and `width()` to blue, green, and 99, respectively. We made an arbitrary choice to set these *after* we told the computer what to do with mouse clicks on the screen (`t.setpos`).

This is fine, because the program keeps running even while it's listening for mouse clicks, so by the time the user clicks for the first time, the screen and pen are correctly colored and sized, as shown in Figure 7-4.

Figure 7-4: A drawing I produced by clicking a few times with TurtleDrawMax.py

Using the setpos() function as the callback for turtle .onscreenclick(), we've built a fun paint program that interacts with the user when they click the mouse by drawing lines to wherever they click. Try customizing the app with different colors, widths, or anything else you can think of to make it your own.

LISTENING FOR KEYBOARD EVENTS: ARROWDRAW

With our turtle drawing program, we saw how listening for mouse clicks can make the user feel like they're more in control of the program. In this section, we'll learn to use keyboard interaction to give the user even more options. We'll also define our own functions to use as event handlers.

In the *TurtleDraw.py* program, we passed t.setpos as the callback function to tell the computer what to do when an onscreenclick() event happened; we wanted to set the turtle's position to the location of that mouse click on the screen. The `setpos()` function is already given to us in the turtle module, but what if we want to create our own functions to handle events? Say we want to build a program that lets the user move the turtle on their screen by pressing the arrow keys instead of clicking the mouse button. How would we do that?

First, we have to build functions for moving the turtle for each arrow keypress on the keyboard, and then we have to tell the computer to listen for those keys to be pressed. Let's write a program that will listen for the up (↑), left (←), and right (→) keyboard arrow keys and let the user move the turtle forward or turn left or right with those keys.

Let's define some functions—up(), left(), and right()—that will move and turn the turtle:

```
def up():
    t.forward(50)
def left():
    t.left(90)
def right():
    t.right(90)
```

Our first function, up(), moves the turtle forward 50 pixels. The second, left(), turns the turtle left 90 degrees. Finally, right() turns the turtle right 90 degrees.

To run each of these functions when the user presses the correct arrow key, we have to tell the computer which function goes with which key and tell it to start listening for keypresses. To set the callback function for a keypress event, we use turtle.onkeypress(). This function usually takes two parameters: the name of the callback function (the event handler functions we created) and the specific key to listen for. To connect each of the three functions to its corresponding arrow key, we would write:

```
turtle.onkeypress(up, "Up")
turtle.onkeypress(left, "Left")
turtle.onkeypress(right, "Right")
```

The first line sets the up() function as the event handler for "Up" arrow keypresses; the function (up) goes first, and "Up" is the name of the up arrow key, ↑. The same goes for the left and right arrow keypresses. The final step is telling the computer to begin listening for keypresses, which we do with this command:

```
turtle.listen()
```

We need this last line for a couple of reasons. First, unlike with mouse clicks, simply pressing a key doesn't ensure that our turtle window will receive the keypress. When you click a window on your desktop, that window moves to the front and receives the *focus*, meaning that window will receive input from the user. When you click the mouse on the turtle window, it automatically makes that window the focus of the screen and of any mouse events that follow. With the keyboard, though, just pressing keys doesn't make a window receive those keypresses; the turtle.listen() command makes sure our turtle's window is the focus of the desktop so that it will be able to hear keypresses. Second, the listen() command tells the computer to start handling keypress events for all keys that we connected to functions with the onkeypress() function.

Here's the complete *ArrowDraw.py* program:

ArrowDraw.py

```
import turtle
t = turtle.Pen()
t.speed(0)
❶ t.turtlesize(2,2,2)
def up():
    t.forward(50)
def left():
    t.left(90)
def right():
    t.right(90)
turtle.onkeypress(up, "Up")
turtle.onkeypress(left, "Left")
turtle.onkeypress(right, "Right")
turtle.listen()
```

At ❶, the only new line in *ArrowDraw.py*, we make the turtle arrow twice as big, and give it a thicker outline with t.turtlesize(2,2,2). The three parameters are the horizontal stretch (2 means to make it twice as wide), the vertical stretch (2 times as tall), and the outline thickness (2 pixels thick). Figure 7-5 shows the result.

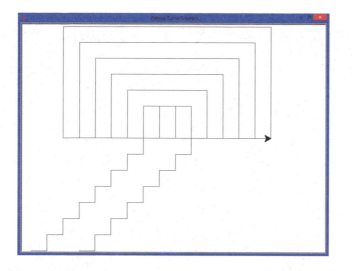

Figure 7-5: The ArrowDraw.py program lets the user draw using the up, right, and left arrow keys. The larger turtle arrow makes it easier to see where the turtle is headed.

This app is a bit like the old Etch-A-Sketch toy: you can draw fun shapes using just those three arrow keys, and you can retrace your steps. Feel free to customize the app with your own colors, pen width, and any other features you'd like to add. One extra feature you could add, which is included as a challenge at the end of this chapter, is the ability to click to move the turtle to a new location. Dream up new features and give them a try—that's the best way to learn something new!

HANDLING EVENTS WITH PARAMETERS: CLICKSPIRAL

In *TurtleDraw.py*, we let the user click to draw by telling the turtle.onscreenclick() listener to call the t.setpos function anytime the user clicked the screen. Let's build a new program named *ClickSpiral.py* that will draw spirals wherever the user clicks, as shown in Figure 7-6.

The onscreenclick() listener passes the x- and y-coordinates of every mouse click as arguments to the callback function we specify. When we want to handle mouse click events with a function of our own, we simply write a function that accepts those values—the x- and y-coordinates of the mouse click—as a pair of parameters.

Figure 7-6: A smiley face drawn using the ClickSpiral.py *app*

RandomSpiralsFunction.py (page 145) contained a function called `random_spiral()` that drew colorful spirals in random places on the screen. Now, however, instead of spirals at random locations, we want a spiral to appear where the user clicks the mouse. To do this, we can rewrite the `random_spiral()` function to take two parameters, x and y, from the `turtle.onscreenclick()` listener. We'll rename the function `spiral(x,y)`:

```python
def spiral(x,y):
    t.pencolor(random.choice(colors))
    size = random.randint(10,40)
    t.penup()
    t.setpos(x,y)
    t.pendown()
    for m in range(size):
        t.forward(m*2)
        t.left(91)
```

In this new version, we change the function's definition to reflect the new name and the two parameters that we will receive to draw at chosen positions on the screen as spiral(x,y). We still choose a random color and size for each spiral, but we have removed the two lines that generate a random x and y, because we will get the x and y as arguments from the onscreenclick() listener. Just as with the random_spiral() function, we move the pen to the correct (*x*, *y*) position and then draw the spiral.

The only step left is to set up our turtle window and the list of colors, and then tell our turtle.onscreenclick() listener to call the spiral function whenever the user clicks the mouse button over the drawing window. Here's the complete program:

ClickSpiral.py

```
import random
import turtle
t = turtle.Pen()
t.speed(0)
turtle.bgcolor("black")
colors = ["red", "yellow", "blue", "green", "orange", "purple",
          "white", "gray"]
def spiral(x,y):
    t.pencolor(random.choice(colors))
    size = random.randint(10,40)
    t.penup()
    t.setpos(x,y)
    t.pendown()
    for m in range(size):
        t.forward(m*2)
        t.left(91)
❶ turtle.onscreenclick(spiral)
```

As in *TurtleDraw.py*, we leave out the parentheses and parameters for our callback function ❶: turtle.onscreenclick(spiral) tells our program that it should call our spiral(x,y) function every time the user clicks the mouse on the screen, and the event listener automatically sends two arguments—the x-position and y-position of that click—to the spiral callback function. The same thing happened in *TurtleDraw.py* with the t.setpos callback, but this time, we created our own function to draw a spiral of a random color and size at the location of the mouse button click.

TAKING IT ONE STEP FURTHER: CLICKANDSMILE

Let's extend this interactive app by making one more change. Instead of drawing a spiral, say we want to draw a smiley face wherever the user clicks the mouse on the drawing screen. The code will look a lot like our *RandomSmileys.py* program from page 151, but instead of a loop that draws 50 smiley faces at random locations on the screen, this program will handle the mouse click event by drawing a smiley at the location the user chooses, as many or as few times as the user wishes to click.

In fact, because our draw_smiley() function already takes two parameters (the x- and y-coordinates of the location where we wish to draw the smiley face), the code for *ClickAndSmile.py* is identical to *RandomSmileys.py*, except for the last section. Just replace the for loop that draws 50 random smileys with a call to turtle.onscreenclick(draw_smiley). Remember how the turtle .onscreenclick() function allows us to pass the name of a function (like setpos) as the event handler for mouse clicks? We can pass it draw_smiley so that when the user clicks, our draw_smiley() function will do its work at the location of the click. We do not include draw_smiley's parentheses, or any arguments, inside the parentheses for turtle.onscreenclick().

ClickAndSmile.py

```python
import random
import turtle
t = turtle.Pen()
t.speed(0)
t.hideturtle()
turtle.bgcolor("black")
def draw_smiley(x,y):
    t.penup()
    t.setpos(x,y)
    t.pendown()
    # Face
    t.pencolor("yellow")
    t.fillcolor("yellow")
    t.begin_fill()
    t.circle(50)
    t.end_fill()
    # Left eye
    t.setpos(x-15, y+60)
    t.fillcolor("blue")
```

```
    t.begin_fill()
    t.circle(10)
    t.end_fill()
    # Right eye
    t.setpos(x+15, y+60)
    t.begin_fill()
    t.circle(10)
    t.end_fill()
    # Mouth
    t.setpos(x-25, y+40)
    t.pencolor("black")
    t.width(10)
    t.goto(x-10, y+20)
    t.goto(x+10, y+20)
    t.goto(x+25, y+40)
    t.width(1)
turtle.onscreenclick(draw_smiley)
```

Now, instead of drawing random smiley faces all over the screen, the user can draw a smiley face wherever they click the mouse; they can even draw a big smiley face out of little smiley faces, as shown in Figure 7-7.

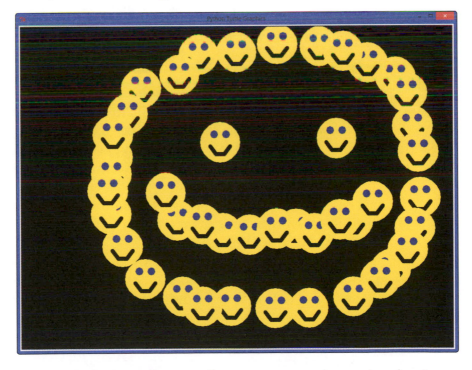

Figure 7-7: We've made our smiley program more interactive, drawing wherever the user clicks.

Whatever kinds of apps you want to build, you're probably going to rely on user interaction to drive the experience. Think of the games or other apps that you spend the most time playing: what they all have in common is that you have some kind of control over what happens and when. Whether you're moving a paddle to hit a ball; pressing the mouse button or touching and dragging to fire something through the air; or clicking, swiping, and tapping to clear a screen, you're generating user events—and the programs you love handle those events by doing something cool. Let's build one more interactive app for practice, and then we'll build even more of the kinds of apps we play with every day.

CLICKKALEIDOSCOPE

Let's combine our ability to create functions and our ability to handle interactive clicks to create an interactive kaleidoscope. The user will be able to click anywhere on the screen, and four reflected spirals of a random shape and color will be drawn starting from the point where the user clicked. The result will look like our *Kaleidoscope.py* program from page 134, but the user will be able to create their own unique patterns using this kaleidoscope.

THE DRAW_KALEIDO() FUNCTION

Let's talk about the challenges in building a customized kaleidoscope program. We know we want to allow the user to click the screen to begin the drawing process, so we'll use the turtle .onscreenclick() function from the previous section. We know that this function will give us an (x, y) location on the screen that we can use in our callback function. And we can look back at our original kaleidoscope program to see that all we have to do is draw a spiral at each of the four points (x, y), (–x, y), (–x, –y), and (x, –y) to achieve the desired reflection effect.

Each of our four reflected spirals should be the same color and size to create the mirror illusion. We will call our function draw_kaleido() and define it as follows:

```
❶ def draw_kaleido(x,y):
❷     t.pencolor(random.choice(colors))
❸     size = random.randint(10,40)
       draw_spiral(x,y, size)
```

```
draw_spiral(-x,y, size)
draw_spiral(-x,-y, size)
draw_spiral(x,-y, size)
```

At ❶, we name our function draw_kaleido, and we allow it to take the two parameters, x and y, from the turtle.onscreenclick() event handler so that our four reflected spirals will start at the (*x*, *y*) location where the user clicked the mouse. Then, at ❷, we randomly choose a pen color for all four reflected spirals in a set from our usual list of colors, colors.

At ❸, we pick a random size for all four reflected spirals and store it in size. Finally, we draw all of the four spirals at their (*x*, *y*), (*−x*, *y*), (*−x*, *−y*), and (*x*, *−y*) locations with a new function we've yet to actually write, called draw_spiral().

THE DRAW_SPIRAL() FUNCTION

Our draw_spiral() function will need to draw a spiral starting at a custom (*x*, *y*) location on the screen. Python's turtle pen will remember the color once it's set, so we don't have to pass that information as a parameter to our draw_spiral() function, but we do need the (*x*, *y*) location and the size of the spiral that we want to draw. So we'll define our draw_spiral() function to take three parameters:

```
def draw_spiral(x,y, size):
    t.penup()
    t.setpos(x,y)
    t.pendown()
    for m in range(size):
        t.forward(m*2)
        t.left(92)
```

This function takes the parameters x and y for the location to start drawing each spiral, and the parameter size to tell us how big to make the spiral. Inside the function, we lift the turtle's pen so that we can move without leaving a trail, we move the pen to the given (*x, y*) location, and we put the pen back down to prepare for the spiral. Our for loop will iterate m over the values from 0 to size, drawing a square spiral up to that side length.

All we'll have to do in our program, besides importing random and turtle and setting up our screen and list of colors, is tell the computer to listen for clicks on the turtle screen and call the draw_kaleido() function whenever a click event happens. We can do that with the command turtle.onscreenclick(draw_kaleido).

PUTTING IT ALL TOGETHER

Here's the full *ClickKaleidoscope.py* program. Type it in IDLE or download it from *http://www.nostarch.com/teachkids/* and run it.

ClickKaleidoscope.py

```
import random
import turtle
t = turtle.Pen()
t.speed(0)
t.hideturtle()
turtle.bgcolor("black")
colors = ["red", "yellow", "blue", "green", "orange", "purple",
          "white", "gray"]
def draw_kaleido(x,y):
    t.pencolor(random.choice(colors))
    size = random.randint(10,40)
    draw_spiral(x,y, size)
    draw_spiral(-x,y, size)
    draw_spiral(-x,-y, size)
    draw_spiral(x,-y, size)
def draw_spiral(x,y, size):
    t.penup()
    t.setpos(x,y)
    t.pendown()
    for m in range(size):
        t.forward(m*2)
        t.left(92)
turtle.onscreenclick(draw_kaleido)
```

We begin with our normal import statements and then set up our turtle environment and list of colors. Next, we define our `draw_spiral()` function, followed by `draw_kaleido()`, and we finish by telling the computer to listen for clicks on the turtle screen and call `draw_kaleido()` when click events occur. Now, whenever the user clicks a location on the drawing window, a spiral will be drawn there and reflected across the x- and y-axes for a total of four spirals of the same random shape and size.

The result is a fully interactive version of our spiral kaleidoscope program that allows the user to control the reflected pattern by clicking only in parts of the screen where they want spirals to appear. Figure 7-8 shows a sample run of the program with reflected patterns made of spirals.

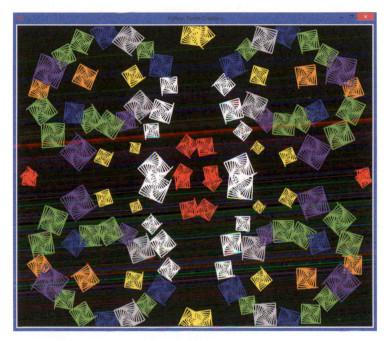

Figure 7-8: With our interactive kaleidoscope program, you can create any reflected pattern you wish!

Try your own patterns (like your first initial!) and take a screenshot of your results (in Windows, hold down the ALT and PRINT SCREEN keys to copy the turtle window and then paste into Word or your favorite drawing program; on a Mac, press and hold the COMMAND [⌘], SHIFT, and 4 keys, then press the spacebar, and then click the turtle drawing window to save a copy of the picture to your desktop as *Screenshot <date and time>.png*). Tweet your best screenshots to me at @brysonpayne on Twitter with the hashtag #kidscodebook, and I'll do my best to respond!

WHAT YOU LEARNED

In this chapter, you learned how to organize chunks of reusable code into functions, call your own functions from anywhere in your programs, pass information as parameters to those functions, and get information back from functions as return values. We wrote our first event-driven programs by telling the computer to listen for mouse clicks and keypresses, and you learned how to write your own callback functions to respond to user events.

We've developed our first fully interactive programs. Using the skills you've gained in this chapter, you're ready to begin writing even more advanced apps. The apps we frequently enjoy give users the experience of being in control of the program by responding to clicks, touches, keypresses, and more.

After mastering the concepts in this chapter, you should be able to do the following:

- Make code more reusable using functions.
- Organize and group code into functions.
- Define functions in Python using the def keyword.
- Call your own functions from programs that you write.
- Define and use functions that accept parameters as input values.
- Write functions that return values when called.
- Convert a mathematical formula into a function that returns the function's value.
- Explain some features of event-driven programs.
- Write a basic event-driven app that uses an event handler.
- Write an app that accepts mouse clicks and draws on the screen.
- Code event handlers for keyboard events.
- Program event handler functions that take parameters.
- Use x- and y-coordinates on the screen to draw specific patterns, such as kaleidoscopes.

PROGRAMMING CHALLENGES

Here are three challenges to extend what you learned in this chapter. For sample answers to these challenges, go to *http://www.nostarch.com/teachkids/*.

#1: MIRRORED SMILEYS

Create a mashup of the programs *ClickAndSmile.py* and *ClickKaleidoscope.py* to draw a smiley face in four mirrored corners of the screen when you click, just like the kaleidoscope program did with spirals. If you'd like an advanced challenge, draw two of the smiley faces flipped upside down so that they really look mirrored across the x-axis.

#2: MORE PING-PONG CALCULATIONS

Modify the Ping-Pong calculator so it asks the user for a number of Ping-Pong balls as input. Have it tell the user both how tall those Ping-Pong balls would be if stacked on top of one another and how much that number of Ping-Pong balls would weigh.

#3: A BETTER DRAWING PROGRAM

Change the *ArrowDraw.py* program to allow the user to turn the turtle in smaller increments—say 45 degrees (or even 30 or 15)—to give them finer control of the turtle. Then, add more key options, like allowing the user to press the greater-than symbol (>) to make the drawing length longer, the less-than symbol (<) to shorten the drawing length, the W key to make the pen wider, and the T key to make the pen thinner. To make it a great drawing program, add feedback in the form of drawing a string on the screen to show the pen width, segment length, and turtle's direction after every change.

For a finishing touch, add the ability to click to reposition the turtle. (Hint: create a function that accepts two parameters (x, y), lifts the turtle's pen, moves to (x, y), then puts the pen back down. Then, pass the name of this function to turtle.onscreenclick() to complete the app.)

8

TIMERS AND ANIMATION: WHAT WOULD DISNEY DO?

One way that I learned to program in my teens was by programming short games and animations, and then changing the code to do something new. I was amazed that I could immediately see my code make graphics appear on the screen, and I think you'll enjoy it as much as I did.

Games and animations have several things in common. First, they're fun! Second, they both involve drawing graphics on the screen and changing those graphics over time to give the illusion of motion. We've been able to draw graphics from the beginning of this book, but the Turtle library is too slow to use for a lot of animation or moving objects. In this chapter, we're going to install and work with a new module, *Pygame*, that lets us draw, animate, and even create arcade-style games using the skills you've picked up so far.

GETTING ALL GUI WITH PYGAME

A *graphical user interface* (*GUI*, sometimes pronounced "gooey") includes all the buttons, icons, menus, and windows that you see on your computer screen; it's how you interact with a computer. When you drag and drop a file or click an icon to open a program, you're enjoying a GUI. In games, when you press keys, move your mouse, or click, the only reason you can expect anything to happen (like running, jumping, rotating your view, and so on) is because a programmer set up the GUI.

Like the Turtle library, Pygame is very visual, perfect for GUIs for games, animations, and more. It's portable to just about every operating system, from Windows to Mac to Linux and beyond, so the games and programs you create in Pygame can run on pretty much any computer. Figure 8-1 shows the Pygame website, where you'll go to download Pygame.

Figure 8-1: Pygame is free, and so are the tutorials and sample games on its website.

To get started, install the pygame module by downloading the installer from the Downloads page at *http://www.pygame.org/*. For Windows, you'll probably want to download *pygame-1.9.1 .win32-py3.1.msi*, but see Appendix B for help if you have any trouble. For Mac and Linux, the installation is more involved; see Appendix B or go to *http://www.nostarch.com/teachkids/* for step-by-step instructions.

You can check that Pygame installed with no errors by entering the following into the Python shell:

```
>>> import pygame
```

If you get a regular >>> prompt in response, you know that Python was able to find the pygame module without error and the Pygame library is ready to use.

DRAWING A DOT WITH PYGAME

Once you have Pygame installed, you can run a short sample program to draw a dot on the screen, like the one in Figure 8-2.

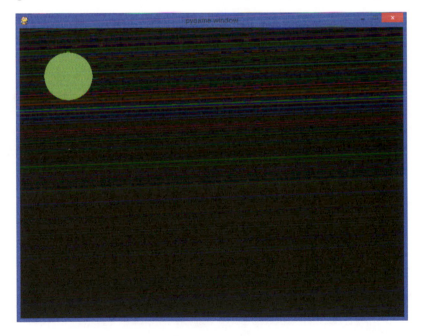

Figure 8-2: The ShowDot.py *program at work*

Type the following in a new IDLE window or download it from *http://www.nostarch.com/teachkids/*:

ShowDot.py

```
import pygame

❶ pygame.init()
❷ screen = pygame.display.set_mode([800,600])

❸ keep_going = True
❹ GREEN = (0,255,0)        # RGB color triplet for GREEN
  radius = 50

❺ while keep_going:
❻     for event in pygame.event.get():
❼         if event.type == pygame.QUIT:
               keep_going = False
❽     pygame.draw.circle(screen, GREEN, (100,100), radius)
❾     pygame.display.update()

❿ pygame.quit()
```

Let's step through this program line by line. First, we import the `pygame` module to gain access to its features. At ❶, we *initialize* Pygame, or set it up for use. The command `pygame.init()` will need to be called every time you want to use Pygame, and it always comes after the `import pygame` command and before any other Pygame functions.

At ❷, `pygame.display.set_mode([800,600])` creates a display window 800 pixels wide by 600 pixels tall. We store it in a variable called `screen`. In Pygame, windows and graphics are called *surfaces*, and the display surface `screen` is the main window where all of our other graphics will be drawn.

At ❸, you might recognize our looping variable, `keep_going`: we used this in our *HighCard.py* and *FiveDice.py* game loops in Chapter 6 as a Boolean flag to tell our program to keep playing. Here in our Pygame example, we use a game loop to continue drawing the graphics screen until the user closes the window.

At ❹, we set up two variables, `GREEN` and `radius`, for use in drawing our circle. The `GREEN` variable is set to the RGB triplet value (0,255,0), a bright green. (*RGB*, or *Red Green Blue*, is one of many ways to specify a color. To pick a color, you choose three numbers, each between 0 and 255. The first number determines how much red is in your color, the second number is the amount of green, and the third is blue. We picked 255 as our value for green and 0 for red and blue, so our RGB color is all green and no red or blue.) Our variable GREEN is a constant. We sometimes write *constants*—variables we don't intend to change—in all caps. Since the color should stay the same throughout our program, we've used all caps for GREEN. We set the radius variable equal to 50 pixels, for a circle 100 pixels in diameter.

The while loop at ❺ is our game loop, and it will keep running the Pygame window until the user chooses to exit. The for loop at ❻ is where we handle all the interactive events that the user can trigger in our program. In this simple example, the only event we're checking for is whether the user clicked the red X to close the window and exit the program ❼. If so, keep_going gets set to False and our game loop ends.

At ❽, we draw a green circle with a radius of 50 on the screen window at position (100,100): right 100 and down 100 pixels from the upper-left corner of the window (see "What's New in Pygame" on page 180 for more information on how Pygame's coordinate system is different from Turtle's). We're using pygame.draw, a Pygame module for drawing shapes like circles, rectangles, and line segments. We pass four arguments to the pygame.draw.circle() function: the surface on which we want to draw the circle (screen), the color for our circle (GREEN), the coordinates of its center point, and the radius. The update() function at ❾ tells Pygame to refresh the screen with the drawing changes.

Finally, when the user exits the game loop, the pygame.quit() command at ❿ clears the pygame module (it undoes all the setup from ❶) and closes the screen window so that the program can exit normally.

You should see an image like the one in Figure 8-2 when you run *ShowDot.py*. Take some time to play around with this dot program—create a different RGB color triplet, draw the dot in a different location on the screen, or draw a second dot. You'll begin to see the power and ease of drawing graphics with Pygame, and you'll have fun along the way.

This first program contains the foundation that we'll build on to create more complex graphics, animation, and, eventually, games.

WHAT'S NEW IN PYGAME

Before we dive deeper into the exciting world of Pygame, it's worth noting some important differences between Pygame and our old friend turtle graphics:

- We have a new coordinate system, as shown in Figure 8-3. Back in turtle graphics, the origin was at the center of the screen, and *y* got larger as we went up the screen. Pygame uses a more common window-oriented coordinate system (we see this in many other GUI programming languages, including Java, C++, and more). The *upper-left corner* of a window in Pygame is the origin, (0, 0). The x-coordinate values still increase as you move to the right (but there are no negative x-coordinate values, as they would be off the screen to the left); y-coordinate values increase as you move down (and negative y-coordinate values would be off the top of the window).

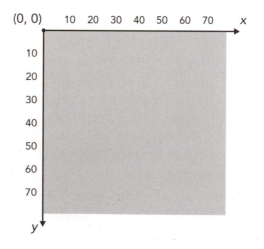

Figure 8-3: Pygame uses a window-oriented coordinate system.

- The game loop is always used in Pygame. In our earlier programs, we used a loop only if we wanted to keep playing or go back and do something again, but Pygame requires the game loop to keep updating the screen and handling events (even if the only event we handle is closing the window).

- We handle events in Pygame by calling `pygame.event.get()` to fetch a list of events that the user has performed. These events could be mouse clicks, key presses, or even window events like the user closing the window. We use a `for` loop to handle everything in this list of events from `pygame.event.get()`. In our turtle programs, we used callback functions to handle events. In Pygame, we can still create functions and call them in our event handler code, but we can process events just using `if` statements for those events that we care to listen for.

These differences make Pygame a new way of solving problems, and that's what we're always looking for! The more tools we have, the more problems we can solve.

THE PARTS OF A GAME

In this section, we'll change our *ShowDot.py* program to display a smiley face image instead of a green circle, as shown in Figure 8-4.

Figure 8-4: ShowPic.py draws the image CrazySmile.bmp on the screen.

As we build our *ShowPic.py* program, we'll learn about the three main parts of a game or animation in Pygame. First, there's the setup, where we import modules we need, create our screen, and initialize some important variables. Then comes the game loop, which handles events, draws graphics, and updates the display. This game loop is a while loop that keeps running as long as the user doesn't quit the game. Finally, we need a way to end the program when the user quits the game.

SETTING UP

First, download the smiley face image and save it in the same folder as your Python programs. Go to *http://www.nostarch.com/teachkids/* to find the source code downloads and save the image *CrazySmile.bmp* to the folder where you've been saving your *.py* files. It doesn't really matter where you keep your *.py* files; just make sure to save the BMP (short for *bitmap*, a common image file format) image file to the same location.

Next, let's take care of the setup:

```
import pygame          # Setup
pygame.init()
screen = pygame.display.set_mode([800,600])
keep_going = True
❶ pic = pygame.image.load("CrazySmile.bmp")
```

As always, we import the pygame module and then initialize using the pygame.init() function. Next, we set up our screen to be a new Pygame window 800×600 pixels in size. We create our Boolean flag keep_going to control our game loop and set it equal to True. Finally, we do something new: at ❶, we use pygame.image.load(), which loads an image from a file. We create a variable for our image file and load *CrazySmile.bmp*, which we'll refer to as pic in our program.

CREATING A GAME LOOP

At this point, we haven't drawn anything, but we've set up Pygame and loaded an image. The game loop is where we'll actually display the smiley face image on the screen. It's also where we'll handle events from the user. Let's start by handling one important event: the user choosing to quit the game.

```
while keep_going:      # Game loop
    for event in pygame.event.get():
❶       if event.type == pygame.QUIT:
            keep_going = False
```

Our game loop will keep running as long as keep_going is True. Inside the loop, we immediately check for events from the user. In advanced games, the user can trigger a lot of events at the same time, like pressing the down arrow on the keyboard while moving the mouse left and scrolling the mouse wheel.

In this simple program, the only event we're listening for is whether the user clicked the close window button to quit the program. We check for this at ❶. If the user triggered the pygame.QUIT event by trying to close the window, we want to tell our game loop to exit. We do this by setting keep_going to False.

We still need to draw our picture to the screen and update the drawing window to make sure everything appears on the screen, so we'll add these two final lines to our game loop:

```
screen.blit(pic, (100,100))
pygame.display.update()
```

The blit() method draws pic, the image that we've loaded from disk (our smiley face), onto our display surface, screen. We'll use blit() when we want to copy pixels from one surface (like the image we loaded from disk) onto another (like the drawing window). Here, we need to use blit() because the pygame.image.load() function works differently than the pygame.draw.circle() function we used earlier to draw our green dot. All pygame.draw functions accept a surface as an argument, so by passing screen to pygame.draw .circle(), we were able to have pygame.draw.circle() draw to our display window. But pygame.image .load() doesn't take a surface as an argument; instead, it automatically creates a new, separate surface for your image. The image won't appear on the original drawing screen unless you use blit().

In this case, we've told `blit()` that we want to draw `pic` at the location (100,100), or right 100 pixels and down 100 pixels from the upper-left corner of the screen (in Pygame's coordinate system, the origin is the upper-left corner; see Figure 8-3 on page 180).

The final line of our game loop is the call to `pygame.display.update()`. This command tells Pygame to show the drawing window with all the changes that have been made during this pass through the loop. That includes our smiley face. When `update()` runs, the window will be updated to show all the changes to our `screen` surface.

So far, we've taken care of our setup code, and we have a game loop with an event handler that listens for the user hitting the close window button. If the user clicks the close window button, the program updates the display and exits the loop. Next, we'll take care of ending the program.

EXITING THE PROGRAM

The last section of our code will exit the program once the user has chosen to quit the game loop:

```
pygame.quit()        # Exit
```

If you leave this line out of your programs, the display window will stay open even after the user tries to close it. Calling `pygame.quit()` closes the display window and frees up the memory that was storing our image, `pic`.

PUTTING IT ALL TOGETHER

Put it all together, and you'll see our *CrazySmile.bmp* image file—as long as you've saved the image in the same directory as your *ShowPic.py* program file. Here's the full listing:

ShowPic.py

```
import pygame        # Setup
pygame.init()
screen = pygame.display.set_mode([800,600])
keep_going = True
pic = pygame.image.load("CrazySmile.bmp")
```

```
while keep_going:     # Game loop
    for event in pygame.event.get():
        if event.type == pygame.QUIT:
            keep_going = False
    screen.blit(pic, (100,100))
    pygame.display.update()

pygame.quit()          # Exit
```

When you click the close window button, the display window should close.

This code has all the basic components we'll build on to make our programs even more interactive. In the rest of this chapter and in Chapter 9, we'll add code to our game loop to respond to different events (for example, making images on the screen move when the user moves the mouse). Now let's see how to create a program that draws an animated bouncing ball!

TIMING IT JUST RIGHT: MOVE AND BOUNCE

We already have the skills needed to create animation, or the illusion of motion, by making one small change to our *ShowPic.py* app. Instead of showing the smiley face image at a fixed location every time through the game loop, what if we change that location slightly every frame? By *frame*, I mean each pass through the game loop. The term comes from one way people make animations: they draw thousands of individual pictures, making each picture slightly different from the one before it. One picture is considered one frame. The animators then put all the pictures together on a strip of film and run the film through a projector. When the pictures are shown one after another very quickly, it looks like the characters in the pictures are moving.

With a computer, we can create the same effect by drawing a picture on the screen, clearing the screen, moving the picture slightly, and then drawing it again. The effect will look a bit like Figure 8-5.

Figure 8-5: In this first attempt at animation, our smiley image will streak off the screen.

We still call each drawing a *frame*, and the speed of our animation is how many *frames per second (fps)* we draw. A video game might run 60–120 frames per second, like high-definition television. Older, standard-definition TVs in the United States run at 30 fps, and many film projectors run at 24 fps (newer high-definition digital projectors can run at 60 fps or higher).

If you've ever made or seen a flip-book animation (in which you draw on the corners of pages in a notebook and then flip through them to create a mini-cartoon), you've seen that the illusion of motion can be created at many different frame rates. We'll aim for a rate around 60 fps, fast enough to create smooth animations.

MOVING A SMILEY

We can create simple motion in our while loop by drawing the smiley face image at different locations over time. In other words, in our game loop, we just need to update the (*x, y*) location of the picture and then draw it at that new location each time through the loop.

We'll add two variables to *ShowPic.py*: picx and picy, for the x- and y-coordinates of the image on the screen. We'll add these at the end of the setup portion of our program and then save the new version of the program as *SmileyMove.py* (the final version is shown on page 190).

```
import pygame           # Setup
pygame.init()
❶ screen = pygame.display.set_mode([600,600])
keep_going = True
pic = pygame.image.load("CrazySmile.bmp")
❷ colorkey = pic.get_at((0,0))
❸ pic.set_colorkey(colorkey)
picx = 0
picy = 0
```

The lines at ❷ and ❸ are an optional fix for a minor issue. If the CrazySmile.bmp image looks like it has square black corners on your screen, you can include these two lines to make sure those corners look transparent.

Notice that we've also changed our window screen to 600×600 pixels to make the window square at ❶. The game loop will begin the same way it did in *ShowPic.py*, but we'll add code to change the picx and picy variables by 1 pixel every time the loop runs:

```
while keep_going:       # Game loop
    for event in pygame.event.get():
        if event.type == pygame.QUIT:
            keep_going = False

    picx += 1           # Move the picture
    picy += 1
```

The += operator adds something to the variable on the left side (picx and picy), so with += 1, we've told the computer we want to change the x- and y-coordinates of the picture, (picx, picy), by 1 pixel every time through the loop.

Finally, we need to copy the image onto the screen at the new location, update the display, and tell our program what to do to exit:

```
    screen.blit(pic, (picx, picy))
    pygame.display.update()
pygame.quit()           # Exit
```

If you run those lines, you'll see our image take off! In fact, you'll have to look fast because it will move right off the screen.

Look back at Figure 8-5 for a glimpse of the smiley image before it slides out of view.

This first version may leave streaks of pixels on the display even when the smiley image has left the drawing window. We can make the animation cleaner by clearing the screen between each frame. The streaking lines we're seeing behind our smiley are the upper-left pixels of the smiley image; every time we move down and over each frame to draw a new version of our image and update the display, we're leaving behind a few stray pixels from the last picture.

We can fix this by adding a screen.fill() command to our drawing loop. The screen.fill() command takes a color as an argument, so we need to tell it what color we'd like to use to fill the drawing screen. Let's add a variable for BLACK (using all uppercase for BLACK to show that it's a constant) and set it equal to black's RGB color triplet, (0,0,0). We'll fill the screen surface with black pixels, effectively clearing it off, before we draw each new, moved copy of our animated image.

Add this line to your setup right after picy = 0 to create the black background fill color:

```
BLACK = (0,0,0)
```

And add this line right before the screen.blit() that draws our pic image on the screen:

```
    screen.fill(BLACK)
```

Our smiley face still speeds off the screen, but this time we're not leaving a trail of pixels behind our moving image. By filling the screen with black pixels, we've created the effect of "erasing" the old image from the screen every frame, before we draw the new image at the new location. This creates the illusion of smoother animation. On a relatively fast computer, though, our smiley flies off the screen way too fast. To change this, we need a new tool: a timer or clock that can keep us at a steady, predictable rate of frames per second.

ANIMATING A SMILEY WITH THE CLOCK CLASS

The final piece to make our *SmileyMove.py* app behave like an animation we might see in a game or movie is to limit the number of frames per second our program draws. Currently, we're moving the smiley image only 1 pixel down and 1 pixel to the right each time through the game loop, but our computer can draw this simple scene so fast that it can produce hundreds of frames per second, causing our smiley to fly off the screen in an instant.

Smooth animation is possible with 30 to 60 frames of animation per second, so we don't need the hundreds of frames zooming past us every second.

Pygame has a tool that can help us control the speed of our animation: the Clock class. A *class* is like a template that can be used to create *objects* of a certain type, with functions and values that help those objects behave in a certain way. Think of a class as being like a cookie cutter and objects as the cookies: when we want to create cookies of a certain shape, we build a cookie cutter that can be reused anytime we want another cookie of the same shape. In the same way that functions help us package reusable code together, classes allow us to package data and functions into a reusable template that we can use to create objects for future programs.

We can add an object of the Clock class to our program setup with this line:

```
timer = pygame.time.Clock()
```

This creates a variable called timer linked to a Clock object. This timer will allow us to gently pause each time through the game loop and wait just long enough to make sure we're not drawing more than a certain number of frames per second.

Adding the following line to our game loop will keep the frame rate at 60 fps by telling our Clock named timer to "tick" just 60 times per second:

```
timer.tick(60)
```

The following code, *SmileyMove.py*, shows the whole app put together. It gives us a smooth, steady animated smiley face slowly gliding off the lower right of the screen.

SmileyMove.py

```
import pygame                        # Setup
pygame.init()
screen = pygame.display.set_mode([600,600])
keep_going = True
pic = pygame.image.load("CrazySmile.bmp")
colorkey = pic.get_at((0,0))
pic.set_colorkey(colorkey)
picx = 0
picy = 0
BLACK = (0,0,0)
timer = pygame.time.Clock()   # Timer for animation

while keep_going:                    # Game loop
    for event in pygame.event.get():
        if event.type == pygame.QUIT:
            keep_going = False

    picx += 1                        # Move the picture
    picy += 1

    screen.fill(BLACK)               # Clear screen
    screen.blit(pic, (picx,picy))
    pygame.display.update()
    timer.tick(60)                   # Limit to 60 frames per second

pygame.quit()                        # Exit
```

The remaining problem is that the smiley still goes all the way off the screen in a few seconds. That's not very entertaining. Let's change our program to keep the smiley face on the screen, bouncing from corner to corner.

BOUNCING A SMILEY OFF A WALL

We've added motion from one frame to the next by changing the position of the image we were drawing on each pass through our game loop. We saw how to regulate the speed of that animation by adding a Clock object and telling it how many times per second to tick(). In this section, we'll see how to keep our smiley on the screen. The effect will look a bit like Figure 8-6, with the smiley appearing to bounce back and forth between two corners of the drawing window.

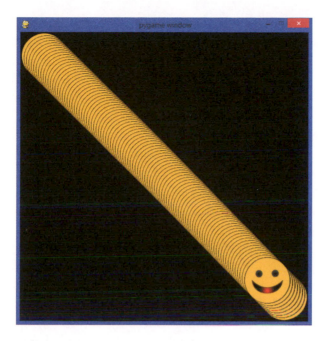

Figure 8-6: Our goal is to keep the smiley "bouncing" between the corners of the screen.

The reason our image ran off the screen before is that we didn't set *boundaries*, or limits, for our animation. Everything we draw on the screen is *virtual*—meaning it doesn't exist in the real world—so things don't really bump into one another. If we want the virtual objects on our screen to interact, we have to create those interactions with programming logic.

HITTING THE WALL

When I say that we want the smiley face to "bounce" off the edge of the screen, what I mean is that when the smiley comes to the edge of the screen, we want to change the direction it's moving so that it looks like it bounces off the solid edge of the screen. To do this, we need to test whether the (picx,picy) location of the smiley has reached the imaginary boundary at the edge of the screen. We call this logic *collision detection* because we're trying to *detect*, or notice, when a *collision* occurs, like the smiley face image "hitting" the edge of the drawing window.

We know that we can test for conditions using an if statement, so we could see if our image is touching, or *colliding* with, the right side of the screen by checking whether picx is greater than some value.

Let's figure out what that value might be. We know our screen is 600 pixels wide because we created our screen with `pygame.display.set_mode([600,600])`. We could use 600 as our boundary, but the smiley face would still go off the edge of the screen because the coordinate pair (`picx`,`picy`) is the location of the top-left pixel of our smiley face image.

To find our logical boundary—that is, the virtual line that `picx` has to reach for our smiley face to look like it has hit the right edge of the `screen` window—we need to know how wide our picture is. Because we know `picx` is the top-left corner of the image and it continues to the right, we can just add the width of our picture to `picx`, and when that sum equals 600, we'll know that the right edge of the image is touching the right edge of the window.

One way to find the width of our image is by looking at the properties of the file. In Windows, right-click the *CrazySmile.bmp* file, select the Properties menu item, and then click the Details tab. On a Mac, click the *CrazySmile.bmp* file to select it, press ⌘-I to get the file info window, and then click More Info. You'll see the width and height of the picture, as shown in Figure 8-7.

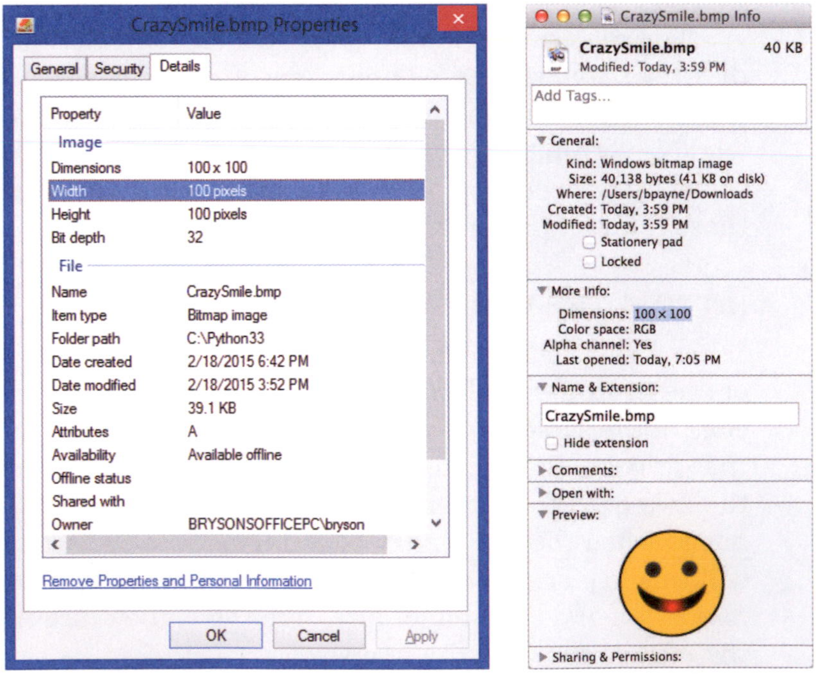

Figure 8-7: To determine our virtual boundaries so our smiley face can bounce off them, we need to know the width of our image file.

Our *CrazySmile.bmp* file measures 100 pixels across (and 100 pixels down). So if our screen is currently 600 pixels wide and the pic image needs 100 pixels to display the full image, our picx has to stay left of 500 pixels in the x-direction. Figure 8-8 shows these measurements.

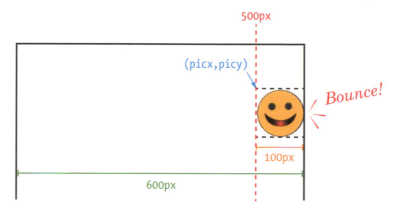

Figure 8-8: Calculating a bounce against the right side of the window

But what if we change our image file or want to handle images of different widths and heights? Fortunately, Pygame has a convenient function in the pygame.image class that our picture variable pic uses. The function pic.get_width() returns the width in pixels of the image stored in the pygame.image variable pic. We can use this function instead of hardcoding our program to handle only an image that measures 100 pixels wide. Similarly, pic.get_height() gives us the height in pixels of the image stored in pic.

We can test whether the image pic is going off the right side of the screen with a statement like this:

```
if picx + pic.get_width() > 600:
```

In other words, if the starting x-coordinate of the picture, plus the picture's width, is greater than the width of the screen, we'll know we've gone off the right edge of the screen, and we can change the image's direction of motion.

CHANGING DIRECTION

"Bouncing" off the edge of the screen means going in the oppo-site direction after hitting that edge. The direction our image is moving is controlled by the updates to picx and picy. In our old *SmileyMove.py*, we just added 1 pixel to picx and picy every time through the while loop with these lines:

```
picx += 1
picy += 1
```

However, these lines kept our image moving right and down 1 pixel every time; there was no "bounce," or changing direction, because we never changed the number added to picx and picy. Those two lines mean we're guaranteed to move right and down at a speed of 1 pixel per frame, every frame, even after the smiley has left the screen.

Instead, we can change the constant value 1 to a variable that will represent the *speed*, or number of pixels the image should move each frame. Speed is the amount of movement in a period of time. For example, a car that moves a lot in a short time is moving at a *high speed*. A snail that barely moves in the same period of time is moving at a *low speed*. We can define a variable called speed in the setup portion of our program for the amount of movement in pixels that we want for each frame:

```
speed = 5
```

Then, all we have to do in our game loop is change `picx` and `picy` by this new speed amount (instead of the constant amount 1) every time through the loop:

```
picx += speed
picy += speed
```

One pixel per frame seemed a bit too slow at 60 frames per second in *SmileyMove.py*, so I've increased the speed to 5 to make it move faster. But we're still not bouncing off the right edge of the screen; we just move off the screen quickly again, because the `speed` variable doesn't change when we hit the edge of the screen.

We can solve that final problem by adding our collision detection logic—that is, our test to see if we've hit the imaginary boundary at the left or right edges of the screen:

```
if picx <= 0 or picx + pic.get_width() >= 600:
    speed = -speed
```

First, we're checking both the left and right boundaries of the screen by seeing if `picx` is trying to draw at a negative x-coordinate value (off the left of the screen where x < 0) or if `picx + pic.get_width()` totals more than the 600-pixel width of the screen (meaning the picture's starting x-coordinate plus its width have gone off the right edge of the screen). If either of these happens, we know we've gone too far and we need to change the direction we're going in.

Notice the trick we're using if either of those boundary tests evaluates to `True`. By setting `speed = -speed`, we're changing the *direction* of the movement in our `while` loop by multiplying `speed` by −1, or by making it the negative of itself. Think of it this way: if we keep looping with `speed` equal to 5 until our `picx` plus the image's width hits the right edge of the screen at 600 pixels (`picx + pic.get_width() >= 600`), setting `speed = -speed` will change speed from 5 to -5 (negative five). Then, whenever our `picx` and `picy` change in the next pass through the loop, we'll add -5 to our location. This is the same as *subtracting* 5 from `picx` and `picy`, or moving *left and up* on our screen. If this works, our smiley face will now bounce off the lower-right corner of the screen and start traveling *backward*, back up to (0, 0) at the upper-left corner of the screen.

But that's not all! Because our `if` statement is also checking for the left screen boundary (`picx <= 0`), when our smiley face looks like it has hit the left side of the screen, it will change `speed` to `-speed` again. If `speed` is `-5`, this will change it to `-(-5)`, or `+5`. So if our negative `speed` variable was causing us to move to the left and up 5 pixels every frame, once we hit `picx <= 0` at the left edge of the screen, `speed = -speed` will turn `speed` back to positive 5, and the smiley image will start moving to the *right and down* again, in the positive x- and y-directions.

PUTTING IT ALL TOGETHER

Try version 1.0 of our app, *SmileyBounce1.py*, to see the smiley face bounce from the upper-left corner of the window to the lower-right corner and back again, never leaving the drawing screen.

SmileyBounce1.py

```
import pygame          # Setup
pygame.init()
screen = pygame.display.set_mode([600,600])
keep_going = True
pic = pygame.image.load("CrazySmile.bmp")
colorkey = pic.get_at((0,0))
pic.set_colorkey(colorkey)
picx = 0
picy = 0
BLACK = (0,0,0)
timer = pygame.time.Clock()
speed = 5

while keep_going:    # Game loop
    for event in pygame.event.get():
        if event.type == pygame.QUIT:
            keep_going = False
    picx += speed
    picy += speed

    if picx <= 0 or picx + pic.get_width() >= 600:
        speed = -speed

    screen.fill(BLACK)
    screen.blit(pic, (picx,picy))
    pygame.display.update()
    timer.tick(60)

pygame.quit()          # Exit
```

With this first version of the program, we have created what looks like a smoothly animated smiley face bouncing back and forth between two corners of a square drawing window. We are able to achieve this effect precisely because the window is a perfect square, 600×600 pixels in size, and because we always change our picx and picy values by the same amount (speed)—our smiley face travels only on the diagonal line where $x = y$. By keeping our image on this simple path, we only have to check whether picx goes past the boundary values at the left and right edges of the screen.

What if we want to bounce off all four edges (top, bottom, left, and right) of the screen, in a window that isn't a perfect square—say, 800×600? We'll need to add some logic to check our picy variable to see if it passes an upper or lower boundary (the top or bottom of the screen), and we'll need to keep track of horizontal and vertical speed separately. We'll do that next.

BOUNCING A SMILEY OFF FOUR WALLS

In *SmileyBounce1.py*, we kept the horizontal (left-right) and vertical (up-down) motion locked so that whenever the image was moving right, it was also moving down, and when it was moving left, it was also moving up. This worked well for our square window because the width and height of the screen were the same. Let's build on that example to create a bouncing animation that rebounds realistically off all four sides of the drawing window. We'll make the window 800×600 pixels in size with screen = pygame.display.set_mode([800,600]) to make the animation more interesting.

HORIZONTAL AND VERTICAL SPEED

First, let's separate the horizontal and vertical components of the speed. In other words, let's create one speed variable, speedx, for the *horizontal* speed (how fast the image is moving to the right or left), and another speed variable, speedy, for the *vertical* speed (how fast the image is moving down or up). We can accomplish this by changing the speed = 5 entry in the setup section of our app to initialize a speedx and speedy as follows:

```
speedx = 5
speedy = 5
```

We can then modify our image position updates in the game loop:

```
picx += speedx
picy += speedy
```

We change `picx` (the horizontal or x-position) by `speedx` (the horizontal speed) and `picy` (the vertical or y-position) by `speedy` (the vertical speed).

HITTING FOUR WALLS

The last part to figure out is the boundary collision detection for each of the four edges of the screen (top and bottom in addition to right and left). First, let's modify the left and right boundaries to match the new screen size (800 pixels wide) and to use the new horizontal speed `speedx`:

```
if picx <= 0 or picx + pic.get_width() >= 800:
    speedx = -speedx
```

Notice that our left-edge-boundary case remains the same at `picx <= 0`, because 0 is still the left boundary value when `picx` is at the left of the screen. This time, though, our right-edge-boundary case has changed to `picx + pic.get_width() >= 800`, because our screen is now 800 pixels wide, and our image still starts at `picx` and then draws its full width to the right. So when `picx + pic.get_width()` equals `800`, our smiley face looks like it is touching the right side of the drawing window.

We slightly changed the action that our left and right boundaries trigger, from `speed = -speed` to `speedx = -speedx`. We now have two components of our speed, and `speedx` will control the left and right directions and speeds (negative values of `speedx` will move the smiley face left; positive values will move it right). So when the smiley hits the right edge of the screen, we turn `speedx` negative to make the image go back toward the left, and when it hits the left edge of the screen, we turn `speedx` back to a positive value to rebound the image to the right.

Let's do the same thing with `picy`:

```
if picy <= 0 or picy + pic.get_height() >= 600:
    speedy = -speedy
```

To test whether our smiley has hit the top edge of the screen, we use `picy <= 0`, which is similar to `picx <= 0` for the left edge. To figure out whether our smiley has hit the bottom edge of the screen, we need to know both the height of the drawing window (600 pixels) and the height of the image (`pic.get_height()`), and we need to see if the top of our image, `picy`, plus the image's height, `pic.get_height()`, totals more than the height of our screen, 600 pixels.

If `picy` goes outside these top and bottom boundaries, we need to change the direction of the vertical speed (`speedy = -speedy`). This makes the smiley face look like it's bouncing off the bottom edge of the window and heading back up, or bouncing off the top and heading back down.

PUTTING IT ALL TOGETHER

When we put the whole program together in *SmileyBounce2.py*, we get a convincing bouncing ball that is able to rebound off all four edges of the screen for as long as we run the app.

SmileyBounce2.py

```
import pygame          # Setup
pygame.init()
screen = pygame.display.set_mode([800,600])
keep_going = True
pic = pygame.image.load("CrazySmile.bmp")
colorkey = pic.get_at((0,0))
pic.set_colorkey(colorkey)
picx = 0
picy = 0
BLACK = (0,0,0)
timer = pygame.time.Clock()
speedx = 5
speedy = 5

while keep_going:      # Game loop
    for event in pygame.event.get():
        if event.type == pygame.QUIT:
            keep_going = False
```

```
    picx += speedx
    picy += speedy

    if picx <= 0 or picx + pic.get_width() >= 800:
        speedx = -speedx
    if picy <= 0 or picy + pic.get_height() >= 600:
        speedy = -speedy

    screen.fill(BLACK)
    screen.blit(pic, (picx, picy))
    pygame.display.update()
    timer.tick(60)

pygame.quit()          # Exit
```

The rebounds look realistic. If the smiley is coming toward the bottom edge at a 45-degree angle down and to the right, it bounces off at a 45-degree angle up and to the right. You can experiment with different values of speedx and speedy (say, 3 and 5, or 7 and 4) to see the angles change for every bounce.

Just for fun, you can comment out the line screen.fill(BLACK) in *SmileyBounce2.py* to see the path traveled by our smiley face as it bounces off each edge of the screen. When you *comment out* a line, you turn it into a comment by putting a hash mark at the beginning, as follows:

```
# screen.fill(BLACK)
```

This tells the program to ignore the instruction on that line. Now the screen is not erased after each smiley face is drawn, and you'll see a pattern created by the trail your animation is leaving behind, like in Figure 8-9. Because each new smiley is drawn over the previous one, the result looks like cool, retro 3-D screensaver artwork as it draws.

Our collision-detection logic has allowed us to create the illusion of a solid smiley face bouncing off all four edges of a solid drawing screen. This is an improvement over our original version, which let the smiley slide off into oblivion. When we create games that allow the user to interact with pieces on the screen, and that allow those pieces to look as if they're interacting with one another—like in Tetris, for example—we're using the same kind of collision detection and boundary checking that we built here.

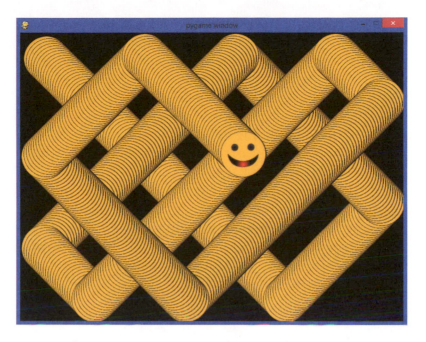

Figure 8-9: If we comment out the line that clears our screen after each frame, our smiley face leaves a bouncing trail behind in a cool pattern.

WHAT YOU LEARNED

In this chapter, you learned how to create the illusion of motion, what we call *animation,* by drawing images in different locations on the screen over time. We saw how the Pygame module can make programming a game or animation much quicker, since it has hundreds of functions that can make almost everything in a game app easier, from drawing images to creating timer-based animation— even checking for collisions. We installed Pygame on our computer so we could use its features to create fun apps of our own.

You learned about the structure of a game or app that we might build in Pygame, with a setup section; a game loop that handles events, updates and draws graphics, and then updates the display; and finally an exit section.

We started our Pygame programming by drawing a simple green dot on the screen at a chosen location, but we quickly moved on to drawing a picture from an image file on disk, saved in the same folder as our program, to our display screen. You learned that Pygame has a different coordinate system from the Turtle library, with the origin (0, 0) in the upper-left corner of the screen and positive y-coordinate values as we move down.

You learned how to create animation by drawing objects on the screen, clearing the screen, and then drawing the objects in a slightly different location. We saw that the `pygame.time.Clock()` object could make our animations steadier by limiting the number of times our animation draws each second, which is called the *frames per second*, or *fps*.

We built our own collision detection to check for objects "hitting" the edge of the screen, and then we added the logic to make objects look like they're bouncing back by changing the direction of their speed or velocity variables (by multiplying them by –1).

Programming the cool apps in this chapter has given us the skills to do the following:

- Install and use the `pygame` module in our own Python programs.
- Explain the structure of a Pygame app, including the setup, game loop, and exit.
- Build a game loop that handles events, updates and draws graphics, and updates the display.
- Draw shapes to the screen using `pygame.draw` functions.
- Load images from disk with `pygame.image.load()`.
- Draw images and objects to the screen with the `blit()` function.
- Create animations by drawing objects to the screen repeatedly in different locations.
- Make animations smooth, clean, and predictable using a `pygame.time.Clock()` timer's `tick()` function to limit the number of frames per second in our animations.
- Check for collision detection by building the `if` logic to check for boundary cases, like a graphic hitting the edge of the screen.
- Control the horizontal and vertical speeds of moving objects on the screen by changing the amount of movement in the x- and y-directions from one frame to the next.

PROGRAMMING CHALLENGES

Here are three challenge problems to extend the skills you developed in this chapter. For sample answers, go to *http://www.nostarch.com/teachkids/*.

#1: A COLOR-CHANGING DOT

Let's explore RGB color triplets further. We worked with some RGB colors in this chapter; remember, green was (0,255,0), black was (0,0,0), and so on. At *http://colorschemer.com/online/*, enter different red, green, and blue values from 0 to 255 to see the colors you can create by combining different amounts of red, green, and blue light from your screen's pixels. Start by choosing your own color triplet to use in the *ShowDot.py* program. Then modify the program to draw the dot larger or smaller and at different locations on the screen. Finally, try creating a random RGB color triplet using random.randint(0,255) for each of the three color components (remember to import random at the top of your program) so that the dot changes colors every time it draws on the screen. The effect will be a color-changing dot. Call your new creation *DiscoDot.py*.

#2: 100 RANDOM DOTS

As a second challenge, let's replace the single dot with 100 dots in random colors, sizes, and locations. To do this, let's set up three arrays capable of storing 100 values each for the colors, locations, and sizes:

```
# Colors, locations, sizes arrays for 100 random dots
colors = [0]*100
locations = [0]*100
sizes = [0]*100
```

Then, fill those three arrays with random color triplets, location pairs, and size/radius values for 100 random dots:

```
import random
# Store random values in colors, locations, sizes
```

continued

```
for n in range(100):
    colors[n] = (random.randint(0,255),random.randint(0,255),
                 random.randint(0,255))
    locations[n] = (random.randint(0,800),
                    random.randint(0,600))
    sizes[n] = random.randint(10, 100)
```

Finally, instead of drawing one dot in our while loop, add a for loop to draw the 100 random dots by using the colors, locations, and sizes arrays:

```
for n in range(100):
    pygame.draw.circle(screen, colors[n], locations[n],
                       sizes[n])
```

Call your new creation *RandomDots.py*. The final app should look something like Figure 8-9 when complete.

Figure 8-9: An advanced version of our dot program, RandomDots.py, gives us 100 dots of random color, location, and size.

#3: RAINING DOTS

Finally, let's take *RandomDots.py* one step further by programming the dots to "rain" off the bottom and right sides of the screen and reappear along the top and left. You've learned in this chapter that we create animation by changing the location of an object over time. We have the location of each dot in an array called `locations`, so if we change each dot's x- and y-coordinates, we can animate our dots. Change the `for` loop from *RandomDots.py* to calculate a new x- and y-coordinates for each dot based on the previous value, like this:

```
for n in range(100):
    pygame.draw.circle(screen, colors[n], locations[n],
                         sizes[n])
    new_x = locations[n][0] + 1
    new_y = locations[n][1] + 1
    locations[n] = (new_x, new_y)
```

This change calculates new x- and y-coordinates (`new_x` and `new_y`) for each dot every pass through the game loop, but it lets the dots fall off the right and bottom edges of the screen. Let's fix this by checking whether each dot's `new_x` or `new_y` is beyond the right or bottom edges of the screen and, if so, move the dot back up or back to the left before we store the new location:

```
if new_x > 800:
    new_x -= 800
if new_y > 600:
    new_y -= 600
locations[n] = (new_x, new_y)
```

The combined effect of these changes will be a steady flow of random dots "raining" down and to the right, disappearing off the bottom right of the screen and popping back up on the top or left edge. Four frames in this sequence are shown in Figure 8-10; you can follow groups of dots as they move down and to the right across the three images.

Save your new app as *RainingDots.py*.

continued

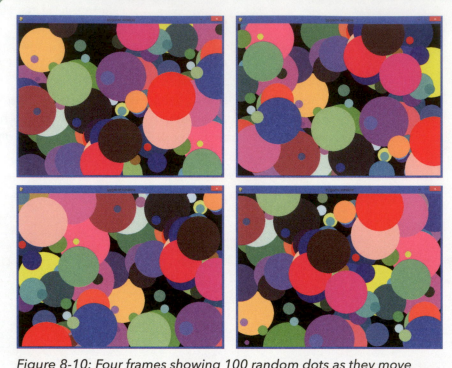

Figure 8-10: Four frames showing 100 random dots as they move right and down across the screen

9

USER INTERACTION: GET INTO THE GAME

In Chapter 8, we used some of the Pygame library's features to draw shapes and images on the screen. We were also able to create animation by drawing shapes in different locations over time. Unfortunately, we weren't able to *interact* with our animated objects like we might in a game; we expect to be able to click, drag, move, hit, or pop objects on the screen to affect or control the elements of a game while it runs.

Interactive programs give us this sense of control in an app or game, because we can move or interact with a character or other object in the program. That's exactly what you'll learn to do in this chapter: we'll use Pygame's ability to handle user interaction from the mouse to make our programs more interactive and more engaging for the user.

ADDING INTERACTION: CLICK AND DRAG

Let's add user interaction by developing two programs that will allow the user to draw interactively on the screen. First, we'll build on our Pygame foundation to handle events like mouse-button clicks and to enable the user to draw dots on the screen. Then, we'll add logic to handle mouse-button presses and releases separately and let the user drag the mouse with the button pressed to draw, like in a paint program.

CLICKING FOR DOTS

We'll build our *ClickDots.py* program using the same steps as in *ShowPic.py* (page 184) with a setup, a game loop, and an exit. Pay extra attention to the event-handling portion of the game loop, since that's where we'll add the if statement that will process mouse clicks.

SETUP

Here are our first few lines of setup. Start a new file and save it as *ClickDots.py* (the final program is shown on page 210).

```
import pygame                              # Setup
pygame.init()
screen = pygame.display.set_mode([800,600])
pygame.display.set_caption("Click to draw")
```

Our setup begins with import pygame and pygame.init() as usual, and then we create a screen object as our drawing window display. This time, though, we've added a title, or *caption*, to the window with pygame.display.set_caption(). This lets the user know what the program is. The argument we pass to set_caption() is a string of text that will appear on the title bar of the window, as shown at the top of Figure 9-1.

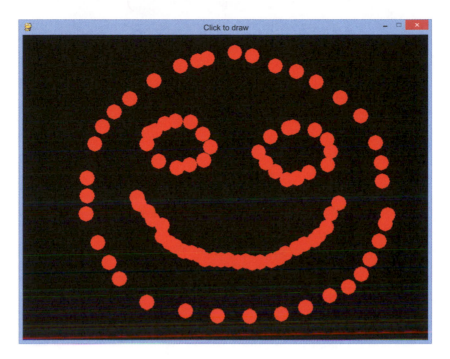

Figure 9-1: The title bar at the top of ClickDots.py *tells the user,*
"Click to draw."

The rest of our setup creates our game loop variable, keep_going;
sets a color constant (we'll draw in red for this program); and creates
a radius for our drawing dots:

```
keep_going = True
RED = (255,0,0)                        # RGB color triplet for RED
radius = 15
```

Now let's move on to our game loop.

GAME LOOP: HANDLING MOUSE CLICKS

In our game loop, we need to tell the program when to quit and
how to handle mouse-button presses:

```
while keep_going:                        # Game loop
    for event in pygame.event.get():     # Handling events
❶       if event.type == pygame.QUIT:
            keep_going = False
❷       if event.type == pygame.MOUSEBUTTONDOWN:
❸           spot = event.pos
❹           pygame.draw.circle(screen, RED, spot, radius)
```

At ❶, we handle the pygame.QUIT event by setting our loop variable keep_going to False.

The second if statement, at ❷, handles a new event type: the pygame.MOUSEBUTTONDOWN event that tells us that the user has pressed one of the mouse buttons. Whenever the user presses a mouse button, this event will appear in the list of events that our program gets from pygame.event.get(), and we can use an if statement both to check for the event and to tell the program what to do when the event occurs. At ❸, we create a variable called spot to hold the x- and y-coordinates of the mouse's position. We can get the location of the mouse-click event with event.pos; event is the current event in our for loop. Our if statement has just verified that this particular event is of type pygame.MOUSEBUTTONDOWN, and mouse events have a pos attribute (in this case, event.pos) that stores the (x, y) coordinate pair telling us where the mouse event occurred.

Once we know the location on the screen where the user clicked the mouse button, at ❹ we tell the program to draw a filled circle on the screen surface, in the RED color from our setup, at the location spot, with the radius of 15 we specified in our setup.

PUTTING IT ALL TOGETHER

The only thing left to do is update the display and tell our program what to do when it's time to exit. Here's the full program for *ClickDots.py*.

ClickDots.py

```
import pygame                                    # Setup
pygame.init()
screen = pygame.display.set_mode([800,600])
pygame.display.set_caption("Click to draw")
keep_going = True
RED = (255,0,0)                                  # RGB color triplet for RED
radius = 15

while keep_going:                                # Game loop
    for event in pygame.event.get():             # Handling events
        if event.type == pygame.QUIT:
            keep_going = False
```

```
        if event.type == pygame.MOUSEBUTTONDOWN:
            spot = event.pos
            pygame.draw.circle(screen, RED, spot, radius)
    pygame.display.update()                     # Update display

pygame.quit()                                   # Exit
```

This program is short but enables the user to draw pictures one dot at a time, as shown back in Figure 9-1. If we want to draw continuously as we drag the mouse with the button pressed, we just need to handle one more type of mouse event, pygame.MOUSEBUTTONUP. Let's give that a try.

DRAGGING TO PAINT

Now let's create a more natural drawing program, *DragDots.py*, that lets the user click and drag to draw smoothly, as with a paint-brush. We'll get a smooth, interactive drawing app, as shown in Figure 9-2.

Figure 9-2: Our DragDots.py *program is a fun way to paint!*

To create this effect, we need to change the logic of our program. In *ClickDots.py*, we handled MOUSEBUTTONDOWN events by just drawing a circle at the location of the mouse button click event. To draw continuously, we need to recognize both the MOUSEBUTTONDOWN and MOUSEBUTTONUP events; in other words, we want to separate mouse button clicks into *presses* and *releases* so that we know when the mouse is being *dragged* (with the button down) versus just being moved with the button up.

One way to accomplish this is with another Boolean flag variable. We can set a Boolean called mousedown to True whenever the user presses the mouse button and to False whenever the user releases the mouse button. In our game loop, if the mouse button is down (in other words, when mousedown is True), we can get the mouse's location and draw a circle on the screen. If the program is fast enough, the drawing should be smooth like in a paintbrush app.

SETUP

Make the setup section of your code look like this:

```
import pygame                                    # Setup
pygame.init()
screen = pygame.display.set_mode([800,600])
❶ pygame.display.set_caption("Click and drag to draw")
keep_going = True
❷ YELLOW = (255,255,0)                           # RGB color triplet for YELLOW
radius = 15
❸ mousedown = False
```

The setup portion of our app looks like *ClickDots.py*, except for the different window caption ❶, the YELLOW color we'll be drawing with ❷, and the very last line ❸. The Boolean variable mousedown will be our flag variable to signal to the program that the mouse button is down, or pressed.

Next, we'll add event handlers to our game loop. These event handlers will set mousedown to True if the user is holding down the mouse and False if not.

GAME LOOP: HANDLING MOUSE PRESSES AND RELEASES

Make your game loop look like this:

```
while keep_going:                              # Game loop
    for event in pygame.event.get():           # Handling events
        if event.type == pygame.QUIT:
            keep_going = False
❶       if event.type == pygame.MOUSEBUTTONDOWN:
❷           mousedown = True
❸       if event.type == pygame.MOUSEBUTTONUP:
❹           mousedown = False
❺   if mousedown:                              # Draw/update graphics
❻       spot = pygame.mouse.get_pos()
❼       pygame.draw.circle(screen, YELLOW, spot, radius)
❽   pygame.display.update()                    # Update display
```

The game loop starts just like our other Pygame apps, but at ❶, when we check to see whether the user has pressed one of the mouse buttons, instead of drawing immediately, we set our mousedown variable to True ❷. This will be the signal our program needs to begin drawing.

The next if statement at ❸ checks whether the user has *released* the mouse button. If so, the line at ❹ changes mousedown back to False. This will let our game loop know to stop drawing whenever the mouse button is up.

At ❺, our for loop is over (as we can see by the indentation), and our game loop continues by checking whether the mouse button is currently pressed (that is, if mousedown is True). If the mouse button is down, the mouse is currently being dragged, so we want to allow the user to draw on the screen.

At ❻, we get the current location of the mouse directly, with spot = pygame.mouse.get_pos(), rather than pulling the position of the last click, because we want to draw wherever the user is dragging the mouse, not just at the location where they first pressed the button. At ❼, we draw the current circle on the screen surface, in the color specified by YELLOW, at the (*x*, *y*) location spot where the mouse is currently being dragged, with the radius of 15 that we specified in the setup section of our code. Finally, we finish the game loop at ❽ by updating the display window with pygame.display.update().

PUTTING IT ALL TOGETHER

The last step is to end the program with `pygame.quit()` as usual. Here's the full program.

DragDots.py

```
import pygame                           # Setup
pygame.init()
screen = pygame.display.set_mode([800,600])
pygame.display.set_caption("Click and drag to draw")
keep_going = True
YELLOW = (255,255,0)                    # RGB color triplet for YELLOW
radius = 15
mousedown = False

while keep_going:                       # Game loop
    for event in pygame.event.get():    # Handling events
        if event.type == pygame.QUIT:
            keep_going = False
        if event.type == pygame.MOUSEBUTTONDOWN:
            mousedown = True
        if event.type == pygame.MOUSEBUTTONUP:
            mousedown = False
    if mousedown:                       # Draw/update graphics
        spot = pygame.mouse.get_pos()
        pygame.draw.circle(screen, YELLOW, spot, radius)
    pygame.display.update()             # Update display

pygame.quit()                           # Exit
```

The *DragDots.py* app is so fast and responsive that it almost feels like we're painting with a continuous brush instead of a series of dots; we have to drag the mouse pretty quickly to see the dots drawn separately. Pygame allows us to build much faster and more fluid games and animation than the turtle graphics we drew in previous chapters.

Even though the `for` loop handles every event during every pass through the `while` loop that keeps our app open, Pygame is efficient enough to do this dozens or even hundreds of times per second. This gives the illusion of instantaneous motion and reaction to our every movement and command—an important consideration as we build animations and interactive games. Pygame is up to the challenge and is the right toolkit for our graphics-intensive needs.

ADVANCED INTERACTION: SMILEY EXPLOSION

One fun animation that my students and my sons enjoy building is a scaled-up version of *SmileyBounce2.py* called *SmileyExplosion.py*. It takes the bouncing smiley to a fun new level by allowing the user to click and drag to create hundreds of bouncing smiley faces of random sizes that travel in random directions at random speeds. The effect looks like Figure 9-3. We'll build this program step by step; the final version is on page 222.

Figure 9-3: Our next app looks like an explosion of smiley face balloons bouncing all over the screen.

As you can see, we will have dozens to hundreds of smiley balloons bouncing all over the screen at any given time, so we're going to need to draw graphics quickly and smoothly for hundreds of objects per frame. To achieve this, we're going to add one more tool to our toolkit: sprite graphics.

SMILEY SPRITES

The term *sprite* goes back to the early days of video games. Moving graphical objects on the screen were called sprites because they floated over the background, like the imaginary fairy sprites they were named after. These light, fast sprite graphics enabled the quick, smooth animation that made video games so popular.

Pygame includes support for sprite graphics through its `pygame.sprite.Sprite` class. Remember from Chapter 8 that a class is like a template that can be used to create reusable objects, each with its own full set of functions and properties. In *SmileyMove.py* on page 190, we used the `Clock` class, along with its `tick()` method, to make our animations smooth and predictable. In the smiley explosion app, we'll use a few handy Pygame classes, and we'll build a class of our own to keep track of each individual smiley face as it moves around the screen.

MORE ON CLASSES AND OBJECTS

In Chapter 8 you learned that classes are like cookie cutters, and objects are like the cookies we create using a particular cookie cutter. Whenever we need several items with similar functions and characteristics (like moving smiley face images with various sizes and locations), and especially when we need each item to contain different information (like the size, location, and speed of each smiley), a class can provide the template to create as many objects of that type as we need. We say that objects are *instances* of a particular class.

The Pygame library has dozens of reusable classes, and each class has its own *methods* (what we call a class's functions) and *attributes* or *data*, the variables and values stored in each object. In the `Clock` class in Chapter 8, the `tick()` method was our function for making animation happen at a certain frame rate. For the floating smiley `Sprite` objects in this app, the attributes we care about are each smiley's location on the screen, its size, and the speed it's moving in the x- and y-directions, so we'll create a `Smiley` class with those attributes. We can create our own classes whenever we need a reusable template.

Breaking a problem or program down into objects, and then building classes that create those objects, is the foundation of *object-oriented programming*. Object-oriented programming is a way of solving problems using objects. It is one of the most popular approaches used in software development, and one reason for that popularity is the concept of code reuse. *Reusability* means that once we write a useful class for one programming project, we can often reuse that class in another program instead of starting from scratch. For example, a game company can write a Card class to represent the cards in a standard deck. Then, every time the company programs a new game—like Blackjack, War, Poker, Go Fish, and so on—it can reuse that Card class, saving time and money by using the same code in future apps.

The Sprite class in Pygame is a great example. The Pygame team wrote the Sprite class to contain many of the features we need when we program a game object, from a running character to a spaceship to a floating smiley face. By using the Sprite class, programmers like us no longer need to write all the basic code to draw an object on the screen, detect when objects collide with one another, and so on. The Sprite class handles many of those functions for us, and we can focus on building the unique qualities of our app on top of that foundation.

Another handy Pygame class we'll use is the Group class. Group is a *container* class that lets us store Sprite objects together as a group. The Group class helps us keep all our sprites together in one place (accessible through a single Group object), and that's important when we have dozens or possibly hundreds of sprites floating around the screen. The Group class also has convenient methods for updating all the sprites in a group (such as moving the Sprite objects to each of their new locations each frame), adding new Sprite objects, removing Sprite objects from the Group, and so on. Let's see how we can use these classes to build our smiley explosion app.

USING CLASSES TO BUILD OUR APP

We're going to create Sprite objects for our smiley face balloons that take advantage of the Sprite class's properties to produce quick animation around the screen, even when hundreds of sprites are being moved in the same frame. I mentioned that Pygame also has support for groups of sprites that can all be drawn and handled as a collection; this group of sprites will be of type pygame.sprite.Group(). Let's look at the setup section of our app:

```
import pygame
import random

BLACK = (0,0,0)
pygame.init()
```

```
screen = pygame.display.set_mode([800,600])
pygame.display.set_caption("Smiley Explosion")
mousedown = False
keep_going = True
clock = pygame.time.Clock()
pic = pygame.image.load("CrazySmile.bmp")
colorkey = pic.get_at((0,0))
pic.set_colorkey(colorkey)
```
❶ `sprite_list = pygame.sprite.Group()`

The setup looks like *SmileyBounce2.py*, but we're adding a variable called sprite_list at ❶ that will contain our group of smiley face sprites. Storing the sprites in a Group will make it faster and easier to do things like draw all the smileys on the screen every frame, move all the smileys for each step of the animation, and even check to see if the smiley sprites are colliding with objects or with one another.

To create sprite objects for complex animations and games, we will create our own Sprite class that *extends*, or builds on, Pygame's Sprite class, adding the variables and functions that we want for our custom sprites. We'll name our sprite class Smiley, and we'll add variables for the position of each smiley (pos), its x- and y-velocity (xvel and yvel; remember *velocity* is another word for speed), and its *scale*, or how big each smiley will be (scale):

```
class Smiley(pygame.sprite.Sprite):
    pos = (0,0)
    xvel = 1
    yvel = 1
    scale = 100
```

Our Smiley class definition starts with the keyword class, followed by the name we want for our class, plus the type we're extending (pygame.sprite.Sprite).

SETTING UP SPRITES

The next step after starting our Smiley class and listing the data variables that we'd like each smiley sprite object to remember is called *initialization*, sometimes also referred to as the *constructor* for our class. This will be a special function that is called every time a new object of our Smiley class is created, or *constructed*, in our program. Just like initializing a variable gives it a starting value, the *initialization function*, __init__(), in our Smiley class will

set up all the starting values we
need in our sprite object. The
two underscores on either side
of the __init__() function name
have special meaning in Python.
In this case, __init__() is the special function name that is used to
initialize a class. We tell Python
how each Smiley object should be
initialized in this function, and
every time we create a Smiley,
this special __init__() function
does its job behind the scenes,
setting up variables and more
for each Smiley object.

There are a number of items we need to set up in our __init__()
function. First, we'll determine what parameters we need to pass
to our __init__() function. For our random smiley faces, we might
pass in a position and the starting x- and y-velocities. Because
our Smiley is a class and all our smiley face sprites will be objects
of the Smiley type, the first parameter in all the functions in the
class will be the smiley sprite object itself. We label this parameter
self, because it connects __init__() and the other functions to the
object's own data. Look at the code for our __init__() function:

```
    def __init__(self, pos, xvel, yvel):
❶       pygame.sprite.Sprite.__init__(self)
❷       self.image = pic
        self.rect = self.image.get_rect()
❸       self.pos = pos
❹       self.rect.x = pos[0] - self.scale/2
        self.rect.y = pos[1] - self.scale/2
❺       self.xvel = xvel
        self.yvel = yvel
```

The four parameters for our __init__() function are the object
itself, self; the position where we want the smiley to appear, pos;
and xvel and yvel, its horizontal and vertical speed values. Next,
at ❶, we call the initialization function for the main Sprite class
so that our object can take advantage of the properties of sprite

graphics without coding them from scratch. At ❷, we set the image of the sprite object (`self.image`) to the `pic` graphic that we loaded from disk (*CrazySmile.bmp*—you'll need to make sure that file is still in the same folder as this new program), and we get the dimensions of the rectangle that contains the 100×100 picture.

At ❸, the statement `self.pos = pos` stores the position that was passed into the __init__() function in the object's own `pos` variable. Then, at ❹, we set the x- and y-coordinates of the sprite's drawing rectangle to the x- and y-coordinates stored in `pos`, shifted by half the size of the image (`self.scale/2`) so that the smiley is centered on the spot the user clicked with the mouse. Finally, we store the x- and y-velocities that were passed to the __init__() function in the object's `xvel` and `yvel` variables (`self.xvel` and `self.yvel`) at ❺.

This __init__() constructor function will set up everything we need for drawing each smiley face on the screen, but it doesn't handle the animation needed to move our sprites around the screen. For that, we'll add another handy function for our sprites, `update()`.

UPDATING SPRITES

Sprites are built for animation, and we've learned that animation means updating the location of a graphic each frame (each time we pass through the game loop). Pygame sprites have an `update()` function built in, and we can *override*, or customize, this function to program the behavior that we want from our custom sprites.

Our `update()` function is pretty simple; the only updates to our bouncing smiley sprites for each frame are changing the position of each sprite according to its speed and checking to see whether it has collided with the edge of the screen:

```
def update(self):
    self.rect.x += self.xvel
    self.rect.y += self.yvel
    if self.rect.x <= 0 or self.rect.x > screen.get_width() - self.scale:
        self.xvel = -self.xvel
    if self.rect.y <= 0 or self.rect.y > screen.get_height() - self.scale:
        self.yvel = -self.yvel
```

The update() function takes one parameter—the sprite object itself, self—and the code for moving the sprite looks a lot like our animation code from *SmileyBounce2.py*. The only real difference is that we refer to the sprite's (*x, y*) location with self.rect.x and self.rect.y, and the x- and y-velocities as self.xvel and self.yvel. Our collision detections for the boundaries of the screen also make use of screen.get_width() and screen.get_height() so they can function for any size window.

BIGGER AND SMALLER SMILEYS

The last feature we'll add to this first version of the app is changing the *scale*, or size, of the image. We'll make this modification to our __init__() function right after setting self.image to pic. First, we'll change our object's scale variable to a random number between 10 and 100 (for a finished smiley sprite that measures between 10×10 and 100×100 pixels in size). We'll apply this change in scale, also known as a *transformation*, by using the pygame.transform.scale() function, as follows:

```
self.scale = random.randrange(10,100)
self.image = pygame.transform.scale(self.image, (self.scale,self.scale))
```

Pygame's transform.scale() function takes an image (our self.image of the smiley graphic) and the new dimensions (our new random self.scale value as the width and height of the transformed image), and it returns the scaled (up or down, bigger or smaller) image, which we're storing as the new self.image.

With this last change, we should now be able to use our Smiley sprite class to draw smiley faces of random sizes and speeds all over our screen with drawing code similar to our *DragDots.py* drawing app, plus a few changes.

PUTTING IT ALL TOGETHER

Here's our full *SmileyExplosion.py* app:

SmileyExplosion.py

```python
import pygame
import random

BLACK = (0,0,0)
pygame.init()
screen = pygame.display.set_mode([800,600])
pygame.display.set_caption("Smiley Explosion")
mousedown = False
keep_going = True
clock = pygame.time.Clock()
pic = pygame.image.load("CrazySmile.bmp")
colorkey = pic.get_at((0,0))
pic.set_colorkey(colorkey)
sprite_list = pygame.sprite.Group()

class Smiley(pygame.sprite.Sprite):
    pos = (0,0)
    xvel = 1
    yvel = 1
    scale = 100

    def __init__(self, pos, xvel, yvel):
        pygame.sprite.Sprite.__init__(self)
        self.image = pic
        self.scale = random.randrange(10,100)
        self.image = pygame.transform.scale(self.image, (self.scale,self.scale))
        self.rect = self.image.get_rect()
        self.pos = pos
        self.rect.x = pos[0] - self.scale/2
        self.rect.y = pos[1] - self.scale/2
        self.xvel = xvel
        self.yvel = yvel

    def update(self):
        self.rect.x += self.xvel
        self.rect.y += self.yvel
        if self.rect.x <= 0 or self.rect.x > screen.get_width() - self.scale:
            self.xvel = -self.xvel
        if self.rect.y <= 0 or self.rect.y > screen.get_height() - self.scale:
            self.yvel = -self.yvel
```

```
while keep_going:
    for event in pygame.event.get():
        if event.type == pygame.QUIT:
            keep_going = False
        if event.type == pygame.MOUSEBUTTONDOWN:
            mousedown = True
        if event.type == pygame.MOUSEBUTTONUP:
            mousedown = False
    screen.fill(BLACK)
❶  sprite_list.update()
❷  sprite_list.draw(screen)
    clock.tick(60)
    pygame.display.update()
    if mousedown:
        speedx = random.randint(-5, 5)
        speedy = random.randint(-5, 5)
❸      newSmiley = Smiley(pygame.mouse.get_pos(),speedx,speedy)
❹      sprite_list.add(newSmiley)

pygame.quit()
```

The code for the game loop in *SmileyExplosion.py* is similar to our drawing app *DragDots.py*, with a few notable changes. At ❶, we're calling the update() function on the list of smiley sprites stored in sprite_list; this single line will call the update function to move every smiley face on the screen and check for edge bounces. Similarly, the code at ❷ will draw every smiley face on the screen in its proper location. It takes only two lines of code to animate and draw potentially hundreds of sprites—that's a huge time savings, and it's just part of the power of sprite graphics in Pygame.

In our mousedown drawing code, we generate a random speedx and speedy for the horizontal and vertical speed of each new smiley face, and at ❸, we create a new smiley face, newSmiley, by calling the constructor for our class Smiley. Notice that we don't have to use the function name __init__(); rather, we use the name of the class, Smiley, whenever we're constructing or creating a new object of the Smiley class or type. We pass the constructor function the position of the mouse, along with the random speed we just created. Finally, at ❹, we take our newly created smiley face sprite, newSmiley, and add it to our Group of sprites called sprite_list.

We've just created a fast, fluid, interactive animation for dozens or even hundreds of smiley face sprite graphics, floating around the screen like balloons of various sizes, traveling at random speeds in every direction. In the final upgrade to this app, we'll see an even more impressive and powerful feature of sprite graphics that handles detecting collisions.

SMILEYPOP, VERSION 1.0

For our closing example, we'll add one crucial bit of fun to the *SmileyExplosion.py* program: the ability to "pop" the smiley balloons/bubbles by clicking the right mouse button (or by pressing the CONTROL key and clicking on a Mac). The effect is like a balloon-popping game or Ant Smasher, Whack-a-Mole, and so on. We'll be able to create smiley balloons by dragging the left mouse button, and we'll pop them (that is, remove them from the screen) by clicking the right mouse button over one or more of the smiley sprites.

DETECTING COLLISIONS AND REMOVING SPRITES

The great news is that the Sprite class in Pygame comes with collision detection built in. We can use the function `pygame.sprite .collide_rect()` to check whether the rectangles holding two sprites have collided; we can use the `collide_circle()` function to check whether two round sprites are touching; and if we're just checking to see whether a sprite has collided with a single point (like the pixel where the user just clicked the mouse), we can use a sprite's `rect.collidepoint()` function to check whether a sprite overlaps, or collides with, that point on the screen.

If we've determined that the user clicked a point that touches one or more sprites, we can remove each of those sprites from our `sprite_list` group by calling the `remove()` function. We can handle all the logic for popping smiley balloons in our MOUSEBUTTONDOWN event handler code. To turn *SmileyExplosion.py* into *SmileyPop.py*, we'll just replace these two lines:

```
if event.type == pygame.MOUSEBUTTONDOWN:
    mousedown = True
```

with the following seven lines of code:

```
  if event.type == pygame.MOUSEBUTTONDOWN:
❶     if pygame.mouse.get_pressed()[0]:    # Regular left mouse button, draw
          mousedown = True
```

❷
❸
❹
❺
```
elif pygame.mouse.get_pressed()[2]:  # Right mouse button, pop
    pos = pygame.mouse.get_pos()
    clicked_smileys = [s for s in sprite_list if s.rect.collidepoint(pos)]
    sprite_list.remove(clicked_smileys)
```

The if statement for MOUSEBUTTONDOWN events remains the same, but now, we're interested in *which* button was pressed. At ❶, we check to see if the *left* mouse button was pressed (the first button, at index [0]); if so, we turn on the mousedown Boolean flag, and the game loop will draw new smiley faces. At ❷, we see if the *right* mouse button is pressed, beginning the logic to check whether the mouse was clicked over one or more smileys in our sprite_list.

First, at ❸, we get the mouse's location and store it in the variable pos. At ❹, we use a programming shortcut to generate a list of sprites from sprite_list that collide with, or overlap, the point the user clicked at pos. If a sprite s in the group sprite_list has a rectangle that collides with the point pos, group it together as a list [s] and store the list as clicked_smileys. That ability to create one list, collection, or array from another based on an if condition is a powerful feature of Python, and it makes our code much shorter for this app.

Finally, at ❺, we call the handy remove() function on our Group of sprites called sprite_list. This remove() function is different from Python's regular remove() function, which removes a single item from a list or collection. The pygame.sprite.Group.remove() function will remove any number of sprites from a list. In this case, it will remove all the sprites from our sprite_list that collide with the point the user clicked on the screen. Once these sprites are removed from sprite_list, when sprite_list is drawn to the screen in our game loop, the clicked sprites are no longer in the list, so they don't get drawn. It's like they've disappeared—or we've popped them like balloons or bubbles!

PUTTING IT ALL TOGETHER

Here's the complete *SmileyPop.py* code.

SmileyPop.py

```python
import pygame
import random

BLACK = (0,0,0)
pygame.init()
screen = pygame.display.set_mode([800,600])
pygame.display.set_caption("Pop a Smiley")
mousedown = False
keep_going = True
clock = pygame.time.Clock()
pic = pygame.image.load("CrazySmile.bmp")
colorkey = pic.get_at((0,0))
pic.set_colorkey(colorkey)
sprite_list = pygame.sprite.Group()

class Smiley(pygame.sprite.Sprite):
    pos = (0,0)
    xvel = 1
    yvel = 1
    scale = 100

    def __init__(self, pos, xvel, yvel):
        pygame.sprite.Sprite.__init__(self)
        self.image = pic
        self.scale = random.randrange(10,100)
        self.image = pygame.transform.scale(self.image, (self.scale,self.scale))
        self.rect = self.image.get_rect()
        self.pos = pos
        self.rect.x = pos[0] - self.scale/2
        self.rect.y = pos[1] - self.scale/2
        self.xvel = xvel
        self.yvel = yvel

    def update(self):
        self.rect.x += self.xvel
        self.rect.y += self.yvel
        if self.rect.x <= 0 or self.rect.x > screen.get_width() - self.scale:
            self.xvel = -self.xvel
        if self.rect.y <= 0 or self.rect.y > screen.get_height() - self.scale:
            self.yvel = -self.yvel
```

```
while keep_going:
    for event in pygame.event.get():
        if event.type == pygame.QUIT:
            keep_going = False
        if event.type == pygame.MOUSEBUTTONDOWN:
            if pygame.mouse.get_pressed()[0]:    # Regular left mouse button, draw
                mousedown = True
            elif pygame.mouse.get_pressed()[2]:  # Right mouse button, pop
                pos = pygame.mouse.get_pos()
                clicked_smileys = [s for s in sprite_list if s.rect.collidepoint(pos)]
                sprite_list.remove(clicked_smileys)
        if event.type == pygame.MOUSEBUTTONUP:
            mousedown = False
    screen.fill(BLACK)
    sprite_list.update()
    sprite_list.draw(screen)
    clock.tick(60)
    pygame.display.update()
    if mousedown:
        speedx = random.randint(-5, 5)
        speedy = random.randint(-5, 5)
        newSmiley = Smiley(pygame.mouse.get_pos(),speedx,speedy)
        sprite_list.add(newSmiley)

pygame.quit()
```

Remember that you'll have to have the *CrazySmile.bmp* image file stored in the same folder or directory as the code to make it work. Once it does work, this program is so much fun to play with, it's almost addictive! In the next chapter, we'll learn about the elements of game design that make games fun, and we'll build a complete game from scratch!

WHAT YOU LEARNED

In this chapter, we combined user interaction with animation to create an explosion of smileys on the screen, and we used sprite graphics to make even hundreds of smiley images easy and fast to animate. We learned how to build our own Sprite class so that we could customize sprites with the features and behaviors we wanted, including data variables, an initialization function, and a custom update function. We also learned how to scale images in Pygame so that our smileys could come in all different shapes and sizes, and we learned the advantages of using pygame.sprite.Group() to store all our sprites for quick updating and drawing on the screen.

In our closing example, we added sprite-based collision detection to see whether the user right-clicked the mouse over one or more smiley sprites. We saw how to check for events on the left mouse button separately from the right mouse button. We learned that Python has powerful features for selecting items out of a list based on an if condition, and we saw how to remove sprites from a Group using the remove() function.

We created fun apps in this chapter, topped off by a SmileyPop app that we'll make even more game-like in Chapter 10. Pygame has given us the final skills we need to program awesome games!

Programming the cool apps in this chapter has given us the skills to do the following:

- Use sprite graphics by customizing the pygame.sprite.Sprite() class.

- Access, modify, update, and draw a list of sprites using pygame.sprite.Group() and its functions.

- Transform an image by applying the pygame.trasform.scale() function to increase or decrease the image's size in pixels.

- Detect sprite collisions using rect.collidepoint() and similar functions from the Sprite class.

- Remove sprites from a Group using the remove() function.

PROGRAMMING CHALLENGES

Here are three challenge problems to extend the skills developed in this chapter. For sample answers to these challenges, go to *http://www.nostarch.com/teachkids/*.

#1: RANDOMLY COLORED DOTS

Start by choosing your own color triplet to use in the *DragDots.py* program. Then modify the program to draw randomly colored dots by creating a triplet of three random numbers between 0 and 255 to use as your colors. Call your new creation *RandomPaint.py*.

#2: PAINTING IN COLORS

Let the user draw in two or more consistent colors using any of the following options:

- Change the current drawing color each time the user presses a key, either to a random color each time or to a specific color for certain keys (like red for R, blue for B, and so on).

- Draw with different colors for each of the mouse buttons (red for the left mouse button, green for the middle button, and blue for the right mouse button, for example).

- Add some colored rectangles to the bottom or side of the screen, and modify the program so that if the user clicks in a rectangle, the drawing color changes to the same color as the rectangle.

Try one approach, or all three, and save your new file as *ColorPaint.py*.

#3: THROWING SMILEYS

Pygame has a function called `pygame.mouse.get_rel()` that will return the amount of *relative* motion, or how much the mouse's position has changed in pixels since the last call to `get_rel()`, in the x- and y-directions. Modify your *SmileyExplosion.py* file to use the amount of relative mouse motion in the x- and y-directions as the horizontal and vertical speeds of each smiley (instead of generating a pair of random `speedx` and `speedy` values). This will look like the user is throwing smileys because they will speed off in the direction the user is dragging the mouse!

To add another realistic effect, slow the smileys slightly by multiplying `xvel` and `yvel` by a number smaller than 1.0 (like 0.95) in the `update(self)` section every time the smileys bounce off an edge of the screen. The smileys will slow down over time, as if friction from each wall bounce is making them move slower and slower. Save your new app as *SmileyThrow.py*.

10

GAME PROGRAMMING: CODING FOR FUN

In Chapter 9, we combined animation and user inter-action to make a fun app. In this chapter, we'll build on those concepts and add elements of game design to create a game from the ground up. We'll combine our ability to draw animations on the screen with our abil-ity to handle user interaction, like mouse movement, to create a classic Pong-type game we'll call *Smiley Pong*.

Games that we enjoy playing have certain *elements of game design*. Here is a breakdown of our Smiley Pong design:

A playing field or game board   A black screen represents half a Ping-Pong board.

Goals and achievements   The player tries to score points and avoid losing lives.

Playing pieces (game characters and objects)   The player has a ball and a paddle.

Rules   The player scores a point if the ball hits the paddle, but the player loses a life if the ball hits the bottom of the screen.

Mechanics   We'll make the paddle move left and right with the mouse, defending the bottom of the screen; the ball may move faster as the game progresses.

Resources   The player will have five lives or turns to score as many points as they can.

Games use these elements to engage players. An effective game has a mix of these elements, making the game easy to play but challenging to win.

BUILDING A GAME SKELETON: SMILEY PONG, VERSION 1.0

Pong, shown in Figure 10-1, was one of the earliest arcade video games, dating back to the 1960s and '70s. More than 40 years later, it's still fun to play.

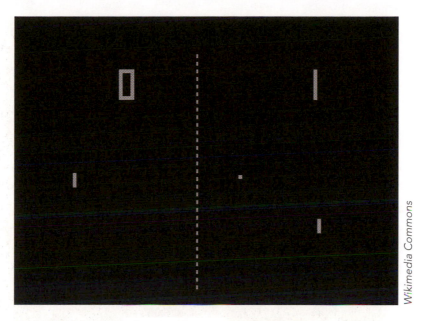

Figure 10-1: Atari's famous Pong game from 1972

The gameplay for a single-player version of Pong is simple. A paddle moves along one edge of the screen (we'll place our paddle at the bottom) and rebounds a ball, in our case a smiley face. Players gain a point each time they hit the ball, and they lose a point (or a life) every time they miss.

We'll use our bouncing smiley face program from Chapter 8 as the foundation for the game. Using *SmileyBounce2.py* (page 199) as our base, we already have a smoothly animated smiley ball bouncing off the sides of the window, and we've already taken care of the while loop that keeps the animation going until the user quits. To make Smiley Pong, we'll add a paddle that follows the mouse along the bottom of the screen, and we'll add more collision detection to see when the smiley ball hits the paddle. The final touch will be to start with zero points and five lives, give the player a point when they hit the ball, and take away a life when the ball bounces off the bottom of the screen. Figure 10-2 shows what we're working toward. When we're finished, our final program will look like the one on page 243.

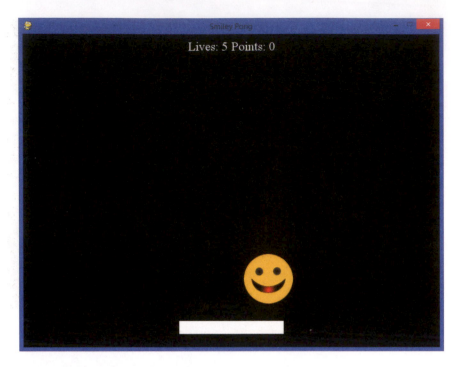

Figure 10-2: The Smiley Pong game we'll build

The first feature we'll add to the former *SmileyBounce2.py* app is the paddle.

DRAWING A BOARD AND GAME PIECES

In our finished game, the paddle will move along the bottom of the screen, following the mouse's movement as the user tries to keep the ball from hitting the bottom edge.

To get the paddle started, we'll add this information to the setup section of our app:

```
WHITE = (255,255,255)
paddlew = 200
paddleh = 25
paddlex = 300
paddley = 550
```

These variables will help us create a paddle that is simply a white rectangle of width 200 and height 25. We'll want the coordinates of its top-left corner to start at (300, 550) so that the paddle starts off slightly above the bottom edge and centered horizontally on the 800 × 600 screen.

But we're not going to draw this rectangle yet. Those variables would be enough to draw a rectangle on the screen the first time, but our paddle needs to follow the user's mouse movements. We want to draw the paddle on the screen centered around where the user moves the mouse in the *x* direction (side to side), while keeping the y-coordinate fixed near the bottom of the screen. To do this, we need the x-coordinates of the mouse's position. We can get the position of the mouse by using `pygame.mouse.get_pos()`. In this case, since we care only about the x-coordinate of `get_pos()`, and since *x* comes first in our mouse position, we can get the x-coordinate of the mouse with this:

```
paddlex = pygame.mouse.get_pos()[0]
```

But remember that Pygame *starts* drawing a rectangle at the (*x*, *y*) position we provide, and it draws the rest of the rectangle to the right of and below that location. To center the paddle where the mouse is positioned, we need to subtract half the paddle's width from the mouse's x-position, putting the mouse halfway through the paddle:

```
paddlex -= paddlew/2
```

Now that we know the center of the paddle will always be where the mouse is, all we need to do in our game loop is to draw the paddle rectangle on the screen:

```
pygame.draw.rect(screen, WHITE, (paddlex, paddley, paddlew, paddleh))
```

If you add those three lines before the `pygame.display.update()` in the `while` loop in *SmileyBounce2.py* and add the paddle color, `paddlew`, `paddleh`, `paddlex`, and `paddley` to the setup section, you'll see the paddle follow your mouse. But the ball won't bounce off the paddle yet because we haven't added the logic to test whether the ball has collided with it. That's our next step.

KEEPING SCORE

Keeping score is part of what makes a game fun. Points, lives, stars—whatever you use to keep score, there's a sense of achievement that comes from seeing your score increase. In our Smiley Pong game, we want the user to gain a point every time the ball hits the paddle and lose a life when they miss the ball and it hits the bottom of the screen. Our next task is to add logic to make the ball bounce off the paddle and gain points, as well as to subtract a life when the ball hits the bottom of the screen. Figure 10-3 shows what your game might look like after a player gains some points. Notice how the point display has been updated to 8.

Figure 10-3: As the smiley ball bounces off the paddle at the bottom, we'll add points to our player's score.

As mentioned earlier, we'll start our game with zero points and five lives in the setup portion of our code:

```
points = 0
lives = 5
```

Next we have to figure out when to add to points and when to take away from lives.

SUBTRACTING A LIFE

Let's start with subtracting a life. We know that if the ball hits the bottom edge of the screen, the player has missed it with the paddle, so they should lose a life.

To add the logic for subtracting a life when the ball hits the bottom of the screen, we have to break our if statement for hitting the top *or* bottom of the screen (if picy <= 0 or picy >= 500) into two parts, top and bottom separately. If the ball hits the top of the screen (picy <= 0), we just want it to bounce back, so we'll change the direction of the ball's speed in the *y* direction with -speedy:

```
if picy <= 0:
    speedy = -speedy
```

If the ball bounces off the bottom (picy >= 500), we want to deduct a life from lives and then have the ball bounce back:

```
if picy >= 500:
    lives -= 1
    speedy = -speedy
```

Subtracting a life is done, so now we need to add points. In "SmileyPop, Version 1.0" on page 224, we saw that Pygame contains functions that make it easier to check for collisions. But since we're building this Smiley Pong game from scratch, let's see how we can write our own code to check for collisions. The code might come in handy in a future app, and writing it is a valuable problem-solving exercise.

HITTING THE BALL WITH THE PADDLE

To check for the ball bouncing off the paddle, we need to look at how the ball might come into contact with the paddle. It could hit the top-left corner of the paddle, it could hit the top-right corner of the paddle, or it could bounce directly off the top of the paddle.

When you're figuring out the logic for detecting collisions, it helps to draw it out on paper and label the corners and edges where you need to check for a possible collision. Figure 10-4 shows a sketch of the paddle and the two corner collision cases with the ball.

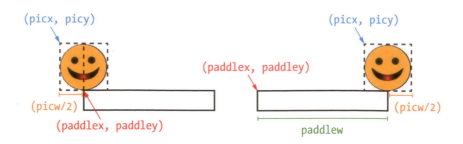

Figure 10-4: Two collision cases between the paddle and our smiley ball

Because we want the ball to bounce realistically off the paddle, we want to check for the cases where the bottom center of the ball just touches the corners of the paddle at the left and right extremes. We want to make sure the player scores a point not only when the ball bounces directly off the top of the paddle but also whenever it bounces off the paddle's corners. To do this, we'll see if the ball's vertical location is near the bottom of the screen where the paddle is, and if so, we'll check whether the ball's horizontal location would allow it to hit the paddle.

First, let's figure out what range of x-coordinate values would allow the ball to hit the paddle. Since the middle of the ball would be half the width of the ball across from its (picx, picy) top-left corner, we'll add the width of the ball as a variable in the setup section of our app:

```
picw = 100
```

As shown in Figure 10-4, the ball could hit the top-left corner of the paddle when picx plus half the width of the picture (picw/2) touches paddlex, the x-coordinate of the left corner of the paddle. In code, we could test this condition as part of an if statement: picx + picw/2 >= paddlex.

We use the *greater than or equal to* condition because the ball can be farther right (greater than paddlex in the x direction) and still hit the paddle; the corner case is just the first pixel for which the player gets a point for hitting the paddle. All the x-coordinate values between the left corner and the right corner of the paddle are valid hits, so they should award the user a point and bounce the ball back.

To find that top-right corner case, we can see from the figure that we're requiring the middle of the ball, whose x-coordinate is `picx + picw/2`, to be less than or equal to the top-right corner of the paddle, whose x-coordinate is `paddlex + paddlew` (or the starting x-coordinate of the paddle plus the paddle's width). In code, this would be `picx + picw/2 <= paddlex + paddlew`.

We can put these two together into a single `if` statement, but that's not quite enough. Those x-coordinates cover the whole screen from the left corner of the paddle to the right corner, from the top of the screen to the bottom. With just the x-coordinates determined, our ball could be anywhere in the *y* direction, so we need to narrow that down. It's not enough to know that our ball is within the *horizontal* limits of the paddle; we also have to know that our ball is within the *vertical* range of y-coordinate values that could allow it to collide with the paddle.

We know that the top of our paddle is located at 550 pixels in the *y* direction, near the bottom of the screen, because our setup includes the line `paddley = 550` and the rectangle begins at that y-coordinate and continues down for 25 pixels, our paddle's height stored in `paddleh`. We know our picture is 100 pixels tall, so let's store that as a variable, `pich` (for picture height), that we can add to our setup section: `pich = 100`.

For our ball's y-coordinate to hit the paddle, the `picy` location plus the picture's height, `pich`, needs to be at least `paddley` or greater for the bottom of the picture (`picy + pich`) to touch the top of the paddle (`paddley`). Part of our `if` statement for the ball hitting the paddle in the *y* direction would be `if picy + pich >= paddley`. But this condition alone would allow the ball to be anywhere greater than `paddley`, even at the bottom edge of the screen. We don't want the user to be able to get points for moving the paddle into the ball after the ball has hit the bottom edge, so we need another `if` condition that sets the maximum y-coordinate value we'll give points for.

A natural choice for the maximum y-coordinate value for earning a point might be the bottom of the paddle, or `paddley + paddleh` (the paddle's y-coordinate, plus its height). But if the bottom of our ball is past the bottom of the paddle, the player shouldn't get a point for hitting the ball, so we want `picy + pich` (the bottom of the ball) to be less than or equal to `paddley + paddleh`—in other words, `picy + pich <= paddley + paddleh`.

There's just one more condition to check. Remember that the ball and paddle are virtual; that is, they don't exist in the real world, don't have actual edges, and don't interact like real game pieces do. We could move our paddle through the ball even when it's bouncing back up from the bottom edge. We don't want to award points when the player has clearly missed the ball, so before awarding a point, let's check to make sure the ball is headed down, in addition to being within the vertical and horizontal range of the paddle. We can tell the ball is headed down the screen if the ball's speed in the y direction (speedy) is greater than zero. When speedy > 0, the ball is moving down the screen in the positive y direction.

We now have the conditions we need to create the two if statements that will check whether the ball hit the paddle:

```
if picy + pich >= paddley and picy + pich <= paddley + paddleh \
    and speedy > 0:
    if picx + picw/2 >= paddlex and picx + picw/2 <= paddlex + \
        paddlew:
```

First, we check whether the ball is within the vertical range to be able to touch the paddle and whether it's heading downward instead of upward. Then, we check whether the ball is within the horizontal range to be able to touch the paddle.

In both of these if statements, the compound conditions made the statement too long to fit on our screen. The backslash character, \, allows us to continue a long line of code by wrapping around to the next line. You can choose to type a long line of code all on a single line, or you can wrap the code to fit the screen by ending the first line with a backslash \, pressing ENTER, and continuing the code on the next line. We have some long lines of logic in the games in this chapter, so you'll see the backslash in several of the code listings. Just remember that Python will read any lines separated by a backslash as a single line of code.

ADDING A POINT

Let's build the logic to bounce the ball and award a point. To complete our paddle logic, we add two more lines right after the two if statements:

```
if picy + pich >= paddley and picy + pich <= paddley + paddleh \
    and speedy > 0:
```

```
if picx + picw/2 >= paddlex and picx + picw/2 <= paddlex + \
   paddlew:
    points += 1
    speedy = -speedy
```

Adding a point is easy: `points += 1`. Changing the direction of the ball so it looks like it bounced off the paddle is easy too; we just reverse our speed in the *y* direction to make it go back up the screen: `speedy = -speedy`.

You can run the program with those changes and see the ball bounce off the paddle. Each time the paddle hits the ball, you're earning a point, and whenever the ball misses the paddle, you're losing a life, but we're not showing those on the screen yet. Let's do that next.

SHOWING THE SCORE

We have the logic we need to add points and subtract lives, but we don't see the points on the screen as we play. In this section, we'll draw text to the screen to give the user feedback while they're playing, as shown in Figure 10-5.

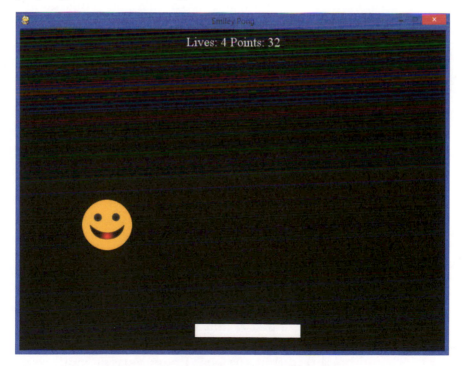

Figure 10-5: Smiley Pong, version 1.0, is becoming a real game!

The first step is putting together the string of text that we want to display. In a typical video game, we'd see our points and how many lives or turns we have left— for example, *Lives: 4, Points: 32.* We already have variables with the number of lives (`lives`) and total points (`points`). All we have to do is use the `str()` function to turn those numbers into their text equivalent (5 becomes "5") and add text to indicate what the numbers mean in each pass through our game loop:

```
draw_string = "Lives: " + str(lives) + " Points: " + str(points)
```

Our string variable will be called `draw_string`, and it contains the text we'd like to draw on the screen to display to users as they play. To draw that text on the screen, we need to have an object or variable that is connected to the text-drawing module `pygame.font`. A *font* is another name for a *typeface*, or the style characters are drawn in, like Arial or Times New Roman. In the setup section of your app, add the following line:

```
font = pygame.font.SysFont("Times", 24)
```

This creates a variable we'll call `font` that will allow us to draw on the Pygame display in 24-point Times. You can make your text larger or smaller, but for now, 24 points will work. Next we'll draw the text; that should be added into the game loop, right after our `draw_string` declaration. To draw the text on the window, we first draw the string on a surface of its own with the `render()` command on the `font` object we created:

```
text = font.render(draw_string, True, WHITE)
```

This creates a variable called text to store a surface that contains the white pixels that make up all the letters, numbers, and symbols of our string. The next step will get the dimensions (width and height) of that surface. Longer strings will render or draw wider, while shorter strings will take fewer pixels to draw. The same goes for larger fonts versus smaller fonts. The text string will be rendered on a rectangular surface, so we'll call our variable text_rect for the rectangle that holds our drawn string:

```
text_rect = text.get_rect()
```

The get_rect() command on our text surface will return the dimensions of the drawn string. Next we'll center the text rectangle text_rect horizontally on the screen, using the .centerx attribute, and position the text rectangle 10 pixels down from the top of the screen so it's easy to see. Here are the two commands to set the position:

```
text_rect.centerx = screen.get_rect().centerx
text_rect.y = 10
```

It's time to draw the text_rect image to the screen. We'll do this using the blit() function like we did for our picture pic:

```
screen.blit(text, text_rect)
```

With those changes, our Smiley Pong game has become like the classic version of the game, but with our smiley face as the ball. Run the app, and you'll see something like Figure 10-5. We're on our way to an arcade-quality game!

PUTTING IT ALL TOGETHER

We've used many coding skills to make this game. Variables, loops, conditions, math, graphics, event handling—almost our full toolkit. Games are an adventure for both the coder and the player. Producing a game is challenging and rewarding; we get to build the gameplay we want, then share it with others. My sons loved version 1.0 of the Smiley Pong game, and they gave me great ideas for extending it to version 2.0.

Here's the full version 1.0, *SmileyPong1.py*:

SmileyPong1.py

```python
import pygame      # Setup
pygame.init()
screen = pygame.display.set_mode([800,600])
pygame.display.set_caption("Smiley Pong")
keepGoing = True
```

```
pic = pygame.image.load("CrazySmile.bmp")
colorkey = pic.get_at((0,0))
pic.set_colorkey(colorkey)
picx = 0
picy = 0
BLACK = (0,0,0)
WHITE = (255,255,255)
timer = pygame.time.Clock()
speedx = 5
speedy = 5
paddlew = 200
paddleh = 25
paddlex = 300
paddley = 550
picw = 100
pich = 100
points = 0
lives = 5
font = pygame.font.SysFont("Times", 24)

while keepGoing:     # Game loop
    for event in pygame.event.get():
        if event.type == pygame.QUIT:
            keepGoing = False
    picx += speedx
    picy += speedy

    if picx <= 0 or picx + pic.get_width() >= 800:
        speedx = -speedx
    if picy <= 0:
        speedy = -speedy
    if picy >= 500:
        lives -= 1
        speedy = -speedy

    screen.fill(BLACK)
    screen.blit(pic, (picx, picy))

    # Draw paddle
    paddlex = pygame.mouse.get_pos()[0]
    paddlex -= paddlew/2
    pygame.draw.rect(screen, WHITE, (paddlex, paddley, paddlew, paddleh))

    # Check for paddle bounce
    if picy + pich >= paddley and picy + pich <= paddley + paddleh \
        and speedy > 0:
```

```
        if picx + picw / 2 >= paddlex and picx + picw / 2 <= paddlex + \
          paddlew:
            points += 1
            speedy = -speedy

    # Draw text on screen
    draw_string = "Lives: " + str(lives) + " Points: " + str(points)

    text = font.render(draw_string, True, WHITE)
    text_rect = text.get_rect()
    text_rect.centerx = screen.get_rect().centerx
    text_rect.y = 10
    screen.blit(text, text_rect)
    pygame.display.update()
    timer.tick(60)

pygame.quit()          # Exit
```

Our gameplay is nearly complete: the ball bounces off the paddle, points are awarded, and players lose a life if they miss the ball and it hits the bottom edge of the screen. All the basic components are there to make this an arcade-style game. Now think about what improvements you would like to see, work out the logic, and try adding code to version 1.0 to make your game even more fun. In the next section, we'll add three more features to create a fully interactive, video game–like experience that we can share with others.

ADDING DIFFICULTY AND ENDING THE GAME: SMILEY PONG, VERSION 2.0

Version 1.0 of our Smiley Pong game is playable. Players can score points, lose lives, and see their progress on the screen. One thing we don't have yet is an end to the game. Another is the sense of greater challenge as the game progresses. We'll add the following features to Smiley Pong, version 1.0, to create a more complete game in version 2.0: a way to show that the game is over when the last life is lost, a way to play again or start a new game without closing the program, and a way to increase the difficulty as the game goes on. We'll add these three features one at a time, winding up with a fun, challenging, arcade-style game! The final version is shown on page 250.

GAME OVER

Version 1.0 never stopped playing because we didn't add logic to handle the game being over. We know the condition to test for: the game is over when the player has no lives left. Now we need to figure out what to do when the player loses their last life.

The first thing we want to do is stop the game. We don't want to close the program, but we do want to stop the ball. The second thing we want to do is change the text on the screen to tell the player that the game is over and give them their score. We can accomplish both tasks with an `if` statement right after the `draw_string` declaration for lives and points.

```
if lives < 1:
    speedx = speedy = 0
    draw_string = "Game Over. Your score was: " + str(points)
    draw_string += ". Press F1 to play again. "
```

By changing `speedx` and `speedy` (the horizontal and vertical speed of the ball, respectively) to zero, we've stopped the ball from moving. The user can still move the paddle on the screen, but we've ended the gameplay visually to let the user know the game is over. The text makes this even clearer, plus it tells the user how well they did this round.

Right now, we're telling the user to press F1 to play again, but pressing the key doesn't do anything yet. We need logic to handle the keypress event and start the game over.

PLAY AGAIN

We want to let the user play a new game when they've run out of lives. We've added text to the screen to tell the user to press the F1 key to play again, so let's add code to detect that keypress and start the game over. First, we'll check if a key was pressed and if that key was F1:

```
if event.type == pygame.KEYDOWN:
    if event.key == pygame.K_F1:    # F1 = New Game
```

In the event handler `for` loop inside our game loop, we add an `if` statement to check if there was a `KEYDOWN` event. If so, we check the key pressed in that event (`event.key`) to see if it's equal to the

F1 key (pygame.K_F1). The code that follows this second if statement will be our *play again* or *new game* code.

NOTE

You can get a full list of the Pygame keycodes, such as K_F1, *at* http://www.pygame.org/docs/ref/key.html.

"Play again" means that we want to start over from the beginning. For Smiley Pong, we started with 0 points, 5 lives, and the ball coming at us at 5 pixels per frame from the top-left corner of the screen, (0, 0). If we reset these variables, we should get the new game effect:

```
points = 0
lives = 5
picx = 0
picy = 0
speedx = 5
speedy = 5
```

Add these lines to the if statement for the F1 key KEYDOWN event, and you'll be able to restart the game anytime. If you'd like to allow restarting only when the game is already over, you can include an additional condition that lives == 0, but we'll leave the if statements as they currently are in our version 2.0 so that the user can restart anytime.

FASTER AND FASTER

Our game lacks one final element of game design: it doesn't get more challenging the longer it's played, so someone could play almost forever, paying less and less attention. Let's add difficulty as the game progresses to engage the player and make the game more arcade-like.

We want to increase the speed of the ball slightly as the game advances, but not too much, or the player might get frustrated. We want to make the game just a bit faster after each bounce. The natural place to do this is within the code that checks for bounces. Increasing the speed means making speedx and speedy greater so that the ball moves farther in each direction each frame. Try changing our if statements for collision detection (where we make the ball bounce back from each edge of the screen) to the following:

```
if picx <= 0 or picx >= 700:
    speedx = -speedx * 1.1
if picy <= 0:
    speedy = -speedy + 1
```

In the first case, when the ball is bouncing off the left and right sides of the screen in the horizontal direction, we increase the horizontal speed, speedx, by multiplying it by 1.1 (and we still change the direction with our minus sign). This is a 10 percent increase in speed after each left and right bounce.

When the ball bounces off the top of the screen (if picy <= 0), we know that the speed will become positive as it rebounds off the top and heads back down the screen in the positive *y* direction, so we can add 1 to speedy after we change the direction with the minus sign. If the ball came toward the top at 5 pixels per frame in speedy, it will leave at 6 pixels per frame, then 7, and so on.

If you make those changes, you'll see the ball get faster and faster. But once the ball starts going faster, it never slows back down. Soon the ball would be traveling so quickly that the player could lose all five lives in just a second.

We'll make our game more playable (and fair) by resetting the speed every time the player loses a life. If the speed gets so high that the user can't hit the ball with the paddle, it's probably a good time to reset the speed to a slower value so the player can catch up.

Our code for bouncing off the bottom of the screen is where we take away one of the player's lives, so let's change the speed after we've subtracted a life:

```
if picy >= 500:
    lives -= 1
    speedy = -5
    speedx = 5
```

This makes the game more reasonable, as the ball no longer gets out of control and stays that way; after the player loses a life, the ball slows down enough that the player can hit it a few more times before it speeds back up.

One problem, though, is that the ball could be traveling so fast that it could "get stuck" off the bottom edge of the screen; after playing a few games, the player will run into a case in which they lose all of their remaining lives on a single bounce off the bottom edge. This is because the ball could move way below the bottom edge of the screen if it's traveling really quickly, and when we reset the speed, we might not get the ball completely back on the screen by the next frame.

To solve this, let's add one line to the end of that `if` statement:

```
picy = 499
```

We move the ball back onto the screen completely after a lost life by setting the `picy` to a value, like `499`, that places the ball completely above the bottom boundary of the screen. This will help our ball move safely back onto the screen no matter how fast it was traveling when it hit the bottom edge.

After these changes, version 2.0 looks like Figure 10-6.

Figure 10-6: Version 2.0 of our Smiley Pong game features faster gameplay, game over, and play again functionality.

Version 2.0 is like a real arcade game, complete with the game over/play again screen.

PUTTING IT ALL TOGETHER

Here's our finished version 2.0, *SmileyPong2.py*. At just under 80 lines of code, it's a full arcade-style game that you can show off to friends and family. You can also build on it further to develop your coding skill.

SmileyPong2.py

```python
import pygame            # Setup
pygame.init()
screen = pygame.display.set_mode([800,600])
pygame.display.set_caption("Smiley Pong")
keepGoing = True
pic = pygame.image.load("CrazySmile.bmp")
colorkey = pic.get_at((0,0))
pic.set_colorkey(colorkey)
picx = 0
picy = 0
BLACK = (0,0,0)
WHITE = (255,255,255)
timer = pygame.time.Clock()
speedx = 5
speedy = 5
paddlew = 200
paddleh = 25
paddlex = 300
paddley = 550
picw = 100
pich = 100
points = 0
lives = 5
font = pygame.font.SysFont("Times", 24)

while keepGoing:         # Game loop
    for event in pygame.event.get():
        if event.type == pygame.QUIT:
            keepGoing = False
        if event.type == pygame.KEYDOWN:
            if event.key == pygame.K_F1:      # F1 = New Game
                points = 0
                lives = 5
                picx = 0
                picy = 0
                speedx = 5
                speedy = 5
```

```python
    picx += speedx
    picy += speedy

    if picx <= 0 or picx >= 700:
        speedx = -speedx * 1.1
    if picy <= 0:
        speedy = -speedy + 1
    if picy >= 500:
        lives -= 1
        speedy = -5
        speedx = 5
        picy = 499

    screen.fill(BLACK)
    screen.blit(pic, (picx, picy))

    # Draw paddle
    paddlex = pygame.mouse.get_pos()[0]
    paddlex -= paddlew/2
    pygame.draw.rect(screen, WHITE, (paddlex, paddley, paddlew, paddleh))

    # Check for paddle bounce
    if picy + pich >= paddley and picy + pich <= paddley + paddleh \
        and speedy > 0:
        if picx + picw/2 >= paddlex and picx + picw/2 <= paddlex + \
            paddlew:
            speedy = -speedy
            points += 1

    # Draw text on screen
    draw_string = "Lives: " + str(lives) + " Points: " + str(points)
    # Check whether the game is over
    if lives < 1:
        speedx = speedy = 0
        draw_string = "Game Over. Your score was: " + str(points)
        draw_string += ". Press F1 to play again. "

    text = font.render(draw_string, True, WHITE)
    text_rect = text.get_rect()
    text_rect.centerx = screen.get_rect().centerx
    text_rect.y = 10
    screen.blit(text, text_rect)
    pygame.display.update()
    timer.tick(60)

pygame.quit()        # Exit
```

You can continue to build on the game elements in this example (see "Programming Challenges" on page 261), or you can use these building blocks to develop something new. Most games, and even other apps, have features like the ones you added in this chapter, and we usually follow a process similar to the one we used to build Smiley Pong. First, map out the skeleton of the game, and then build a working *prototype*, or a version 1.0. Once that's working, add features until you get the final version you want. You'll find *iterative versioning*—adding features one at a time to create new versions—useful as you build more complex apps.

ADDING MORE FEATURES: SMILEYPOP V2.0

We'll follow our iterative versioning process one more time by adding features that my son Max and I wanted to see in the SmileyPop app in Chapter 9. First, he wanted a sound effect whenever a smiley face bubble (or balloon) was popped by a mouse click. Second, we both wanted some kind of feedback and display (maybe how many bubbles had been created and how many had been popped), and I wanted some sign of progress, like the percentage of bubbles we'd popped. The SmileyPop app was already fun, but these elements could make it even better.

Look back at *SmileyPop.py* on page 226; we'll start with this version of the app, and we'll build our second version (v2.0, short for version 2.0) by adding code. The final version, *SmileyPop2.py*, is shown on page 257.

We'll begin by adding Max's request: the popping sound.

ADDING SOUND WITH PYGAME

At *http://www.pygame.org/docs/*, you'll find modules, classes, and functions that can make your games more fun to play and easier to program. The module we need for sound effects is `pygame.mixer`. To use this mixer module to add sound to your game, you first need a sound file to use. For our popping sound effect, download the *pop.wav* file from *http://www.nostarch.com/teachkids/* under the source code and files for Chapter 10.

We'll add these two lines to the setup section of *SmileyPop.py*, right below `sprite_list = pygame.sprite.Group()`:

```
pygame.mixer.init()     # Add sounds
pop = pygame.mixer.Sound("pop.wav")
```

We begin by initializing the mixer (just like we initialize Pygame with `pygame.init()`). Then we load our *pop.wav* sound effect into a `Sound` object so we can play it in our program.

The second line loads *pop.wav* as a `pygame.mixer.Sound` object and stores it in the variable `pop`, which we'll use later when we want to hear a popping sound. As with image files, you'll need *pop.wav* saved in the same directory or folder as your *SmileyPop.py* program for the code to be able to find the file and use it.

Next we'll add logic to check whether a smiley was clicked and play our `pop` sound if a smiley was popped. We'll do this in the event handler section of our game loop, in the same `elif` statement that processes right-mouse-button events (`elif pygame.mouse.get_pressed()[2]`). After the `sprite_list.remove(clicked_smileys)` that removes clicked smileys from the sprite_list, we could check to see if there were actually any smiley collisions, then play a sound.

The user could right-click the mouse in an area of the screen with no smiley faces to pop, or they might miss a smiley when trying to click. We'll check whether any smileys were actually clicked by seeing `if len(clicked_smileys) > 0`. The `len()` function tells us the length of a list or collection, and if the length is greater than zero, there were clicked smileys. Remember, `clicked_smileys` was a list of the smiley sprites that collided with or were drawn overlapping the point where the user clicked.

If the `clicked_smileys` list has smiley sprites in it, then the user correctly right-clicked at least one smiley, so we play the popping sound:

```
if len(clicked_smileys) > 0:
    pop.play()
```

Notice that both lines are indented to align correctly with the other code in our `elif` statement for handling right-clicks.

These four lines of added code are all it takes to play the popping sound when a user successfully right-clicks a smiley. To make these changes and hear the result, make sure you've downloaded the *pop.wav* sound file into the same folder as your revised *SmileyPop.py*, turn your speakers to a reasonable volume, and pop away!

TRACKING AND DISPLAYING PLAYER PROGRESS

The next feature we want to add is some way to help the user feel like they're making progress. The sound effects added one fun kind of feedback (the user hears a popping sound only if they actually clicked a smiley sprite), but let's also track how many bubbles the user has created and popped and what percentage of the smileys they've popped.

To build the logic for keeping track of the number of smileys the user has created and the number they've popped, we'll begin by adding a font variable and two counter variables, count_smileys and count_popped, to the setup section of our app:

```
font = pygame.font.SysFont("Arial", 24)
WHITE = (255,255,255)
count_smileys = 0
count_popped = 0
```

We set our font variable to the Arial font face, at a size of 24 points. We want to draw text on the screen in white letters, so we add a color variable WHITE and set it to the RGB triplet for white, (255,255,255). Our count_smileys and count_popped variables will store the number of created and popped smileys, which both start at zero when the app first loads.

SMILEYS CREATED AND POPPED

First, let's count smileys as they're added to the sprite_list. To do that, we go almost to the bottom of our *SmileyPop.py* code, where the if mousedown statement checks whether the mouse is being dragged with the mouse button pressed and adds smileys to our sprite_list. Add just the last line to that if statement:

```
if mousedown:
    speedx = random.randint(-5, 5)
    speedy = random.randint(-5, 5)
    newSmiley = Smiley(pygame.mouse.get_pos(), speedx, speedy)
    sprite_list.add(newSmiley)
    count_smileys += 1
```

Adding 1 to `count_smileys` every time a new smiley is added to the `sprite_list` will help us keep track of the total number of smileys drawn.

We'll add similar logic to the `if` statement that plays our popping sound whenever one or more smileys have been clicked, but we won't just add 1 to `count_popped`—we'll add the real number of smileys that were clicked. Remember that our user could have clicked the screen over two or more smiley sprites that are overlapping the same point. In our event handler for the right-click event, we gathered all these colliding smileys as the list `clicked_smileys`. To find out how many points to add to `count_popped`, we just use the `len()` function again to get the correct number of smileys the user popped with this right-click. Add this line to the `if` statement you wrote for the popping sound:

```
if len(clicked_smileys) > 0:
    pop.play()
    count_popped += len(clicked_smileys)
```

By adding `len(clicked_smileys)` to `count_popped`, we'll always have the correct number of popped smileys at any point in time. Now, we just have to add the code to our game loop that will display the number of smileys created, the number popped, and the percentage popped to measure the user's progress.

Just like in our Smiley Pong display, we'll create a string of text to draw on the screen, and we'll show the numbers as strings with the `str()` function. Add these lines to your game loop right before `pygame.display.update()`:

```
draw_string = "Bubbles created: " + str(count_smileys)
draw_string += " - Bubbles popped: " + str(count_popped)
```

These lines will create our draw_string and show both the number of smiley bubbles created and the number popped.

PERCENTAGE OF SMILEYS POPPED

Add these three lines, right after the two draw_string statements:

```
if (count_smileys > 0):
    draw_string += " - Percent: "
    draw_string += str(round(count_popped/count_smileys*100, 1))
    draw_string += "%"
```

To get the percentage of smileys popped out of all the smileys that have been created, we divide count_popped by count_smileys (count_popped/count_smileys), then multiply by 100 to get the percent value (count_popped/count_smileys*100). But we'll have two problems if we try to show this number. First, when the program starts and both values are zero, our percentage calculation will produce a "division by zero" error. To fix this, we'll show the percentage popped only if count_smileys is greater than zero.

Second, if the user has created three smileys and popped one of them—a ratio of one out of three, or 1/3—the percentage will be 33.33333333. . . . We don't want the display to get really long every time there's a repeating decimal in the percentage calculation, so let's use the round() function to round the percentage to one decimal place.

The last step is to draw the string in white pixels, center those pixels on the screen near the top, and call screen.blit() to copy those pixels to the game window's drawing screen:

```
text = font.render(draw_string, True, WHITE)
text_rect = text.get_rect()
text_rect.centerx = screen.get_rect().centerx
text_rect.y = 10
screen.blit (text, text_rect)
```

You can see the effect of these changes in Figure 10-7.

The smaller smileys are more difficult to catch and pop, especially when they're moving fast, so it's hard to pop more than 90 percent. That's exactly what we want. We've used this feedback and challenge/achievement component to make the app feel more like a game we might play.

Figure 10-7: The SmileyPop app is more like a game now that we've added sound and a progress/feedback display.

The popping sound and progress display feedback have made SmileyPop feel like a mobile app. As you're popping smiley faces by right-clicking, you can probably imagine tapping the smileys with your finger to pop them on a mobile device. (To learn how to build mobile apps, check out MIT's App Inventor at *http://appinventor .mit.edu/*.)

PUTTING IT ALL TOGETHER

Here's the complete code for SmileyPop, version 2.0. Remember to keep the *.py* source code file, the *CrazySmile.bmp* image file, and the *pop.wav* sound file all in the same folder.

At almost 90 lines, this app might be a bit too long to type by hand. Go to *http://www.nostarch.com/teachkids/* to download the code, along with the sound and picture files.

SmileyPop2.py

```
import pygame
import random

BLACK = (0,0,0)
WHITE = (255,255,255)
```

```python
pygame.init()
screen = pygame.display.set_mode([800,600])
pygame.display.set_caption("Pop a Smiley")
mousedown = False
keep_going = True
clock = pygame.time.Clock()
pic = pygame.image.load("CrazySmile.bmp")
colorkey = pic.get_at((0,0))
pic.set_colorkey(colorkey)
sprite_list = pygame.sprite.Group()
pygame.mixer.init()        # Add sounds
pop = pygame.mixer.Sound("pop.wav")
font = pygame.font.SysFont("Arial", 24)
count_smileys = 0
count_popped = 0

class Smiley(pygame.sprite.Sprite):
    pos = (0,0)
    xvel = 1
    yvel = 1
    scale = 100

    def __init__(self, pos, xvel, yvel):
        pygame.sprite.Sprite.__init__(self)
        self.image = pic
        self.scale = random.randrange(10,100)
        self.image = pygame.transform.scale(self.image,
                                        (self.scale,self.scale))
        self.rect = self.image.get_rect()
        self.pos = pos
        self.rect.x = pos[0] - self.scale/2
        self.rect.y = pos[1] - self.scale/2
        self.xvel = xvel
        self.yvel = yvel

    def update(self):
        self.rect.x += self.xvel
        self.rect.y += self.yvel
        if self.rect.x <= 0 or self.rect.x > screen.get_width() - self.scale:
            self.xvel = -self.xvel
        if self.rect.y <= 0 or self.rect.y > screen.get_height() - self.scale:
            self.yvel = -self.yvel

while keep_going:
    for event in pygame.event.get():
        if event.type == pygame.QUIT:
            keep_going = False
```

```
        if event.type == pygame.MOUSEBUTTONDOWN:
            if pygame.mouse.get_pressed()[0]:     # Left mouse button, draw
                mousedown = True
            elif pygame.mouse.get_pressed()[2]:  # Right mouse button, pop
                pos = pygame.mouse.get_pos()
                clicked_smileys = [s for s in sprite_list if
                                   s.rect.collidepoint(pos)]
                sprite_list.remove(clicked_smileys)
                if len(clicked_smileys) > 0:
                    pop.play()
                    count_popped += len(clicked_smileys)
        if event.type == pygame.MOUSEBUTTONUP:
            mousedown = False
    screen.fill(BLACK)
    sprite_list.update()
    sprite_list.draw(screen)
    clock.tick(60)
    draw_string = "Bubbles created: " + str(count_smileys)
    draw_string += " - Bubbles popped: " + str(count_popped)
    if (count_smileys > 0):
        draw_string += " - Percent: "
        draw_string += str(round(count_popped/count_smileys*100, 1))
        draw_string += "%"

    text = font.render(draw_string, True, WHITE)
    text_rect = text.get_rect()
    text_rect.centerx = screen.get_rect().centerx
    text_rect.y = 10
    screen.blit (text, text_rect)

    pygame.display.update()
    if mousedown:
        speedx = random.randint(-5, 5)
        speedy = random.randint(-5, 5)
        newSmiley = Smiley(pygame.mouse.get_pos(), speedx, speedy)
        sprite_list.add(newSmiley)
        count_smileys += 1

pygame.quit()
```

The more programs you write, the better you'll get at coding. You may start by coding games that you find interesting, writing an app that solves a problem you care about, or developing apps for other people. Keep coding, solve more problems, and get better and better at programming, and you'll soon be able to help create products that benefit users around the world.

Whether you're coding mobile games and apps; writing programs that control automobiles, robots, or drones; or building the next social media web application, coding is a skill that can change your life.

You have the skills. You have the ability. Keep practicing, keep coding, and go out there and make a difference—in your own life, in the lives of the people you care about, and in the world.

WHAT YOU LEARNED

In this chapter, you learned about elements of game design, from goals and achievements to rules and mechanics. We built a single-player Smiley Pong game from scratch and turned our SmileyPop app into a game we could picture playing on a smartphone or tablet. We combined animation, user interaction, and game design to build two versions of the Smiley Pong game and a second version of SmileyPop, adding more features as we went.

In Smiley Pong, we drew our board and game pieces, added user interaction to move the paddle, and added collision detection and scoring. We displayed text on the screen to give the user information about their achievements and the state of the game. You learned how to detect keypress events in Pygame, added "game over" and "play again" logic, and finished version 2.0 by making the ball speed up as the game progressed. You now have the framework and parts to build more complex games.

In SmileyPop, we started with an app that was already fun to play with, added user feedback in the form of a popping sound using the pygame.mixer module, and then added logic and a display to keep track of the user's progress as more bubbles are created and popped.

The apps you'll create with your programming skills will also start with a simple version, a *proof of concept*, that you can run and use as a foundation for new versions. You can begin with any program and add features one at a time, saving each new version along the way—a process called *iterative versioning*. This process helps you debug each new feature until it works correctly, and it helps you keep the last good version of a file even when the new code breaks.

Sometimes a new feature will be a good fit, and you'll keep it as the foundation of the next version. Sometimes your new code won't work, or the feature won't be as cool as you expected. Either way, you build your programming skills by trying new things and solving new problems.

Happy coding!

After mastering the concepts in this chapter, you should be able to do the following:

- Recognize common game design elements in games and apps that you use.

- Incorporate game design elements into apps that you code.

- Build a skeleton of a game by drawing the board and playing pieces and adding user interaction.

- Program collision detection between game pieces and keep score in an app or game.

- Display text information on the screen using the `pygame.font` module.

- Write game logic to determine when a game is over.

- Detect and handle keypress events in Pygame.

- Develop the code to start a new game or play again after a game ends.

- Use math and logic to make games progressively more difficult

- Add sounds to your apps with the `pygame.mixer` module.

- Display percentages and rounded numbers to keep users informed of their progress in a game.

- Understand the process of iterative versioning: adding features to an app one at a time and saving it as a new version (1.0, 2.0, and so on).

PROGRAMMING CHALLENGES

For sample answers to these challenges, and to download the sound files for this chapter, go to *http://www.nostarch.com/teachkids/*.

#1: SOUND EFFECTS

One feature we could add to Smiley Pong, version 2.0, is sound effects. In the classic Pong console and arcade game, the ball made a "blip" noise when players scored a point and a "buzz" or "blap" noise when they missed. For one of your

continued

final challenges, use the skills you learned in version 2.0 of the SmileyPop app to upgrade Smiley Pong v2.0 to v3.0 by adding sound effects to the point and miss bounces. Save this new file as *SmileyPong3.py*.

#2: HITS AND MISSES

To make the SmileyPop app even more game-like, add logic to keep track of the number of hits and misses out of the total number of clicks. If the user hits any smiley sprites when they right-click, add 1 to the number of hits (1 hit per click—we don't want to duplicate count_popped). If the user right-clicks and doesn't hit any smiley sprites, record that as a miss. You could program the logic to end the game after a certain number of misses, or you could give the user a certain number of total clicks to get the highest percentage they can. You might even add a timer and tell the player to create and pop as many smiley bubbles as they can in, say, 30 seconds. Save this new version as *SmileyPopHitCounter.py*.

#3: CLEAR THE BUBBLES

You might want to add a "clear" feature (or cheat button) to pop all the bubbles by hitting a function key, sort of like our "play again" feature in Smiley Pong. You could also make the bouncing smiley faces slow down over time by multiplying their speed by a number less than 1 (like 0.95) every time they bounce off an edge. The possibilities are endless.

A

PYTHON SETUP FOR WINDOWS, MAC, AND LINUX

This appendix will walk you through each step of installing Python on Windows, Mac, or Linux. Depending on your operating system version, what you see here might be slightly different from what's on your screen, but these steps should get you up and running.

If you're installing Python on a computer at school or work, you may need help or permission from the IT department to perform the installation. If you run into issues installing Python at school, ask for IT help and let them know you're studying programming.

PYTHON FOR WINDOWS

For Windows, we'll use Python version 3.2.5 so that our Pygame installation (in Appendix B) for the programs in Chapters 8 to 10 will be easier.

DOWNLOAD THE INSTALLER

1. Go to *http://python.org/*, and hover your mouse over the **Downloads** link. You'll see a drop-down list of options, as shown in Figure A-1.

Figure A-1: Hover your mouse over Downloads *to display a list of options.*

2. In the drop-down list, click the **Windows** link. This will take you to a Python Releases For Windows page, as shown in Figure A-2.

Figure A-2: The Python downloads page for Windows

3. Scroll down until you see the link that begins with *Python 3.2.5*. Under that link, you'll see several items, as shown in Figure A-3.

Figure A-3: Under Python Releases For Windows, find the Python 3.2.5 installer.

4. Under Python 3.2.5, click **Windows x86 MSI installer**. This will download the installer program.

RUN THE INSTALLER

1. Wait until the download finishes, then open your *Downloads* folder. You should see the *python-3.2.5* Windows Installer program file, as shown in Figure A-4.

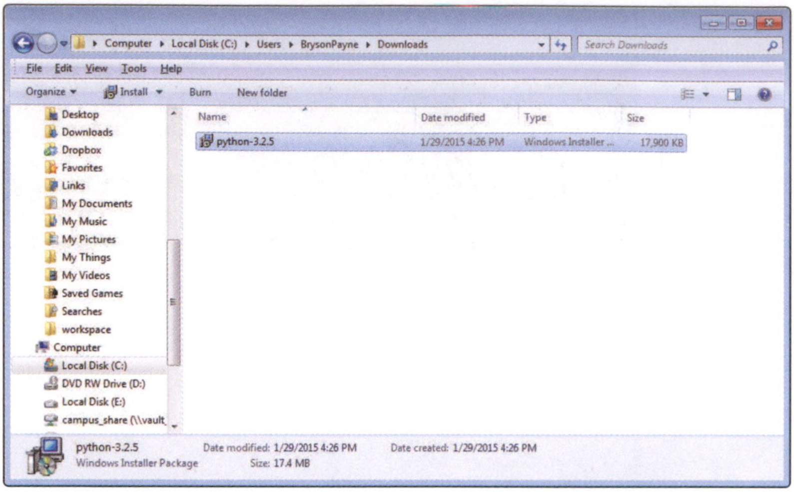

Figure A-4: Double-click the installer in your Downloads *folder.*

2. Double-click the *python-3.2.5* Windows Installer program file to begin installation.

3. A Security Warning dialog might come up, as shown in Figure A-5. If you see a Security Warning window, click **Run**; Windows is just letting you know the software is trying to install something on your computer.

*Figure A-5: Click **Run** to allow the installation.*

4. The installer may ask if you would like to install Python for all users or just yourself, as shown in Figure A-6. It's usually best to choose **Install for all users**, but if that isn't allowed at your school or office, or if you can't get it to work, try **Install just for me**. Then click **Next >**.

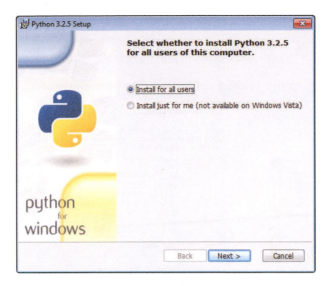

Figure A-6: Install for all users.

5. Next you'll see a Select Destination Directory window like the one shown in Figure A-7. This is where you can choose which folder to install Python in. The program will try to install on your *C:* drive under a folder called *Python32*, and this should work for your laptop or home PC. Click **Next >** to keep installing. (If you're installing at school or work and run into trouble, your IT staff might tell you to install in a different folder, like *User* or *Desktop*.)

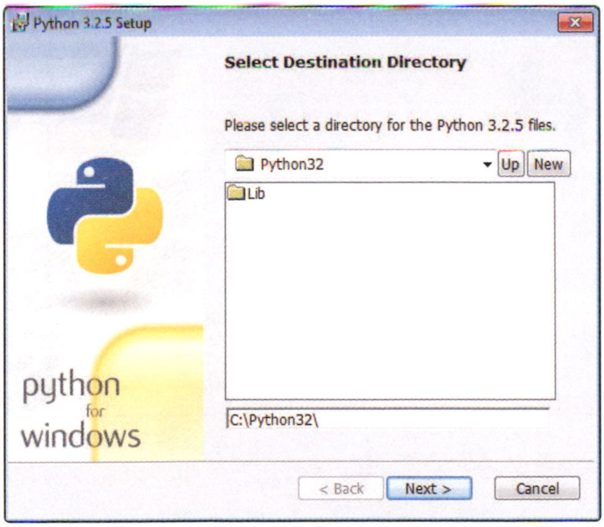

Figure A-7: Choose a folder to install Python in.

6. Now you'll see a window like the one shown in Figure A-8 asking you to customize Python. You don't need to change anything here. Just click **Next >**.

Figure A-8: Don't change anything; just click **Next >**.

7. You're now finished with the installer, and you should see a window like the one shown in Figure A-9. Click **Finish**.

Figure A-9: Click **Finish** to exit the installer.

You've installed Python! Next, you can try it out to make sure it works properly.

TRY OUT PYTHON

1. Go to **Start ▸ Programs ▸ Python 3.2 ▸ IDLE (Python GUI)**, as shown in Figure A-10. (On Windows 8 and later, you can click the Windows/Start button, go to the Search tool, and type **IDLE**).

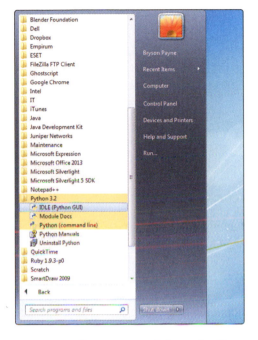

Figure A-10: Open IDLE from the Start menu.

2. The Python shell editor screen should appear. This Python shell program is where you can enter code and see results right away. If you're curious, you can start trying out some code. Type **print("Hello, Python!")** and press ENTER. The Python shell should respond with Hello, Python!, as shown in Figure A-11. Try an addition statement, like **2 + 3**. Press ENTER, and Python will respond with the answer!

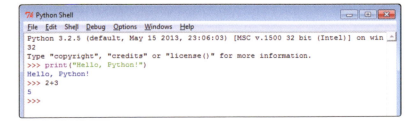

Figure A-11: Trying some commands in the Python shell

3. Finally, you may want to change the size of the text in IDLE to make it easier to read. Go to **Options ▸ Configure IDLE...**. Under **Fonts/Tabs**, as shown in Figure A-12, change the **Size** option to **18** or whatever size is easiest for you to read. You can also check the Bold checkbox to make the text thicker. Customize the font so it's comfortable for your eyes.

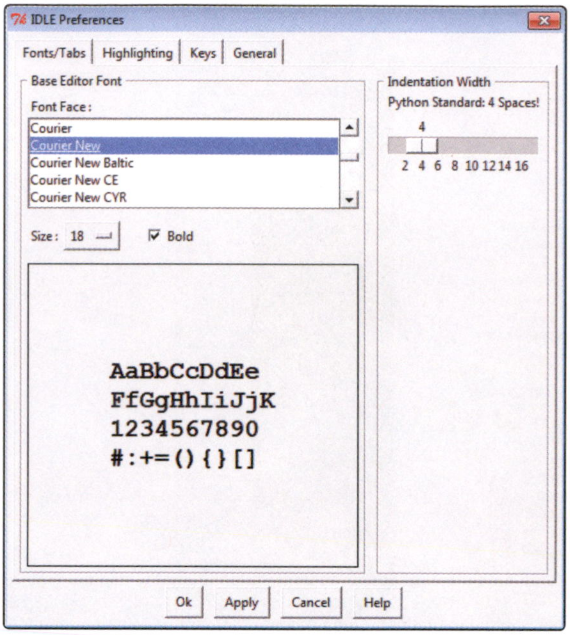

Figure A-12: Configuring preferences in IDLE

4. Once you've chosen font and size options to make your IDLE input easy to read, click **Apply**, and then click **Ok** to return to the IDLE Python shell screen. Now when you type, you should see text appear in the font and size you chose.

Now you're ready to tackle Chapters 1 through 7. To use the programs from Chapters 8 through 10, go to Appendix B and follow the steps to install Pygame. Happy coding!

PYTHON FOR MAC

Most Apple computers come with an earlier version of Python already installed, but we want to install version 3.4.2 to use the new features of Python 3 to run the sample code from the book.

DOWNLOAD THE INSTALLER

1. Go to *http://python.org/*, and hover your mouse over the **Downloads** link to see a drop-down list of options. You'll see Mac OS X on this list, as shown in Figure A-13.

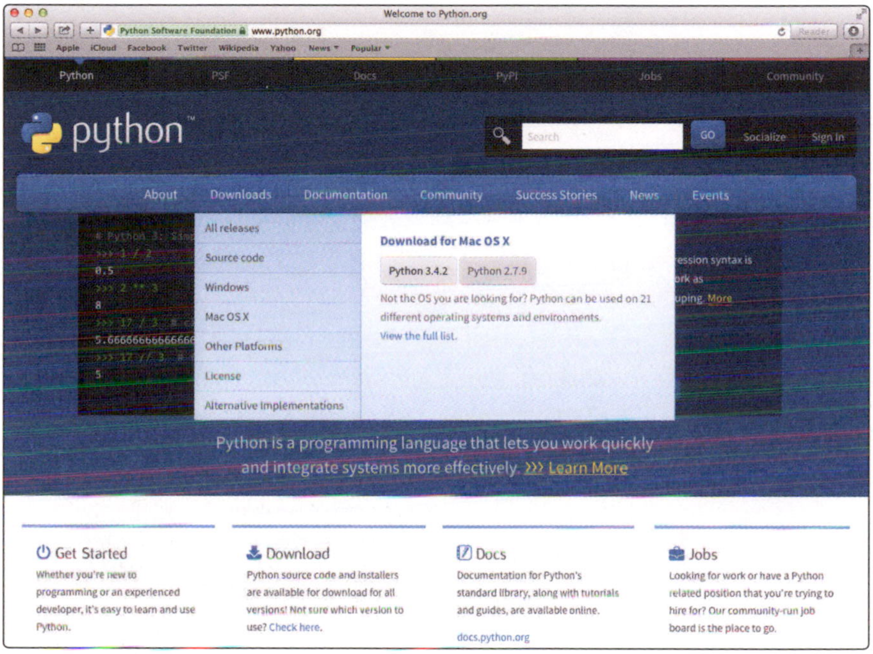

Figure A-13: Hover your mouse over the Downloads link. You should see a Mac OS X link in the drop-down list.

2. Click the **Mac OS X** link in the drop-down list. This will take you to a Python Releases For Mac OS X page.

3. On the Python Releases For Mac OS X page, find the link that starts with *Python 3.4.2* and click it. This will download the installer program.

RUN THE INSTALLER

1. Wait for the download to finish. Then open your *Downloads* folder to find the *python-3.4.2* Mac Installer program file, as shown in Figure A-14. Double-click the file to begin installation.

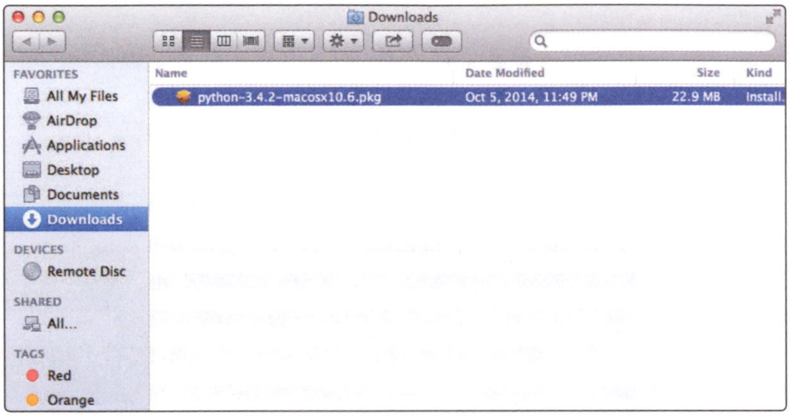

Figure A-14: Double-click the installer in your Downloads *folder.*

2. Double-clicking the installer file will open an Install Python window. You'll see a welcome screen like the one shown in Figure A-15. Click **Continue**.

*Figure A-15: Click **Continue** on the welcome screen.*

3. Read and click **Agree** on the software license pop-up dialog, as shown in Figure A-16.

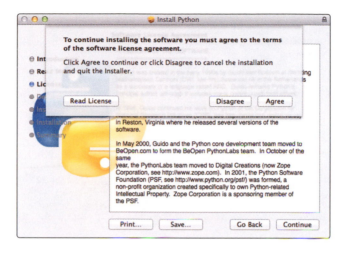

Figure A-16: Read and click *Agree* on the software license dialog.

4. You'll be taken to a Select a Destination screen, as shown in Figure A-17, where you'll choose which disk to install Python on. The program will usually be installed on your Mac HD hard drive, and this should work for your MacBook or home Mac. Click **Continue** to keep installing. (If you're installing at school or work and run into trouble, your IT staff may tell you to install in a different folder; ask them for help if needed.)

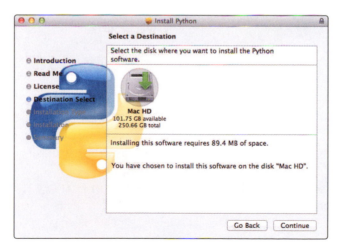

Figure A-17: Click *Continue* to keep installing.

5. Click **Install** on the next screen, as shown in Figure A-18.

Figure A-18: Click *Install*.

6. You should see a screen confirming that the installation is complete, like the one shown in Figure A-19. Click **Close** to exit the installer.

Figure A-19: To exit the installer, click *Close*.

You've installed Python! Next, you can try it out to see if it works.

TRY OUT PYTHON

1. Go to your Launchpad and click **IDLE**, or go to **Finder ▸ Applications**, double-click the *Python 3.4* folder, and double-click **IDLE** to open the Python shell, as shown in Figure A-20.

Figure A-20: Open IDLE from Launchpad (left) or the Applications folder (right).

2. The Python shell editor screen should appear. You're ready to try coding in the shell. Type **print("Hello, Python!")** and press RETURN; the Python shell should respond with Hello, Python!, as shown in Figure A-21. Try an addition statement, like **2 + 3**. Press RETURN, and Python will respond with the answer.

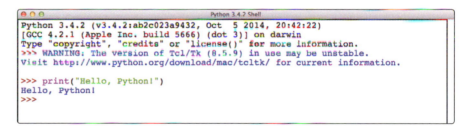

Figure A-21: Trying some commands in the Python shell

3. You may want to change the size of the text in the IDLE window to make it easier to read on your computer. Go to **IDLE ▸ Preferences...**. Under **Fonts/Tabs**, change the **Size** option to **20**, as shown in Figure A-22, or adjust it larger or smaller until it's easy to read. You can check the Bold checkbox to make the text thicker if it helps. Customize the font to anything that's comfortable for your eyes.

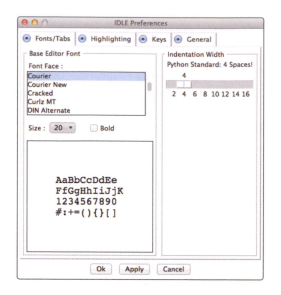

Figure A-22: Configuring preferences in IDLE

Now you're ready to tackle Chapters 1 through 7. To use the programs from Chapters 8 through 10, go to Appendix B and follow the steps to install Pygame. Happy coding!

PYTHON FOR LINUX

Most Linux distributions, including Ubuntu and even the Linux OS that comes installed on the Raspberry Pi, come with an earlier version of Python already installed. However, most of the apps in this book require Python 3. To install Python 3 on Linux, follow these steps:

1. In the Dash menu, go to System Tools and run the Ubuntu Software Center or similar application for your version of Linux. Figure A-23 shows the Software Center running on Lubuntu.

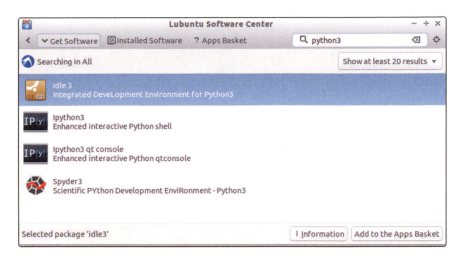

Figure A-23: Installing Python 3 on a computer running Lubuntu Linux

2. Search for *python3* and find *Idle 3*. Click **Add to the Apps Basket**.

3. Open the Apps Basket tab and click **Install Packages**, as shown in Figure A-24.

Lubuntu Software Center			
‹ ⌄ Get Software ⊙ Installed Software ? Apps Basket (1)			
? Apps Basket			
Package	To Download	To Install	Version
Idle3	3,172	55.3 k	3.4.2-1
dh-python (requested by idle3)	52.2 k	316 k	1.20140511-1
idle-python3.4 (requested by idle3)	32.4 k	208 k	3.4.2-1
python3 (requested by idle3)	8,786	102 k	3.4.2-1
python3-tk (requested by idle3)	23.7 k	109 k	3.4.2-1
python3.4-tk (requested by idle3)	unknown	unknown	unknown
python3:any (requested by idle3)	unknown	unknown	unknown
1 package marked, 120 k to download, 791 k to install		Discard	Install Packages

Figure A-24: Install the Idle 3 package, which includes Python 3.

4. After the installation completes, open a file window, select **Applications**, then **Programming**, and you should see **IDLE (using Python-3.4)**, as shown in Figure A-25.

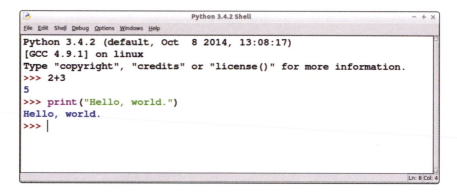

Figure A-25: IDLE, the Python shell program

5. Test IDLE by running it and typing **2 + 3** and pressing ENTER. Type **print("Hello, world.")** and press ENTER. IDLE should respond as shown in Figure A-26.

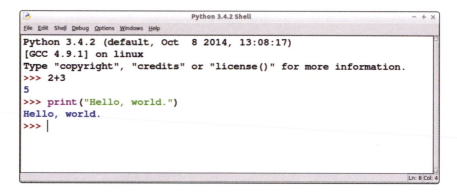

Figure A-26: Test Python by running IDLE. You're ready to code!

You're ready to try all the programs from Chapters 1 through 7. To use the programs from Chapters 8 through 10, see Appendix B on how to install Pygame for Linux. Happy coding!

B
PYGAME SETUP FOR WINDOWS, MAC, AND LINUX

After installing Python (see Appendix A), you'll want to install Pygame to run the animations and games in Chapters 8 through 10. This appendix will get you up and running. If you're installing Pygame on a computer at school or work, you may need help or permission from the IT department to perform the installation. If you run into issues, ask IT for help.

PYGAME FOR WINDOWS

For Windows, we'll use Pygame 1.9.2 for Python 3.2 (see Appendix A for help setting up Python 3.2.5).

1. Go to *http://pygame.org/* and click the **Downloads** link on the left, as shown in Figure B-1.

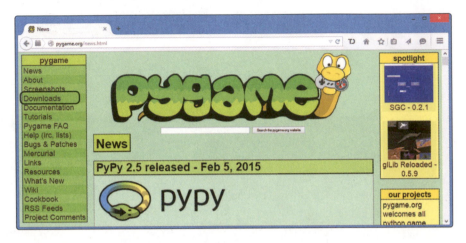

*Figure B-1: Click the **Downloads** link.*

2. Under the Windows section, find the link for *pygame-1.9.2a0 .win32-py3.2.msi* and click it to download the installer program, as shown in Figure B-2.

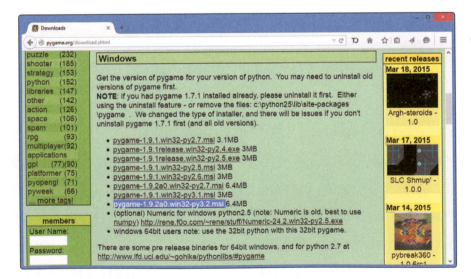

Figure B-2: Download the installer program for Windows.

3. When the download finishes, open your *Downloads* folder to find the *pygame-1.9.2a0.win32-py3.2* Windows Installer program file, as shown in Figure B-3. Double-click the file to begin installation. If a Security Warning window comes up, click **Run**. Windows is just letting you know the software is trying to install on your computer.

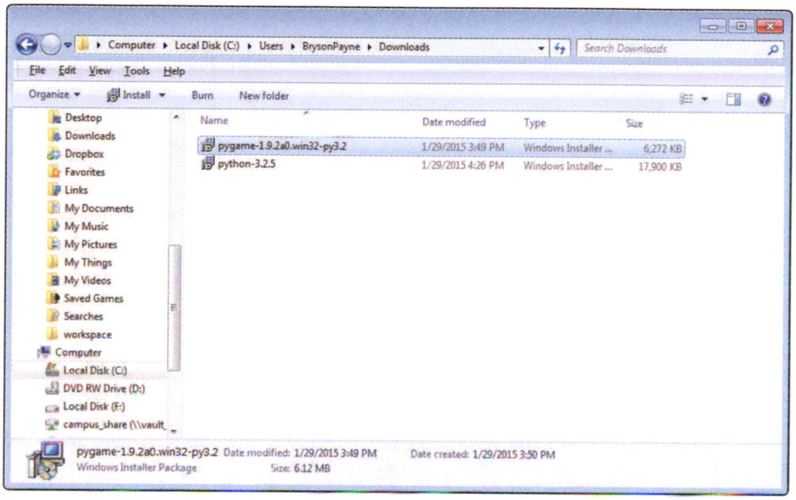

Figure B-3: Double-click the installer in your Downloads folder.

4. The installer might ask if you would like to install Pygame for all users or just for yourself. It's usually best to choose **Install for all users**, but if that isn't allowed at your school or office or you can't get it to work, try **Install just for me**. Click **Next >**, as shown in Figure B-4.

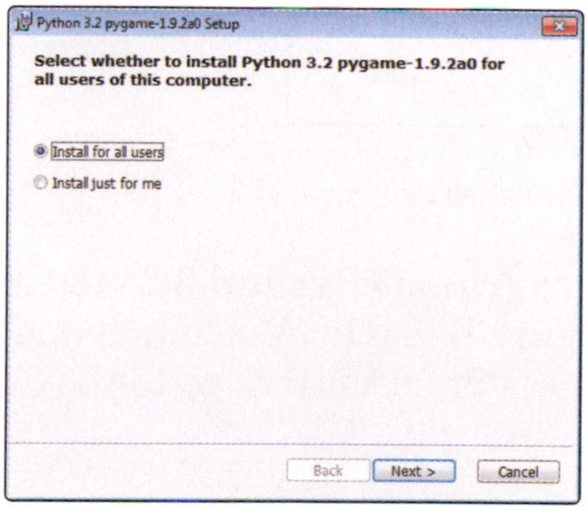

Figure B-4: Install for all users.

5. The program should find your Python 3.2.5 installation from Appendix A. Select **Python 3.2 from registry**. Click **Next >** to keep installing, as shown in Figure B-5. (If you're installing at school or work and run into trouble, your IT staff may need to select the option for Python from another location.)

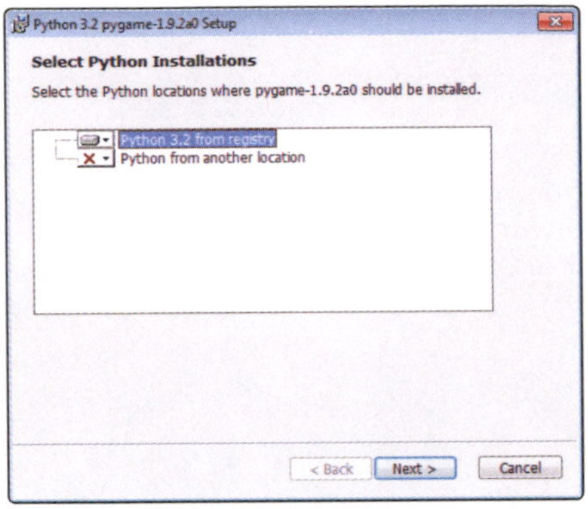

Figure B-5: Select **Python 3.2 from registry***.*

6. Once you've completed the installer, click **Finish** to exit, as shown in Figure B-6.

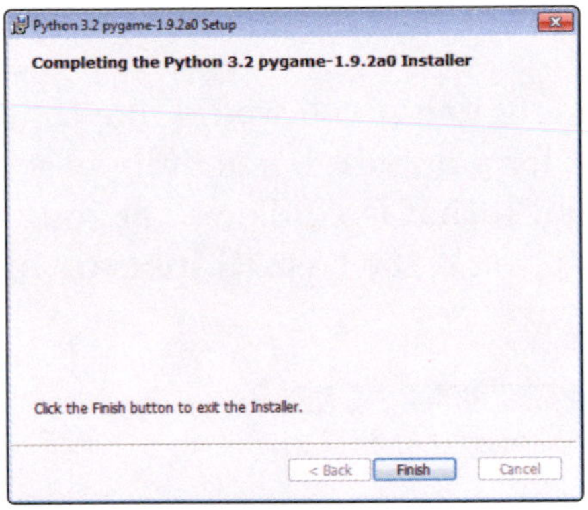

Figure B-6: Click **Finish** *to exit.*

7. Go to **Start ▸ Programs ▸ Python 3.2 ▸ IDLE (Python GUI)**, as shown in Figure B-7. (On Windows 8 and later, you can press the Windows/Start button, go to the Search tool, and type **IDLE**).

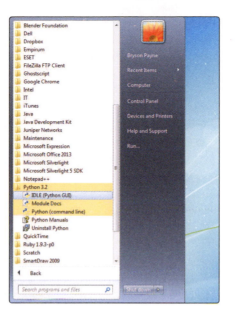

Figure B-7: Open IDLE from the
Start menu.

8. In the Python shell editor, type `import pygame` and press
    ENTER. The Python shell should respond with >>>, as shown
    in Figure B-8. If it does, then you know Pygame installed
    correctly and is ready to use.

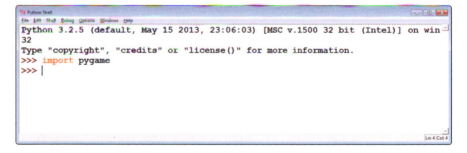

Figure B-8: Import Pygame in the Python shell.

Now you're ready to run the programs from Chapters 8
through 10. Happy coding!

PYGAME FOR MAC

Installing Pygame on a Mac is more complicated than on a PC. You have three options:

1. If you have access to a Windows PC, you may find it easier to install the Windows versions of Python and Pygame in order to run the programs from Chapters 8 through 10. If you choose this option, follow the steps in "Python for Windows" on page 264. Then follow the steps in "Pygame for Windows" on page 280.

2. You can install an older version of Python, like Python 2.7.9, along with Pygame 1.9.2 for OS X in order to run the Pygame programs in Chapters 8 through 10. Installing Python 2.7.9 and Pygame 1.9.2 is easier than making Pygame work with Python 3.4.2. But there are differences between Python 2 and 3, so for Chapters 1 through 7, I recommend sticking to Python 3.4.2 to make sure the examples work. Then, for Chapters 8 through 10, you can use Python 2.7 and Pygame 1.9.2 to run the Pygame examples. If you choose this option, follow the steps under "Python 2.7 and Pygame 1.9.2" in the next section.

3. To install Pygame for Python 3.4 on your Mac, see the instructions online at *http://www.nostarch.com/teachkids/*. If you're doing this at school or work, you will almost certainly need IT support. Give your IT professional the online instructions to use as a guide.

PYTHON 2.7 AND PYGAME 1.9.2

Newer Macs come with a version of Python 2.7 preinstalled by Apple as part of OS X. But the version of Python that Apple provides may not work with the Pygame installer. I recommend installing the latest version of Python 2.7 from *http://python.org/* before you try to install Pygame.

1. To install Python 2.7 on your Mac, go back to Appendix A and start following the steps under "Python for Mac" on page 271 again. But this time, instead of downloading the 3.4.2 installer from the Mac downloads page at *http://python.org/*, download and run the 2.7 installer (2.7.9 as of this writing), as shown in Figure B-9.

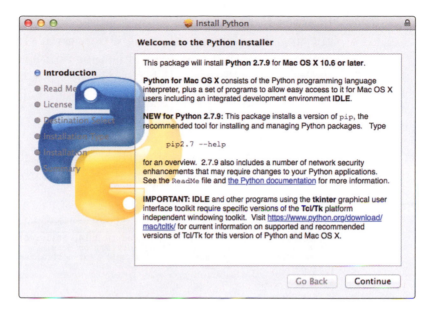

Figure B-9: Install Python 2.7.

2. The installation process for Python 2.7 should be similar to the installer for 3.4. Continue following the steps under "Python for Mac" in Appendix A until you complete the installation.

3. Check your *Applications* folder. There should now be a *Python 2.7* folder in addition to your *Python 3.4* folder, as shown in Figure B-10.

Figure B-10: You should have both Python 2.7 and Python 3.4.

4. Go to *http://pygame.org/,* go to the Downloads page, and download the Pygame 1.9.2 installer for Python 2.7: *pygame-1.9.2pre-py2.7-macosx10.7.mpkg.zip.*

5. Run the Pygame installer by holding down the CONTROL key, clicking the file, and selecting **Open with ▸Installer** from the pop-up menu that appears. The steps will be similar to those for installing Python: click **Continue** a few times, accept the license, and choose the installation drive. Click **Close** when the installer finishes.

6. To test your Pygame installation, go to your *Applications* folder, select Python 2.7, and open IDLE. In IDLE for Python 2.7, type `import pygame`. IDLE should respond with >>>, as shown in Figure B-11.

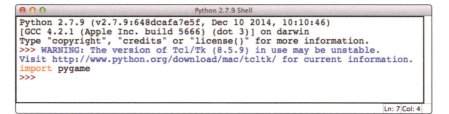

Figure B-11: Import Pygame in the Python shell.

7. You might get a pop-up notice like the one in Figure B-12 saying that you need to install X11, a windowing system used by Pygame. Click **Continue** to go to the XQuartz website, *http://xquartz.macosforge.org/*. Download *XQuartz-2.7.7.dmg*, open the file, and run the installer package.

Figure B-12: Click **Continue** to install X11.

8. To run the Pygame programs in Chapters 8 through 10, use Python 2.7 IDLE instead of Python 3.4 IDLE.

NOTE *On newer Macs with Retina displays, using Pygame with Python 2.7 looks a bit different than it does on other computers because Retina displays use a higher screen resolution. Your programs should work fine, but they will appear in a smaller area of the screen.*

PYGAME FOR LINUX

Similar to installing Pygame on a Mac, you have two options for Pygame on Linux:

1. You can install Pygame for Python 2, the version of Python that is likely to have come pre-installed as part of your version of Linux. For Chapters 1 through 7, you'll need to use Python 3, so follow the instructions in Appendix A and use that version of IDLE for the apps in the first seven chapters. Then, for Chapters 8 through 10, you can use Pygame for Python 2 to run the Pygame examples in those chapters. If you choose this option, follow the steps under "Pygame for Python 2" in the next section.

2. To install Pygame for Python 3.4 on Linux, see the instructions online at *http://www.nostarch.com/teachkids/*. If you're doing this at school or work, you will likely need IT support. Give your IT professional the online instructions to use as a guide.

PYGAME FOR PYTHON 2

Most Linux operating systems come with Python installed already, usually Python 2. The game-based and graphical apps in Chapters 8 through 10 can run just fine on this older version of Python. The following steps will get Pygame up and running on your Linux system.

1. In the Dash menu, go to System Tools and run the Synaptic Package Manager or similar application for your version of Linux. Figure B-13 shows the package manager running on Lubuntu.

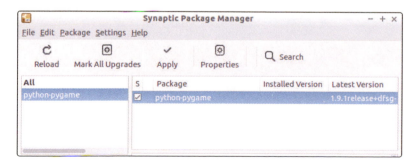

Figure B-13: Installing Pygame for Python 2 on Linux

2. Search for *python-pygame*. Check the box next to *python-pygame* in the search results and click **Apply** to complete the installation.

3. Run **System Tools ▸ Terminal** (or **XTerm** or a similar application for your version of Linux). You can start Python 2 by entering `python2` in the terminal window. Then test your Pygame installation by entering `import pygame` at the >>> prompt as shown in Figure B-14. Python should reply with >>> to let you know that Pygame was successfully imported.

Figure B-14: You can test your installation of Pygame for Python 2 from the Linux command line terminal.

4. You can use the Software Center (as shown in "Python for Linux" on page 276) or the Synaptic Package Manager shown in Figure B-13 to search for and install IDLE for Python 2. Use this version of IDLE when running the Pygame apps from Chapters 8 through 10.

C

BUILDING YOUR OWN
MODULES

Throughout this book, you've imported modules like
turtle, random, and pygame into your programs to add
functions for drawing, generating a random number,
and animating graphics without having to code them
from scratch. But did you know that you can also
write your own modules and import them into your
programs? Python makes it easy to build modules so
you can save useful code and use it in many programs.

To create a reusable module, we write the module in IDLE's file editor window just like other program files we've built, and we save it as a new *.py* file with the name of the module as the filename (for example, *colorspiral.py* might be the filename for a module that draws color spirals). We define functions and variables in our module. Then, to reuse them in another program, we import the module into the program by typing import and the name of the module (for example, import colorspiral would let a program use the code in *colorspiral.py* to draw color spirals).

To practice writing our own module, let's create an actual colorspiral module and see how it saves us from having to rewrite code.

BUILDING THE COLORSPIRAL MODULE

Let's create a colorspiral module to help us draw spirals quickly and easily in our programs just by calling import colorspiral. Type the following code into a new IDLE window and save it as *colorspiral.py*.

colorspiral.py

```
❶ """A module for drawing colorful spirals of up to 6 sides"""
   import turtle
❷ def cspiral(sides=6, size=360, x=0, y=0):
❸     """Draws a colorful spiral on a black background.

       Arguments:
       sides -- the number of sides in the spiral (default 6)
       size -- the length of the last side (default 360)
       x, y -- the location of the spiral, from the center of the screen
       """
       t=turtle.Pen()
       t.speed(0)
       t.penup()
       t.setpos(x,y)
       t.pendown()
       turtle.bgcolor("black")
       colors=["red", "yellow", "blue", "orange", "green", "purple"]
       for n in range(size):
           t.pencolor(colors[n%sides])
           t.forward(n * 3/sides + n)
           t.left(360/sides + 1)
           t.width(n*sides/100)
```

This module imports the `turtle` module and defines a function called `cspiral()` for drawing colorful spirals of different shapes, sizes, and locations. Let's look at differences between this module and the other programs we've written. First, at ❶, we have a special comment called a *docstring*. A docstring is a way of adding documentation to files that we intend to reuse or share with others; in Python, modules should have docstrings to help future users understand what the module does. The docstring will always be the first statement in a module or function, and each docstring starts and ends with *triple double quotes* (""", three double quotes in a row with no spaces in between). After the docstring, we import the turtle module—yes, we can import modules into our modules!

At ❷, we define a function called `cspiral()` that accepts up to four arguments—`sides`, `size`, `x`, and `y`—for the number of sides in the spiral, the size of the spiral, and the (*x*, *y*) location of the spiral starting from the center of the turtle screen. A docstring for the `cspiral()` function begins at ❸; this multiline docstring provides more specific information about the function. The first line of the docstring begins with triple double quotes and describes the function overall. Next we leave a blank line, followed by a list of the arguments accepted by the function. With this documentation, a future user can easily read which arguments are accepted by the function and what each one means. The rest of the function is the code to draw a colorful spiral, similar to code from Chapters 2, 4, and 7.

USING THE COLORSPIRAL MODULE

Once we've completed *colorspiral.py* and saved it, we can use it as a module by importing it into another program. Create a new file in IDLE and save it as *MultiSpiral.py* in the same folder as *colorspiral.py*.

MultiSpiral.py

```
import colorspiral
colorspiral.cspiral(5,50)
colorspiral.cspiral(4,50,100,100)
```

This three-line program imports the `colorspiral` module we created and uses the module's `cspiral()` function to draw two spirals on the screen, as shown in Figure C-1.

Figure C-1: Two colorful spirals created with a three-line program, thanks to the colorspiral.py *module*

With the colorspiral module, anytime a programmer wants to create colorful spirals, all they have to do is import the module and call colorspiral.cspiral()!

REUSING THE COLORSPIRAL MODULE

Let's reuse the colorspiral module to draw 30 random, colorful spirals. To do that, we'll import another module we've used before, random. Type the following eight lines of code into a new file in IDLE and save the file as *SuperSpiral.py*.

SuperSpiral.py

```python
import colorspiral
import random
for n in range(30):
    sides = random.randint(3,6)
    size = random.randint(25,75)
    x = random.randint(-300,300)
    y = random.randint(-300,300)
    colorspiral.cspiral(sides, size, x, y)
```

This program begins with two import statements: one for the colorspiral module we created and the other for the random module we've used throughout the book. The for loop will run 30 times. The loop generates four random values for the number of sides (between 3 and 6), the size of the spiral (between 25 and 75), and the x- and y-coordinates to draw the spiral on the screen, between (–300, –300) and (300, 300). (Remember that the turtle's origin, (0, 0), is at the center of the drawing screen.) Finally, each pass through the loop calls the colorspiral.cspiral() function from our module, drawing a colorful spiral with the randomly generated attributes from the loop.

Although this program is only eight lines long, it produces stunning graphics like Figure C-2.

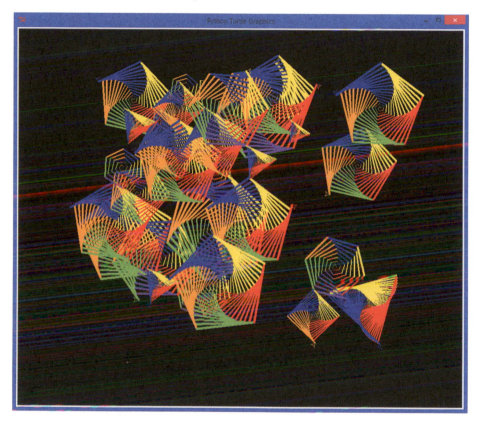

Figure C-2: The colorspiral *module allows* SuperSpiral.py *to produce a lovely multispiral collage with only eight lines of code.*

The ability to create reusable modules means that you can spend more time solving new problems and less time recoding previous solutions. Whenever you build a useful function or set of functions that you want to use over and over, you can create a module to use for yourself or share with fellow coders.

ADDITIONAL RESOURCES

The official documentation for Python at *http://docs.python.org/3/* includes more information on modules and the Python language. The Python Tutorial has a section on modules at *http://docs .python.org/3/tutorial/modules.html*. As you learn new Python programming skills, make use of these resources to add to your coding tool set.

GLOSSARY

Many of the terms you encounter in learning to code are everyday words that you already understand. Some terms, though, are brand new or have special meaning to computer programmers. This glossary defines several of the newer terms you'll come across in the book, as well as familiar words that take on new meanings in the world of coding.

algorithm   A set of steps for performing a task, like a recipe.

animation   The illusion of motion created when similar images are displayed quickly one after the other, as in a cartoon.

app   Short for *application*, a computer program that does something useful (or fun!).

append   To add something to the end; for example, adding letters onto the end of a string or adding elements to the end of a list or array.

argument   A value passed to a function; in the statement range(10), 10 is an argument.

array   An ordered list of values or objects, usually of the same type, accessed by their *index*, or position in the list.

assignment   Setting the value of a variable, as in x = 5, which assigns the value 5 to the variable x.

block   A group of programming statements.

Boolean   A value or expression that can be either true or false.

class   A template defining the functions and values to be contained in any objects of that type.

code   Statements or instructions written by a programmer in a language that computers can understand.

collision detection   Checking to see if two virtual objects are touching, or *colliding*, on the screen, like the ball and paddle in Pong.

concatenate   To combine two strings of text into a single string.

conditional expression   A statement that allows the computer to test a value and perform different actions depending on the outcome of that test.

constant   A named value in a computer program that stays the same, like math.pi (3.1415...).

declaration   A statement or group of statements that tell a computer what a variable or function name means.

element   A single item in a list or array.

event   An activity that a computer can detect, like a mouse click, value change, keypress, timer tick, and so on. Statements or functions that respond to events are called *event handlers* or *event listeners*.

expression   Any valid set of values, variables, operators, and functions that produces a value or result.

file   A collection of data or information stored by a computer on some kind of storage device, like a hard disk, DVD, or USB drive.

for loop   A programming statement that allows a block of code to be repeated for a given range of values.

frame   A single image in a moving sequence for animation, video, or computer graphics.

frames per second (fps)   The rate or speed that images are drawn on the screen in an animation, video game, or movie.

function   A named, reusable set of programming statements to perform a specific task.

import   To bring reusable code or data into a program from another program or module.

index   An element's position in a list or array.

initialize   To give a variable or object its first, or *initial*, value.

input   Any data or information entered into a computer; input can come from a keyboard, mouse, microphone, digital camera, or any other input device.

iterative versioning   Repeatedly making small changes or improvements to a program and saving it as a new version, like *Game1*, *Game2*, and so on.

keyword   A special, reserved word that means something in a particular programming language.

list   A container for an ordered group of values or objects.

loop   A set of instructions that is repeated until a condition is reached.

module   A file or set of files with related variables, functions, and classes that can be reused in other programs.

nested loop   A loop inside another loop.

object   A variable containing information about a single instance of a class, such as a single sprite from the Sprite class.

operator   A symbol or set of symbols that represents an action or comparison and returns a result, such as +, -, *, //, <, >, ==, and so on.

parameter   An input variable to a function, specified in the function's definition.

pixel   Short for *picture element*, the small dots of color that make up images on a computer screen.

program   A set of instructions written in a language computers can understand.

pseudorandom   A value in a sequence that seems to be random or unpredictable, and is random enough to simulate rolling dice or flipping coins.

random numbers   An unpredictable sequence of numbers evenly distributed over a certain range.

range   An ordered set of values between a known start and end value; in Python, the range function returns a sequence of values, such as 0 through 10.

RGB color   Short for *red-green-blue color*, a way of representing colors by the amount of red, green, and blue light that can be mixed to re-create each color.

shell   A text-based command line program that reads commands from the user and runs them; IDLE is Python's shell.

sort   To put elements of a list or array in a certain order, such as alphabetical order.

string   A sequence of characters, which can include letters, numbers, symbols, punctuation, and spacing.

syntax   The spelling and grammar rules of a programming language.

transparency   In graphics, the ability to see through portions of an image.

variable   In a computer program, a named value that can change.

while loop   A programming statement that allows a block of code to be repeated as long as a condition is true.

INDEX

Note: Page numbers followed by *f*, *n*, or *t* indicate figures, notes, and tables, respectively.

SYMBOLS

+= (addition and assignment operator), 100, 187
+ (addition operator), 35, 35t
\ (backslash), 240
/ (division operator), 35, 35t, 39
= (equal sign), 32
== (equal to operator), 62, 79–80, 82–83, 82t
> (greater than operator), 62, 82–83, 82t
>= (greater than or equal to operator), 82–84, 82t
( ) (grouping operator), 35, 35t
(hash mark), 6
// (integer division operator), 49–50, 114, 156
< (less than operator), 62, 82–84, 82t
<= (less than or equal to operator), 82–83, 82t
% (modulo [mod] operator), 21–22, 49–50, 88–89, 156
* (multiplication operator), 35, 35t
!= (not equal to operator), 62, 82t, 83
** (power [exponent] operator), 35t
" (quotation marks), 32
' (single quotation marks), 80
[ ] (square brackets), 46
- (subtraction operator), 35, 35t

A

addition and assignment operator (+=), 100, 187
addition operator (+), 35, 35t
algorithms, defined, 20, 41, 296
American Standard Code for Information Interchange (ASCII) values, 97, 98t
and (logical operator), 93–94, 93t
animation, 175–206. *See also* drawing
bouncing
changing direction, 194–196
off four walls, 197–201
off one wall, 190–197
speed, 194–199
boundaries, 191–193, 198
collision detection, 191, 195, 198, 200, 221, 224–225, 237–240, 238f, 247–248
defined, 296
frames, 185–186
game loop, 182–184
movement, 186–190
Pygame, 176–181
append( ) function, 66
appending, 65, 97, 296
applications (apps; programs), defined, 2, 296

arguments, 43, 110, 146, 296
arrays, 119–122, 122t, 126–128
defined, 119, 296
ArrowDraw.py program, 161–163, 163f, 173
ASCII (American Standard Code for Information Interchange) values, 97, 98t
assignment, of values to variables, 32
defined, 296
AtlantaPizza.py program, 39–42, 42f
attributes, defined, 216

B

backslash (\), 240
bgcolor( ) function, 23, 159
binary search, 108
BLACK variable, 188
blit( ) function, 183, 188, 243, 256
BMP format, 182
Boolean (conditional) expressions, 62, 79, 81–85
comparison operators, 81–84
defined, 296
Boolean numbers, 34
bouncing (animation)
changing direction, 194–196
off four walls, 197–201
off one wall, 190–197
speed, 194–199
boundaries, for animations, 191–193, 198

C

Caesar cipher, 95, 95f
callback functions, 158
calling functions,
        defined, 144
canvas size, determining,
        113–114
Cartesian coordinates,
        111–112, 111f,
        133, 133f
case sensitivity, 33
characters, 97–99
choice() function, 110, 115,
        116, 120–121
chr() function, 100
ciphers, 95–100
circle() function, 17–19,
        54–55, 57, 148,
        179, 183
CircleSpiral1.py program,
        17–19, 18f
CircleSpiralInput.py
        program, 52
classes, 216–219. *See also*
        names of specific
        classes
    constructed, 218
    container, 217
    defined, 189, 296
    extending, 218
ClickAndSmile.py program,
        166–167, 167f, 173
ClickDots.py program,
        208–211, 209f
ClickKaleidoscope.py
        program, 170–171,
        171f, 173
ClickSpiral.py program,
        163–165, 164f
close window button (event),
        182–184
Clock class, 188–190
coding, defined, 1
collide_circle()
        function, 224
collidepoint() function, 224

collide_rect() function, 224
collision detection, 191,
        195, 198, 200, 221,
        224–225, 237–240,
        238f, 247–248
    defined, 296
ColorCircleSpiral.py
        program, 23–24, 52
ColorMeSpiralled.py
        program, 52
ColorPaint.py program, 229
colors, 19
    changing background, 23
    using multiple, 20–22
colors argument, 110
colorspiral module
    building, 290–291
    reusing, 292–293
    using, 291–292
ColorSpiralInput.py
        program, 47–48,
        48f, 52
ColorSpiral.py program, 25,
        26f, 27–28
ColorSquareSpiral.py
        program, 21–22, 21f
colors variable, 20–21, 46
comments, 13
    defined, 6
    docstrings, 291
    usefulness of, 40–41
comparison operators,
        62–63, 81–84,
        82t, 83f
complex conditions, 92–94
complex numbers, 34
compound if statements, 93
concatenation, 97, 296
conditional expressions,
        defined, 296.
        See also Boolean
        expressions;
        conditions
conditions, 77–103
    Boolean expressions, 62,
        79, 81–85
    ciphers, 95–100

complex, 92–94
    elif statements, 91–92,
        118, 253
    else statements, 85–91
    if statements. *See* if
        statements
    while statements, 62–64
constants, 179, 188, 296
constructors, 218
container classes, 217
convert_in2cm() function,
        153–156
convert_lb2kg() function,
        154–156
count_popped variable,
        254–256
count_smileys variable,
        254–256
cspiral() function, 291–293

D

declaring (defining)
        functions, 143–144,
        150–151
    defined, 296
def keyword, 143
Descartes, René, 111
diameter, 19
DiscoDot.py program, 203
division operator (/), 35,
        35t, 39
docstrings, 291
downloading Python, 4–5
DragDots.py program,
        211–214, 211f, 228
drawing, 11–29. *See also*
        animation
    circles, 17–19
    colors, 19
        changing
            background, 23
        using multiple, 20–22
    dots, 177–180
    multi-sided spirals, 25–26
    square spirals
        adjusted, 16–17
        basic, 12–15

draw_kaleido() function, 168–169, 171
draw_smiley() function, 146, 150–151, 166
draw_spiral() function, 169–171
draw_string variable, 242
driving_age variable, 85f

E

element, defined, 297
elif statements, 91–92, 118, 253
else statements, 85–91
EncoderDecoder.py program, 99–100, 102–103
end_fill() function, 148
end keyword, 43
equal sign (=), 32
equal to operator (==), 62, 79–80, 82–83, 82t
eval() function, 28, 40, 48
evaluation, 28, 40
event, defined, 297
event handlers (event listeners), 157–158, 160–165, 183–184
close window button, 182–184
defined, 157
keyboard events, 160–163, 246–247
mouse clicks, 158–160, 163–171, 209–210
mouse presses and releases, 213
parameters, 163–171
in Pygame, 181
exponent (power) operator (**), 35t
expressions
Boolean, 62, 79, 81–85
defined, 36, 297
in shell, 36, 36f
extending classes, 218

F

False value, 83–84
fillcolor() function, 148
fill() function, 148, 188
FiveDice.py program, 129–131, 130f
flags, 123–124, 212, 225
floating-point numbers, defined, 34–35
focus, 162
fonts (typefaces), 242–243
for loops, 14, 55–59, 65, 80, 135, 142, 144, 179, 214
defined, 297
forward() function, 13–15, 17, 142–143
frames, 185–186, 297
frames per second (fps), 186, 297
functions, 141–173. *See also names of specific functions*
callback, 158
calling, 144
defined, 17, 297
defining, 143–144, 150–151
interaction, 157–171
parameters, 146
returning values from, 153–154
using return values in programs, 154–157
utility of, 142

G

game keycodes, 247
game loops, 61–62, 108, 130, 135, 181
animation, 182–184
handling mouse clicks, 209–210
handling mouse presses and releases, 213
ongoing play, 123–124

game programming, 231–262. *See also names of specific games*
adding difficulty, 247–249
adding points, 240–241
board and pieces, 234–241
displaying score, 241–245
elements of design, 232
game over, 246
hitting ball with paddle, 237–240
playing again, 246–247
sound, 252–254
subtracting lives, 236–237
tracking and displaying progress, 254–257
get() function, 181, 210
get_height() function, 193, 199, 221
get_pos() function, 213, 235
get_pressed() function, 253
get_rect() function, 243
get_rel() function, 229
get_width() function, 193, 195, 221
goto() function, 150
greater than operator (>), 62, 82–83, 82t
greater than or equal to operator (>=), 82–84, 82t
GREEN variable, 178–179
Group class, 217–218
grouping operator (( )), 35, 35t
GuessingGame.py program, 107–109, 108f
guess variable, 108

H

hash mark (#), 6
heading() function, 69–70, 139

Pygame, *continued*
  surfaces, 178
  turtle graphics vs.,
      180–181, 214
  update() function, 220
pygame.draw module, 179, 183
pygame module, 177–179, 182
Python
  defined, 4
  documentation for, 294
  downloading, 4–5
  installing, 5
      for Linux, 276–278
      for Mac, 271–274
      for Windows, 264–268
  setup
      for Linux, 278
      for Mac, 275–276
      for Windows, 269–270
  website, 4f, 5

Q

QUIT event, 183, 210
quit() function, 179,
      184, 214
quotation marks ("), 32

R

radius, 17–18
RainingDots.py program,
      205, 206f
randint() function, 106–107,
      109, 115
RandomDots.py program,
      203–205, 204f
random module, 106
  choice() function, 110,
      115, 116, 120–121
  importing, 106
  randint() function,
      106–107, 109, 115
  randrange() function,
      114–115, 152
randomness, 105–139
  Hi-Lo guessing game,
      106–109

kaleidoscope mirror
      effect, 132–136
random spirals, 109–116
  choosing random
      colors, 110
  coordinates, 111–112
  determining canvas
      size, 113–114
Rock-Paper-Scissors
      game, 116–118
War-style card game,
      119–125
  building deck of cards,
      119–120
  continuing play,
      123–125
  counting cards,
      121–123
  dealing cards, 120–121
Yahtzee-style game,
      126–132
  probabilities, 131–132
  setting up, 126–127
  sorting dice, 127–128
  testing dice, 128–129
RandomPaint.py
      program, 228
RandomSmileys.py function,
      146–152, 146f,
      153f, 166
random_spiral() function,
      164–165
  calling, 144–145
  defining, 143–144
RandomSpiralsFunction.py
      program,
      143–145, 164
RandomSpirals.py program,
      109–116, 109f, 132,
      142–143
randrange() function,
      114–115, 152
range, defined, 298
range() function, 17, 23,
      55–56, 58, 59–60
remove() function,
      224–225, 253

render() function, 242
returning (to new line), 44
return statement, 154
return values, 153–157
reusing code, 13, 142–143,
      145, 189, 216–217,
      292–293
RGB color triplets, 178,
      188, 203, 298
right() function, 161
Rock-Paper-Scissors game,
      116–118
RockPaperScissors.py
      program,
      116–118, 118f
Rosette4.py program, 56–57
Rosette6.py program, 58–59,
      59f, 74
RosetteGoneWild.py
      program, 60–61,
      61f, 74
Rosette.py program, 54, 54f
RosettesAndPolygons.py
      program, 88–89, 90f,
      91, 102
rotations, 95
round() function, 156, 256
RubberBandBall.py
      program, 28, 29f
running programs, 6–7

S

SayMyName.py program,
      42–44, 44f
SayOurNames.py program,
      63–65, 64f
scale() function, 221
score
  adding points, 240–241
  displaying in game,
      241–245
  subtracting lives,
      236–237
screenshots, 171
self parameter, 219–221
set_caption() function, 208
setheading() function, 70–71

306   INDEX

set_mode() function, 178,
192, 197
setpos() function, 112,
148–150, 158–160,
163, 166
setx() function, 70
sety() function, 70–71
shell, 5f, 269, 275
defined, 5, 298
doing math in, 36, 36f
syntax errors, 37–38, 37f
variables in, 38–39, 38f
ShowDot.py program,
177–180, 177f, 203
ShowPic.py program,
181–185, 181f
sides variable, 25, 26f,
27–28, 138
single quotation marks
('), 80
size variable, 115–116
SmileyBounce1.py program,
190–197, 191f, 192f
SmileyBounce2.py program,
197–200, 201f,
233–234
Smiley class, 218–219
SmileyExplosion.py
program, 215–224,
215f, 229
SmileyMove.py program,
186–190
SmileyPong1.py program,
233–245, 234f, 236f,
238f, 241f
SmileyPong2.py program,
245–252, 249f,
261–262
SmileyPong3.py
program, 262
SmileyPopHitCounter.py
program, 262
SmileyPop.py program,
224–227
SmileyPop2.py program,
252–259

SmileyThrow.py
program, 229
sorting, defined, 298
sort() function, 127, 131
sound, adding with Pygame,
252–254
speed, 194–199
speed() function, 135
SpiralFamily.py program,
65–67, 67f, 75
spiral() function, 165
SpiralMyName.py program,
44–45, 46f, 52
SpiralRosettes.py program,
74, 74f
spot variable, 210
Sprite class, 216–218
sprites
defined, 215
removing, 224–225
scaling, 221
setting up, 218–220
updating, 220–221
square brackets ([ ]), 46
square spirals
adjusted, 16–17
basic, 12–15
SquareSpiral1.py program,
12–15, 12f
SquareSpiral2.py program,
16–17, 16f
SquareSpiral3.py program,
19–20, 19f
statements
defined, 37
syntax errors, 37–38
str() function, 242, 255
strings, 32, 42–44, 96–97
defined, 20, 42, 298
subtraction operator (-),
35, 35t
SuperSpiral.py program,
292–293, 293f
surfaces, 178

symmetric ciphers
(symmetric
codes), 95
symmetry, 95
syntax
defined, 37, 298
errors, 37–38, 37f

T

textinput() function,
44–45, 44f
text variable, 242
ThankYou.py program,
33, 34f
tick() method, 190, 216
timer variable, 189
transformation, defined, 221
transparency, defined, 299
true division, 39
True value, 83–84
TurtleDrawMax.py program,
159–160, 160f
TurtleDraw.py program,
158–159, 159f,
163, 165
turtle graphics, 11–29
circles, 17–19
colors, 19
changing
background, 23
using multiple, 20–22
defined, 11–12
multi-sided spirals, 25–26
Pygame vs., 180–181
setting random
positions, 112
square spirals
adjusted, 16–17
basic, 12–15
website, 20
turtle module, 12–13.
See also drawing;
functions; loops;
randomness
circle() function, 147

Teach Your Kids to Code is set in Century Schoolbook, TheSansMono Condensed, Avenir, and Housearama Kingpin. The book was printed and bound by Versa Printing in East Peoria, Illinois. The paper is 70# Evergreen Skyland. The book uses a layflat binding, so when open, the book lies flat and the spine doesn't crack.

UPDATES

Visit *http://www.nostarch.com/teachkids/* for updates, errata, program files for the projects and programming challenges, and other information.

MORE SMART BOOKS FOR CURIOUS KIDS!

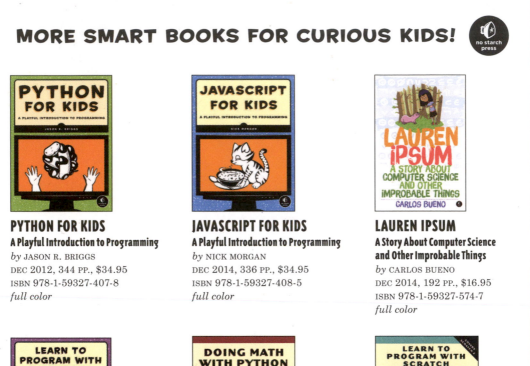

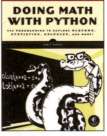